ZICKZACK neu

2

Teacher's Book

Paul Rogers, Lawrence Briggs, Bryan Goodman-Stephens

Nelson

Thomas Nelson and Sc Ltd
Nelson House Mayfir Road
Walton-on-Thames rrey
KT12 5PL UK

Nelson Blackie
Wester Cledden Road
Bishopbriggs
Glasgow
G64 2NZ U

Thomas Nelson (Hong Kong) Ltd
Toppan Building 10/F
22A Westlands Road
QuarryBay Hong Kong

Thomas Nelson Australia
102 Dodds Street
South Melbourne Victoria 3205
Australia

Nelson Canada
1120 Birchmount Road
Scarborough Ontario
M1K 5G4 Canada

I(T)P Thomas Nelson is an International Thomson
Publishing Company

I(T)P is used under licence.

ISBN 0-17-439797-6
NPN 9 8 7 6 5 4 3 2 1

Printed in Great Britain

Acknowledgements

Gerold Deffner
Klaus May
Jeanne McCarthy
Herbert Nagel
Monika and Michael Schätzle
Christian Schweiger
Anna Timm
Jane Tuppen

Contents

Aims

- To provide an enjoyable and stimulating language-learning experience for students of all levels of ability.
- To develop the ability to use German effectively for the purposes of practical communication both within and outside the classroom.
- To establish the skills, language and attitudes required to promote and facilitate further study of German.
- To develop a knowledge and understanding of, and positive attitude towards, speakers of German throughout the world.
- To raise awareness of multicultural and gender issues.
- To establish an awareness of the language-learning process and thereby facilitate the learning of other languages.
- To promote a range of learning styles, including collaborative work with peers and independent learning.
- To contribute to the general education of the learners.
- To develop students' communication skills in general.
- To make a useful contribution to other areas of the curriculum, especially IT, Humanities, Health Education and Personal and Social Education.

Course components

The course consists of four stages, which encompass all aspects of the National Curriculum and Standard Grade.

Stage 2 comprises the following:

- Students' Book
- Teacher's Book, containing teacher's notes and transcripts
- Audio cassettes
- Copymasters
- Flashcards
- Activity Box for independent learning, containing activity cards and audio cassette (duplicating master)
- Video cassettes
- Computer software
- Language Master Cards
- Assessment Support Pack

Core and complementary materials

The material can be broadly divided into two types: core (i.e. a common body of work which all students will follow) and complementary (providing opportunities for extension, revision and supported self-study).

All notes on complementary material in the Teacher's Book are indicated by boxes or by flags at three levels, GOLD, ROT and SCHWARZ (see below). Everything else, therefore, relates to core material.

The core material consists of:

- the first six pages and *auf einen Blick* in each chapter of the Students' Book;
- most of the recordings on cassette;
- some of the copymasters;
- the flashcards;
- many activities explained in the teacher's notes but not involving printed or recorded materials;
- the video cassettes, if possible.

The core provides an acceptable common basis of language for each topic area, thus ensuring that students will not be asked at a later stage to build on something they have not been taught. This is not to say that the core is enough in itself. Students need flexibility to practise, develop, revise and use what they have learned in the core. This is where the rich variety of complementary material comes into its own. It is intended that the majority of students should be able to cover the core material in each of the ten chapters in under four weeks during lesson time. Stage 2 should therefore conveniently provide a year's work.

The complementary material consists of:

- the *Selbstbedienung* pages towards the end of each chapter of the Students' Book;
- some of the recordings on cassette;
- some copymasters;
- various activities and games described only in the teacher's notes;
- the Activity Box cards and related audio cassette;
- the computer software;
- the Language Master Cards;
- the Assessment Support Pack.

All complementary materials are graded to match three levels of difficulty as follows:

GOLD: simple but stimulating activities, attractively presented, designed primarily with low attainers in mind, but likely to appeal to all students, either for consolidation or just for fun.

ROT: interesting and imaginative materials suitable for the majority of students.

SCHWARZ: challenging material and activities for students who enjoy more demanding tasks. Some SCHWARZ activities are more difficult because they include unknown vocabulary. Frequently, however, they are more challenging because students are required to manipulate known lexis and make a logical deduction or series of deductions in order to solve a problem or puzzle.

The categorisation of activities in this way is intended to be a helpful guide for students and teachers. It is recognised, however, that perceived levels of difficulty do not always apply with equal force to all students. In certain cases, therefore, the teacher will be the most appropriate person to match students to tasks.

The Students' Book

The students' book is divided into ten chapters, nine of which are of equal length. Each of these chapters is then subdivided into two related *Lernziele*, each dealing with a different aspect of the topic in question. Chapter 10 is slightly longer and is not subdivided, but introduces the perfect tense for the first time.

Independent learning

The final section of each chapter is called *Selbstbedienung*. This provides a selection of additional differentiated activities for self-access, and is a springboard for other self-access extension material in the Activity Box. A special index to the instructions given in the *Selbstbedienung* sections is given on page 144 of the students' book. Solutions to all activities are provided on copymaster and should be made available to students.

Acquisition of vocabulary

Since great emphasis is placed upon independent learning, it is essential that students should develop good dictionary and reference skills from the outset. The students' book has an easy-to-use glossary (German–English and English–German) and a step-by-step approach to the presentation and explanation of grammar. Together, these help students to gradually develop the skills necessary to cope with unknown vocabulary encountered either in reading or in listening to texts required for oral or written tasks.

Students are encouraged throughout *Zickzack neu* to develop strategies to increase their word power, and also to cope in situations where they are faced with unknown vocabulary. Techniques such as brainstorming, speculation and deduction are frequently used, as are games, puzzles and problem-solving activities.

A substantial part of language learning consists of acquiring new vocabulary. In addition to the vocabulary taught in both core and complementary activities, *Zickzack neu* offers students another way of learning some new words associated with topics covered: *Bildvokabeln*. These labelled pictures, which are in most chapters, can either be used by students themselves to select the words they may need, or used systematically by the teacher to introduce new vocabulary. The same pictures are provided on copymaster, and can be used to help students learn by copying the vocabulary, or even for testing. Why not encourage students to label as many other things in the picture as they can?

Songs and poems

In most chapters of the students' book you will find either a song or a poem. The songs are recorded on cassette. They are designed to be easily learnable and fun to sing along with. Having played the song to the class, get students to sing it line by line, either all together or in groups. If there are musicians in the class, a final stage could be to abandon the tape and let students perform it in their own way. Why not record these performances? Add actions and mime, and there are no limits to how these might be developed.

The poems in their turn are designed not only to be accessible, but to stimulate students to produce their own versions along similar lines.

Cartoons

A relevant cartoon strip also features in most chapters. These are not intended for detailed exploitation, but to encourage students to read for their own interest. You may like to read through them together initially. Students may well be inspired by these to produce cartoons of their own.

Grammar

An awareness of structure is considered of vital importance for students of all levels of ability if they are to be able to take language encountered in one situation and transfer it to another. For many pupils a familiarity with some of the German language patterns will help them generate their own phrases or sentences by using known vocabulary and structures creatively. For these reasons, grammar is treated systematically from the beginning of the course and can be represented as follows:

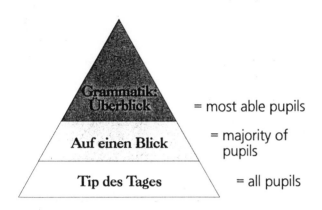

Tip des Tages: a presentation of the main structures without explanation, to support communicative activities and to focus students' attention on core language.

Auf einen Blick: a collation, without explanation, of the core structures presented in each chapter under functional headings. Students should be encouraged to begin to identify the emergence of general patterns. Since all structures are translated into English, this section clarifies meanings, supports independent learning, aids revision and serves as a point of reference if students have been absent.

Grammatik: Überblick: a summary of all the main structures in the book within a largely functional framework, with increased focus on grammatical forms. Verbs, for example, are dealt with person by person rather than in full conjugation. This has the advantage of retaining the functional context, whilst emphasising the simplicity of the patterns. This reference section is intended for those students who require more information about the way German is structured. All explanations are, therefore, presented clearly, and grammatical terminology is defined in simple terms before it is used.

Further practice on many points of grammar is provided on copymasters 75-81.

Activity Box

The cards in the Activity Box contain a wealth of activities for autonomous learning. These are differentiated at the three levels of difficulty: GOLD, ROT and SCHWARZ. All the material is specially written to be directly accessible to students and to reflect their interests. Answers, where appropriate, are provided to encourage self-correction and assessment, and students should feel free to choose material at any level.

There are no teacher's notes accompanying the differentiated Activity Box, but the instructions to the students are unambiguous. Students may work independently, in pairs or in groups; this offers an opportunity for further development in the range of learning styles. All material is fully integrated with the core material and fun to do.

The Teacher's Book

Zickzack neu has been designed to expose students to the maximum amount of both spoken and written German as a normal means of communication within the classroom. To this end, a suggested sequence of language to set up each activity is provided in addition to other strategies such as mime, gesture, use of visuals, written clues and demonstration. This support is not, however, intended to be prescriptive. Indeed, many experienced teachers or teachers with German as their specialist subject may prefer to use other language or techniques to set up or practise activities.

Whilst the teacher's notes provide the language necessary to set up all activities, it is also suggested that a number of *Dolmetscher(innen) des Tages* be nominated for each lesson, through whom questions about new vocabulary can be channelled. They can be given the responsibility of looking up new words when the need arises. A card or badge designating these official interpreters can add fun to the process.

Another useful strategy, suggested occasionally in the teacher's notes, is to outline the task to be performed privately to one or two students in advance so that they can be part of a demonstration.

In order to convey to students the fundamental importance of using German to communicate in the classroom, it is vital that an early start be made to activities which require students to listen to and understand instructions. From there the next all-important step, of course, is for students to begin using the phrases themselves. The classroom language copymaster from Stage 1 is an essential component in this process. It should be given to students or displayed permanently, preferably enlarged on a photocopier or rewritten by the students by hand or on computer once the language shown has been encountered.

A list of suggested games to help familiarise students with classroom instructions is given on page 8. Students will enjoy frequent short-burst practice of such classroom language, providing it takes the form of action or mime games and involves the use of phrases they hear regularly during lessons.

Students' familiarity with classroom vocabulary will also be greatly increased if parts of the room and items of equipment are labelled in German: *die Tür, das Fenster, der Stuhl, der Tisch, die Tafel, der Kassettenrecorder, der Tageslichtprojektor, der Vorhang, die Jalousie, der Bildschirm, die Kreide, die Filzstifte, die Bücher, die Hefte,* etc.

Assessment material

The skills involved in each activity are clearly identified in the teacher's notes. Several activities which involve predominately oral production have been designed for use in an assessment mode once students can confidently produce the required structures and lexis without the support of written cues. When students are being assessed, the written cues on a copymaster can be either folded under or cut off and teachers can either assess students performing in pairs or conduct face-to-face interviews. Such strategies make it relatively straightforward for students and teachers to keep a continuous record of progress. This formative assessment should provide valuable diagnostic information to guide future learning and teaching.

For student self-assessment throughout the course, assessment profile sheets called *Personalakte* are available on copymasters 84–85. These relate to the topics covered in each chapter of the book, and give students the opportunity to record what they can do, which topics they enjoyed most and how easy or difficult they found them.

In addition, the separate Assessment Support Pack provides detailed guidance on formative and summative assessment and a battery of tests in all skills. There are tests to cover the contents of each chapter, as well as more demanding cumulative tests to cover groups of chapters. Each of these tests is easy to administer and mark, and is linked to the student profile sheets.

Video cassettes

The video cassettes provide further practice in the structures and topics covered in each chapter, as well as showing the language being used in context in German-speaking countries. Full details are given in the notes that accompany the cassettes.

Computer software

Zickzack neu offers a wide range of possibilities for the integration of IT into the teaching and learning of German. Textfiles are available to run on the popular Fun with Texts program. These provide valuable practice at all levels and in all skills, but especially in reading and writing. Full details are available with the package. In addition, there are suggestions for the use of information technology in the chapter-by-chapter notes which follow.

Language Master Cards

The Language Master card system is an audio-visual component which develops basic skills and encourages independent work. It offers practice in a variety of areas – for example listening, pronunciation, reading, consolidation of vocabulary and, if students are allowed to create their own cards, writing too.

Students feed the Language Master card with its pre-recorded magnetic strip into the machine and hear the recording while looking at the words. They can then record the same words on a separate track on the magnetic strip. They can listen to the master track and re-record on the student track as often as they like in order to learn the particular item on the card.

Additional practical points

- For open-ended tasks, there may be a range of possible answers. This is made clear in the teacher's notes and a range of suggested solutions is offered for reference.

- Frequent reference is made to the value of displaying flashcards and students' work. Many activities provide opportunities to produce work for display.

- Many of the games on copymaster, especially those which are graded GOLD, are best copied onto card, and if possible laminated, to make them more durable. In certain cases, especially for students with impaired vision, copymasters could be enlarged beforehand.

- When photocopying reading material, choose pastel backgrounds, preferably yellow, apricot or pink if possible. Evidence has shown that this is the most helpful combination for slow readers.
- In many instances it can be useful to make an OHT of some copymasters, either to demonstrate activities to the whole class or to check solutions. Such OHTs could be coloured in order to emphasize and clarify.
- Each page of the students' book is numbered in figures and words in order to help the students.
- It is advisable to re-record the listening items on the Activity Box cassette in separate batches so that short cuts can be used by students to access the item they need more easily.

Games cupboard

There are many games which can be used effectively to promote language learning. The following can be used at various stages in the year to stimulate the production of a wide range of vocabulary and structures, and should be used as often as you feel is appropriate. Where a game is particularly relevant to practise a specific area of language, it has also been included within the body of the teacher's notes at the appropriate point for easy reference. When selecting games, it is usually preferable to choose those which practise language recognition before those which need language production.

As a general rule in all of the games, students should be encouraged to take over the teacher's role as soon as possible. In elimination games, it is advisable to give students several lives in order to prevent those who are eliminated from losing interest.

Games to practise classroom language

Macht mit! The German equivalent of 'Simon says' – perfect for classroom commands. This game can be used time and time again when new language has been introduced. To keep the students alert, you can start or end selected commands with the key words *Macht mit!*

Zeigt auf! This also lends itself to the early stages of language acquisition, as it enables students to demonstrate comprehension without speaking. Once language has been introduced through the use of visuals, students can be expected to point quickly to appropriate cards or objects to show they have understood.

Auf die Jagd. A pretext for giving students a seemingly difficult series of directions or instructions

to be followed, then marvelling at their recall. The activity can be performed using past tenses, without putting them off – for example: *Zuerst habe ich das Fenster geöffnet, dann habe ich die Tür geschlossen, den Bleistift auf den Tisch gestellt, den Tageslichtprojektor eingeschaltet und auf die Leinwand gesehen.*

Jetzt bist du dran. One student has to mime or obey an instruction without speaking, then give another instruction of their own to the next student in line. To make the activity more demanding and enjoyable, it can be made cumulative. In this case each student has to recall and carry out all the instructions given by previous players as well as that given by his or her immediate predecessor. Group support should be encouraged here to keep pace and involvement to the maximum.

Ich bin der Lehrer/die Lehrerin. An opportunity for students to assume the role of teacher and give commands or instructions to the rest of the group or class – surely irresistible, especially if they are allowed to use your chair!

Games for vocabulary learning

Englisch/Deutsch. Students make their own cards with a German word or phrase on one side and its English equivalent on the other. Tell them to choose words they find hard to remember. These cards can then be used in two ways:

1 Two or more students shuffle their cards together, then deal them out in a large circle on the table, English side up. They then take turns, starting from a given card, to say the German for each card. If they get it right they keep the card and try the next one as well, going on in this way until they get to one they can't do or get wrong. Then it is the next player's turn. Any word that a player gets wrong comes up again, of course, so there is a great incentive to learn words they don't know the first time round.

2 Alternatively, students play in pairs taking half the pack each. They take turns to lay their top card English side up, and their partner has to say the German equivalent. Each time one of them gets it wrong, he or she has to pick up the whole pile and put it under his/her other cards so that they recur later. The winner is the first player to get rid of all his/her cards.

Pelmanism. In pairs or small groups, students make, say 20 cards, writing German words or phrases on ten of them and the English equivalents on the others. This can either be prescribed vocabulary or, for revision purposes, the choice can be left to students. Once they get used to these games they will get into the habit of not choosing words their partners are likely to find too easy! The cards should be shuffled and laid face down. Each student turns over two cards and keeps them if they are a pair. If not, they are put back in place. As the focus in this game is on remembering where cards are, students can, if they wish, always help each other with the words themselves. The winner is the player who gains the most cards.

Games to practise numbers

Lotto. At its most complicated, the teacher can prepare 'lotto' cards and provide counters. At its simplest, students can write down a selection of numbers and cross them out as you call them. Students could be asked to read them back in German. This game also provides excellent practice for other vocabulary.

Platsch! Write the numbers to be practised on the board in the form of stepping stones across a river, for example:

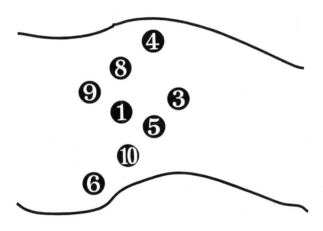

Ask a volunteer to 'cross the river' using the stepping stones. A sequential route could be included, but students are free to choose their own path. If there is a hesitation or a mistake, the rest of the class shouts Platsch! as the volunteer 'falls in the river'.

Zuviel/Zuwenig. Think of a number and ask the class to guess it. The only clue you give them is whether the number they have suggested is zuviel or zuwenig. This game works best with a wide range of numbers.

Welche Zahl? Write the numbers haphazardly all over the board. Divide the class into two teams and ask a representative from each one to come to the board. Call out a number, and the first one to circle it with a piece of chalk wins a point for his/her team.

Dirigent. Divide the class into two teams: 'vorwärts' and 'rückwärts'. Call out a number. The 'vorwärts' team always has to give the next number, the 'rückwärts' team always has to give the previous number. Play one team against another, giving a point for a correct response.

Zählt mal so. Start by saying *Zählt mal so*, and begin to count in a particularly way – for example: forward; backward; alternate numbers; or in multiples of 2 or 3 etc. Students join in as soon as they can with the right sequence, and are out if they give a wrong number. Change the sequence at intervals by saying *Zählt mal so* and beginning again. A group version of this can be played in which you point at a specific group to count. If the group makes a mistake, or fails to join in after the first three or four numbers are called, they are out. Students may assume the role of caller once they are familiar with the rules.

Wach auf! Give each student a number or a word at the beginning of a week. At any time during the lessons for that week call out a number or word and wait for the correct student to stand up. Students could be divided into teams and awarded points for correct responses.

Abwischen. Write numbers in random order on the board. Then invite two students to come to the front. The first student to rub out the number you call earns a point. You can also play this by just pointing at the next student or at groups or teams of students. In the latter case, it is advisable to write two sets of numbers on each half of the board and provide two board rubbers. If the numbers are required for further practice, they could be ringed in coloured chalk instead of being rubbed off.

This game can also be played with other vocabulary, for example pictures of objects or a series of words.

Würfelspiel. Students throw dice in pairs or groups and say aloud the total number. They could also add up their scores over a series of five or six throws.

Die Leiter. Draw two or more six-rung ladders with a number on each rung. Each team or group throws a dice and reads out the number. If it is the next on the ladder, it is crossed off and the team moves up to the next rung. This game can also be used to practise new vocabulary.

Quadratzahlen. Draw a square like the one on page 10 on the board or OHP. Students have to say the numbers against the clock, incurring a five-second penalty for any incorrect number. This could be played with pictures or symbols to practise other vocabulary.

	A	B	C	D	E
Anfang →	5	15	61	27	84
	55	30	13	60	99
	43	12	100	8	11
Ziel	26	48	18	90	72

Games using flashcards

Making and using flashcards.

Students generally respond well to visuals, and home-made flashcards can inject humour and increase motivation and comprehension. Cut-outs from magazines, simple line drawings, symbols and photographs can all make good flashcards. Pictures may be glued onto card or put into plastic wallets to make them more durable.

Various types of flashcard design:

- A picture on one side only with the text on the other.
- Related pictures on both sides, for example *er ist glücklich/traurig.*
- Related pictures on one or more flashcards, for example a sequence of events. This sequence can be described in the present or past.
- Folded cards with one part hidden when folded.
- A card with a flap which can be used to change the picture. *Normalerweise komme ich zu Fuß nach Hause. Heute aber fahre ich mit dem Rad.*
- A concertina of pictures which can be used to tell a story.

Flashcards can be used to cue a wide range of vocabulary and structures. The activities below can be used at any stage during the course.

Flashcards can be used to encourage creative use of language – for example, to see how many sentences relating to one picture the class can make up in a limited time. A kitchen timer can be used to set the time. Encourage the class to compete against itself and to try to improve on its previous best score. Flashcards can help with reading and writing. Display several flashcards, clearly numbered for all students to see. Write on the board a number of sentences, one relating to each card but in a different order. The students then write down the number of each card and the sentence which relates to it.

Richtig oder falsch? A group game. One student has a pile of flashcards. At random he/she picks up a card and says something about it. The others decide if it is richtig or falsch.

Gedächtnisspiel. Blu-tack ten flashcards to the board and write a number next to each. Remove the flashcards one at a time and call out, for example, a sentence relating to a missing flashcard and ask the students to say the correct number. Later this process can be reversed by calling out a number and asking students to make an appropriate comment.

Was waren das? Show about ten related cards and then ask the class to try and remember what they were. When they can remember all of them, remove one and ask them which is missing.

Ohne Worte. Show a picture of an object and ask a student to mime it for others to guess.

Die Hälfte der Klasse weiß Bescheid. Once the students know which cards you have in your hands, select one card and show it to half of the class. The other half must then ask questions to find out what it is.

Fünf Fragen. Hold a card so that the class cannot see it. Give a clue, for example: *Ich habe ein Tier.* Students have five attempts to guess which animal is on the card.

Das stimmt nicht. Show four cards. Ask the students to decide which is the odd one out. This game is useful for the revision of vocabulary from other areas.

Was war drauf? Challenge students by showing a card for a split second only. Then ask them to describe the picture, for example:

Teacher: *Was war drauf?*

Student: *Ein Mann.*

Teacher: *Ein Mann oder zwei Männer?*

Allow the students to speculate before showing them the card properly. Such speculation can also be encouraged by blurring slides of overhead transparency drawings and inviting students to work out what is depicted. The image should only be brought into focus when each stage of questioning has been exhausted.

Was ist das? A game to be played with any group of flashcards depicting nouns. The flashcards are shuffled and a plain piece of paper placed on top to hide the image. The caller looks under the paper to see what the top card is and asks: *Was ist das?* Other students reply: *Das ist ein(e) ...* , and the student who guesses correctly comes out and acts as caller. He removes the top card and looks at the next before asking: *Was ist das?*

Was machst du? This game is similar to the above, using flashcards depicting actions.

Eins, zwei, drei. Display a large number of flashcards depicting a range of vocabulary areas. Point to a student, who should point to three related flashcards as fast as possible and say, for example: *ein Kaffee, eine Limonade und ein Orangensaft; eine Katze, ein Hund und ein Goldfisch.*

Richtig oder falsch? This is a version of 'Simon Says'. From a pile of flashcards, pick one and show it to the group, making a statement about it in German. If the statement is *richtig*, everyone repeats it, but if it is *falsch* they keep quiet. Anyone speaking in the wrong place, or failing to repeat a true statement, is out. The winner takes over the role of caller.

Other games

Das ist falsch! A game played by two teams. Each team has ten cards. A student in one team says what is on his/her card. The other team say whether they think this is true or false. Points can be awarded.

Ja und nein. A student comes to the front of the class and the teacher asks him/her questions. The student has to answer without simply using the words ja or nein. A score can be kept of the number of questions each student manages to answer. As well as being fun, this game helps familiarise students with phrases like *hoffentlich, das stimmt, selbstverständlich, klar.* Questions like *Trinkst du gern Cola?* can be answered with *Ich trinke sehr gern Cola.* A good way of catching students out is to ask a question that requires a factual answer, and then to repeat their answer for confirmation – for example:

Teacher: *Wann hast du Geburtstag?*
Student: *Am vierzehnten Juli.*
Teacher: *Am vierzehnten?*
Student: *Ja.*

Schlachtschiffe. The game of battleships can be adapted to practise various items of language. In its simplest form, give students the area of vocabulary to be practised – for example, parts of a verb, numbers, days of the week – or put a set of flashcards on display as a reminder. Each student writes down any three of the alternatives. Each in turn guesses what his/her partner has written, and if the guess is correct the partner must cross it out. The first one to eliminate all three of his/her partner's items is the winner.

Woran denke ich? The basic guessing game in which someone thinks of a word within a given range for others to guess by asking *Ist das ein(e) ... ?* This can also be played by asking *Woran denke ich? Das beginnt mit B ...* to provide alphabet practice as well.

Im Rampenlicht. A group game in which students take it in turn to answer for 30 seconds any questions fired at them. Initially the questions to be used can be written on the board.

Unser Geheimnis. Select a student in advance of the lesson with whom you agree a secret code. For example, when you point to the chosen item, it might be the next item after you point to, say, *die Katze*, or something black or green, etc. A number code can be used referring to a set sequence so that 3529 would indicate that the 3rd, 5th, 2nd and 9th in any 'go' is the correct answer.

During the lesson, appear to select that student at random and ask him/her to leave the room. The others then choose an object or flashcard in the room. When the student returns, say the name of an object or flashcard around the room and ask, for example, *Ist das es?* The student replies *Nein.* Continue in this way until you use the secret code to indicate the selected object, at which point the student can readily appear to guess the item.

How long you continue before revealing the secret code is a matter of discretion. Once one technique has been revealed (or guessed), switch to another using a different student.

Flüstere es mir. Students must pass a message along a row of players. Each student must remain seated, and only a quiet whisper is allowed. The message can be an instruction to do something, and the student at the end of the row carries out the instruction. This is best done as a race between rows.

Bist du wach? Give each student in the class a number or a word at the beginning of the week, and write a full list on a notice at the side of the blackboard. At any odd time during the German lessons for that week, call out a number and word, and the correct student should stand up. If not, he/she is out and crossed off the list. At the end of the week those left on the list could perhaps be given a team point.

Kannst du einen Satz bilden? A particulary good game for practising word order and/or conjugation of verbs. Divide the class into two equal teams. Write a selection of words (see below for examples) on plain paper, making two copies of each group of words, one for each team. Before the game begins these can be used to demonstrate the word order/conjugation point being practised, by sticking them in various combinations to the board and pegging them in a line, or by getting students to stand in front of the class holding them.

The students physically change places when a new component forces a change to the word order, and this helps make the point graphically – similarly with inversion for questions.

In order to play the game, distribute one set of word-cards to each team. A good, clear space will be needed in the classroom. Say a sentence in English. The aim is for each team to compose the sentence in German by getting students with the appropriate word-cards to stand in a line in front of the class. The first team to compose the sentence correctly gets a point. The game can become rather frantic, of course, but in order to arouse in students a passionate desire to get word order right this seems a fair price.

Below is an example of 15 word cards (two sets of which would serve a class of 30) that could be used to practise both conjugation and word order. You can quickly manufacture your own sets of workcards to suit the occasion.

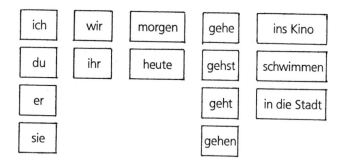

NB In order to get all students involved, it is advisable to write a list of words used and tick them off as they are required.

A variation of this is to have two-sided workcards, thus increasing the possibilities – and the panic!

Useful addresses

Austrian Government Tourist Office:
30 St George Street, London W1R 9FA
German Government Tourist Office:
61 Conduit Street, London W1R 0EN
Swiss Government Tourist Office:
1 New Coventry Street, London W1V 8EE
Austrian Embassy:
18 Belgrave Mews, London SW1X 8HU
German Embassy:
23 Belgrave Square, London SW1X 8HW
Swiss Embassy:
16-18 Montagu Place, London W1H 2BQ
Lufthansa:
23/28 Piccadilly, London W1V 0EJ
CILT (Centre for Information on Language Teaching and Research): 20 Bedfordbury, London WC2N 4LB
Goethe Institut:
50 Princes Gate, Exhibition Road, London SW7 2PH
CBEVE (Central Bureau for Educational Visits and Exchanges): Seymour Mews House, Seymour Mews, London W1H 9PE

Key to icons

Icon	Meaning
	Students' book page 44
	Copymaster 20 – complementary material at level GOLD (for example)
	Flashcards 11-15
	Cassette recording
	Board/OHP
SCHWARZ	Complementary material at level SCHWARZ (for example)
	Pairwork/Partnerarbeit
	IT suggestion

List of copymasters

List of cassette recordings

Kapitel 1
Meine Stadt

Wo wohnst du?

Wo ist das, bitte?

Stadtrundfahrt

Stadtrundgang

Im Verkehrsamt

Ich kenne die Stadt nicht

Wi findest du Osnabrück?

Kapitel 2
Wo ist hier die nächste Post?

Stadtplan

Wegbeschreibungen

Die Post? Das ist ganz einfach

Wo ist das, bitte?

Ist das weit von hier?

Wo ist das Schwimmbad?

Touristen

Kapitel 3
Beim Einkaufen

Kann ich Ihnen helfen?

Ralf der Räuber

Wo treffen sie sich vielleicht?

Das Einkaufslied

Was kaufen die Leute im Geschäft?

Radiorezepte

Ladendieb!

Kapitel 4
Wie kommst du dahin?

Sonntags bin ich immer müde

Entschuldigung ... ich suche den Bahnhof

Welche Linie ist das?

München Hauptbahnhof

Einmal nach Pfarrkirchen, bitte

Auskunft

Zurückbleiben, bitte

Kapitel 5
Gruppenfoto

Was hältst du von Asla?

Teenager

Was hältst du von Elke?

Sag mir jemand, wer sie war

Kapitel 6
Kommst du?

Tut mir leid

Die Clique am Samstagabend

Wir gehen aus

Ausreden

Kapitel 7
Ich habe Kopfschmerzen ... Mein Fuß tut weh

Was wird hier gespielt?

Die neue Turnhalle

Partnerarbeit. Was fehlt dir?

Ich kann nicht ... ich bin krank

Allergien

Krank im Urlaub

In der Apotheke

Wundermittel

Was meinen Sie, Herr Doktor Schweiger?

Hypochonderlied

Kapitel 8
Wohin fahren sie?

Wie kommt die Familie Müller nach Spanien?

Mit dem Flugzeug nach Helgoland

Wir fahren nach England

Helgoland – Inselparadies!

Welcher Campingplatz?

Camping ist billig, oder?

Urlaubszeit

Kapitel 9
Wegweiser

Ich hätte gern ...

Billig oder teuer?

Vor Weihnachten im Kaufhaus

Frank und Erika im Kaufhaus

Wo bekomme ich Briefmarken?

Auf der Post

Was kaufen sie auf der Post?

Kleiner Mensch

Kapitel 10
Sabines Jahr

Was hast du heute gekauft?

Was hast du zum Geburtstag bekommen?

Was hast du an deinem Geburtstag gemacht?

Hast du die Betti kennengelernt?

Wie war die Reise?

Katjas Tagebuch

List of Flashcards

The following flashcards are provided for use with *Zickzack neu* stages 1 and 2:

Pets
1 dog (with lead)
2 cat
3 budgie
4 horse (with saddle)
5 mouse
6 guinea pig
7 hamster
8 goldfish
9 rabbit
10 tortoise

Housing
11 *Wohnung*
12 *Reihenhaus*
13 *Einfamilienhaus*
14 *Doppelhaus*
15 *Bungalow*

Breakfast and other meals
16 rolls; *Schwarzbrot*; loaf of bread
17 jar of marmalade/jam; jar of *Nutella*; jar of honey
18 packet of cornflakes; muesli packet
19 glass of milk; packet
20 cup of coffee; cup of tea; cup of cocoa
21 carton of orange juice; apple juice
22 cheeses
23 platter of cold meats
24 butter (packet); margarine (tub)
25 boiled egg; box of eggs
26 *Quark*; yoghurt
27 chips; mayonnaise
28 sugar (granules + cubes)
29 onions; red/green peppers
30 salt; pepper
31 cut of beef; any other meat
32 bottle of cooking oil
33 noodles; spaghetti
34 (cooked) chicken
35 bottle of coca cola; bottle of lemonade
36 rissoles
37 potatoes
38 tomatoes (tinned + fresh)

Activities
39 watching TV
40 computer
41 record player; radio; cassette player
42 football; basketball
43 friends meeting/greeting
44 tennis; table tennis
45 cycling; rollerskates
46 going shopping
47 eating at table at home
48 homework
49 guitar; flute; clarinet; recorder; piano
50 comic; book
51 chess board + pieces
52 *Jugendzentrum*
53 *Disco*; gymnastics/dance
54 cooking
55 cinema
56 strolling
57 slouching on a sofa
58 stamp collection

More food and quantities
59 *Hamburger*
60 *(Brat)wurst*; tube of mustard; curry sauce
61 *ein belegtes Brot* (cheese + ham)
62 crisps
63 *Schaschlik*
64 crate of beer; litre of wine
65 carton/box (of chocolates); bag of sweets; (Mars) bar
66 *100 Gramm/200 Gramm/500 Gramm/1 Pfund*

In town
67 *Dom*
68 *Rathaus*
69 *Schloß; Stadtmauer*
70 *Restaurant; Café*
71 *Stadthalle*
72 office blocks; high-rise flats
73 swimming pool (indoor + outdoor)
74 sports stadium
75 post office (main)
76 campsite
77 *Verkehrsamt*
78 harbour

79 railway station

80 hospital

81 car park

82 bank

83 museum

Shops

84 *Metzgerei* (backed with meats: *Wurst, Schinken* etc.)

85 *Bäckerei* (backed with bread)

86 *Drogerie* (backed with toothpaste, cosmetics etc.)

87 *Apotheke* (backed with medicines)

88 *Konditorei* (backed with pastries)

89 *Buchhandlung* (backed with books)

90 *Sportgeschäft* (backed with sports equipment)

91 *Schuhgeschäft* (backed with footwear)

92 *Kleidergeschäft* (backed with clothes on rails)

93 *Kaufhaus* (backed with floor plan, records, consumer goods etc.)

94 *Supermarkt* (backed with tins, washing powder, biscuits etc.)

95 *Markt* (backed with fruit and vegetables etc.)

Purchases

96 postcard; stamps

97 T-shirt

98 souvenirs (doll, beer mug etc.)

99 writing block; writing paper; envelopes

100 purse/wallet

101 rubber; pencil; pen; ink

102 flowers; plants

Means of transport

103 on foot

104 bicycle

105 *Mofa*; motorbike; moped

106 car

107 bus

108 tram

109 train (*S-Bahn*)

110 underground

111 ferry

112 aeroplane

Outline of contents and language

Kapitel 1: Willkommen!
Lernziele
1 *Was gibt es hier zu sehen?* (Saying what there is to do and see in different towns)
2 *Wie findest du deine Stadt?* (Opinions about places)
Language presented:
- *Es gibt* (+ accusative)
- *Was gibt es zu sehen?*
- *Man kann ...*
- *Haben Sie?* (+ accusative)
- *Gern*
- *Links, rechts, geradeaus*
- Places to see or visit in town
- Adjectives describing towns
- Items available from a tourist office

Kapitel 2: Wo denn?
Lernziele
1 *Wo ist hier die Post?* (Asking the way)
2 *Wo ist das genau?* (Saying whereabouts and how far away something is)
Language presented:
- *Wo ist hier ...?*
- *Erste, zweite, dritte*
- Prepositions with dative (*in, an, hinter, vor*)
- *Auf der linken/rechten Seite*
- *In der -straße*
- *Ich suche* (+ accusative)
- *Mit dem Bus, zu Fuß*
- Giving and understanding directions

Kapitel 3: Beim Einkaufen
Lernziele
1 *Wo kauft man das?* (Shops and what they sell)
2 *Wieviel ist das?* (Shopping for food and drink)
Language presented:
- *Man*
- Shops
- *In* + accusative/dative (with shops)
- Further items of food and drink
- Weights, quantities and containers

Kapitel 4: Wie fährt man?
Lernziele
1 *Verkehrsmittel* (Modes of transport)
2 *Wie komme ich dahin?* (Travel by bus and train)

Language presented:
- *Mit dem/der*
- Modes of transport
- *Wie kommst du zum/zur/nach ...?*
- *Einfach/hin und zurück*
- *Von welchem Gleis?*
- *Abfahren/ankommen*
- *Welche Linie ist das?*
- Language for bus and railway travel

Kapitel 5: Kleider machen Leute!
Lernziele
1 *Sieht schön aus!* (Describing people)
2 *Tolle Typen!* (Opinions about people)

Language presented:
- *Aussehen/tragen*
- Colours
- Clothing vocabulary
- Adjectives of appearance and character
- Adjectival agreement with the accusative case
- Accusative pronouns *ihn/sie*

Kapitel 6: Willst du mitkommen?
Lernziele
1 *Kommst du mit?* (Making and declining invitations and suggestions about what to do)
2 *Wo treffen wir uns?* (Arranging when and where to met)

Language presented:
- *Mitkommen*
- *Hast du Lust, ... zu ...?* + infinitive
- Further activities language
- Prepositions with the dative case (*hinter, neben, vor, an*)

Kapitel 7: Mir ist schlecht
Lernziele
1 *Krankheiten und Verletzungen* (Parts of the body, illness, injury and allergy)
2 *Medikamente* (Seeking advice and going to the chemist's)

Language presented:
- Parts of the body
- Illness, injury and allergy vocabulary
- *Mir ist ...*
- *Was fehlt dir?*
- *Weh tun*
- *Ich habe* + illness
- *Ich bin allergisch gegen*
- *Ich darf nicht*
- *Haben Sie etwas gegen ...?*
- Medicaments vocabulary

Kapitel 8: Bald sind Ferien
Lernziele
1 *Wohin?* (Planning a journey)
2 *Camping macht Spaß!* (Staying at a campsite)

Language presented:
- *Ich will/Wir wollen* + infinitive
- *Das ist zu* + adjective
- *Lieber/Am besten*
- *Wohin?*
- *Wie lange?*
- Travel vocabulary
- Vocabulary for holiday activities
- Camping vocabulary

Kapitel 9: Was kaufst du?
Lernziele
1 *Im Kaufhaus* (Shopping in a department store)
2 *Schenken und Schicken* (Buying presents and stamps)

Language presented:
- *Billig/teuer*
- *Im ersten/zweiten Stock* etc.
- *Für* + accusative
- *Gefallen*
- Gifts vocabulary
- *Eine Briefmarke zu ...*

Kapitel 10: Ein tolles Jahr!
(Talking about what you've done and where you've been during the year)

Language presented:
- The perfect tense with *haben* and *sein*
- *war/waren*

Main teaching points

Lernziel 1: Saying what there is to do and see in different towns
Lernziel 2: Opinions about places

Language presented:

- *Es gibt* (+ accusative)
- *Was gibt es zu sehen?*
- *Man kann ...*
- *Haben Sie?* (+ accusative)
- *gern*

- *links, rechts, geradeaus*
- Places to see or visit in town
- Adjectives describing towns
- Items available from a tourist office

Before beginning work on this chapter, check where the video material, Activity Box cards and Assessment Support Pack tasks will be most appropriate.

Lernziel 1
Was gibt es hier zu sehen?

Presentation of language (places in town)

Listening
Speaking

Use the flashcards initially to present places to see or visit in town. Present the places in groups of two or three, using choral and individual repetition. You can also play a number of flashcard games to reinforce the new vocabulary.

Teacher: *Was ist das? Das ist der Dom.* (To one student:) *Bitte wiederhol: ‚der Dom‘.*
Student: *Der Dom.*
Teacher: (To another student:) *Was ist das?*
Student: *Der Dom.*

In meiner Stadt

Speaking
Reading
Writing

A copy of some of the places in town presented on flashcards. The copymaster is designed for cutting up and can be used in a variety of ways, including Pelmanism (turning two cards over in an attempt to find a match between text and visual). Students could also stick the visuals in their exercise books and label them in their own hand or with the printed text supplied.

Meine Stadt

Listening
Speaking
Reading
Writing

Five teenagers talking about their home town/village. Revise locations, including points of the compass. Then refer students to the printed text and tell them they are going to hear people describing briefly where they live. The outline map in the students' book shows the location only of the five towns and villages, which are unnamed. Students must, therefore, work out where each of the teenagers lives. Then ask students to follow the texts and repeat parts of each chorally and/or individually. Revise the difference between *Stadt* and *Dorf* by assuming the role of some of the teenagers and asking questions.

Teacher: *Seht euch die Bilder an und hört gut zu. Fünf Jugendliche sprechen über ihre Stadt oder ihr Dorf. Wer wohnt wo? Seht euch die Landkarte an und hört gut zu. Zum Beispiel, ich heiße Susi. Wohne ich in einer Stadt oder in einem Dorf? Und wo ist das? In welchem Land?*

 Meine Stadt

1 – Ich wohne in Osnabrück – das ist eine Stadt in Nordwestdeutschland. Für Touristen gibt es hier viel zu sehen ... den Dom, das Rathaus ..., und wir haben auch ein Schloß. Osnabrück ist eine alte Stadt ... der Dom ist sehr alt ... wir haben eine Mauer rund um die Stadt. Das Stadtzentrum ist aber modern, und die Stadthalle ist auch modern. Hier gibt es manchmal Popkonzerte.

2 – Ich wohne in Braunau. Das ist eine Stadt in Österreich – im Norden an der Grenze mit Deutschland. Es gibt hier ein schönes Jugendzentrum und ein Kino. Es gibt auch ein Hallenbad, eine Sporthalle und einen Sportplatz. Es gibt viel für junge Leute, finde ich.

3 – Ich wohne in Horn. Das ist ein Dorf in der Schweiz. Es gibt nichts da! Absolut nichts. Es ist stinklangweilig! Aber Zürich ist ganz in der Nähe. Da gibt's alles: Discos, Kinos, Schwimmbäder, Tennishallen, ein großes Fußballstadion, alles.

4 – Ich wohne in Passau in Süddeutschland. Die Stadt ist ganz gut für junge Leute. Wir haben Kinos, und es gibt auch ein Jugendzentrum, Squash- und Tennishallen, ein Schwimmbad, Discos, Cafés, alles. Ich wohne ganz gern hier.

5 – Ich wohne in Krempe. Das ist eine kleine Stadt in Norddeutschland, in der Nähe von Kiel. Es gibt nicht viel für junge Leute. Es gibt eine große Sporthalle, aber das ist auch alles. Wir haben keine Disco und kein Jugendzentrum. Nichts. Im Winter kann man auf dem See vor der Schule Schlittschuh laufen.

Solution:

A Osnabrück **B** Passau **C** Krempe **D** Horn
E Braunau

Richig oder falsch?

Reading

Students can now complete the true/false activity based on the five texts.

Teacher: *Lest die Sätze und schreibt ‚richtig' oder ‚falsch'.*

Solution:

1 falsch **2** richtig **3** falsch **4** falsch **5** richtig

Was gibt es in deiner Stadt zu sehen?

Listening
Speaking
Reading

Display the flashcards in turn, presenting the nominative case once more, but moving quickly onto the accusative construction following *es gibt*.

Teacher: *Das ist der Dom. Was gibt es in deiner Stadt zu sehen?* (Write up the question and the start of the reply *Es gibt ...*, then prompt:) *den Dom.* (To student:) *Was gibt es in deiner Stadt zu sehen?*
Student: *Den Dom.*
Teacher: *Prima. Den Dom. Es gibt den Dom. Es gibt einen Dom.* (Write up and continue the process with the answers featuring in three columns, thus:)

Es gibt	den	die	das
	einen	eine	ein
	Dom	Stadthalle	Rathaus

To reinforce the point you could now replay the cassette version of *Meine Stadt* and ask students to write *einen, eine* and *ein* and tick them as and when they hear them in the text. Check their answers first by finding out how many ticks they have for each category, and then by asking them to suggest what each *einen, eine* and *ein* is followed by in the text.

Teacher: *Schreibt auf: ‚einen‘, ‚eine‘ und ‚ein‘. Hört gut zu und kreuzt an. Zum Beispiel* (play the first statement and tick accordingly to demonstrate:) *Wieviel für ‚einen‘? Und für ‚eine‘?*

Partnerarbeit. Stadtspiel

Listening
Speaking
Reading

A pairwork activity based on the facilities/amenities available in a number of towns. Talk students through the key, so that they will be able to take it in turns to choose a town without naming it and challenge their partner to find out the name by asking questions. Practise pronunciation of the fictitious town names. Some students could also look up the meanings of these names.

Teacher: *Partnerarbeit. Seht euch diese Städte an* (go through the names). *Und diese Bilder. Was gibt es in diesen Städten? Partner(in) A wählt eine Stadt. Partner(in) B stellt Fragen. A antwortet mit ‚ja‘ oder ‚nein‘. Zum Beispiel* (go through the model dialogue).

Wo wohnst du?

Listening
Reading

A number of interviews with young people about the facilities available where they live, building on the language introduced in *Meine Stadt*. Ask students to listen to the cassette and fill in the grid by placing a cross in the appropriate boxes. Talk students through the example on the copymaster.

Teacher: *Hört gut zu. Sechs junge Leute sprechen über ihre Stadt oder ihr Dorf. Was gibt es dort für junge Leute? Kreuzt die richtigen Spalten an. Zum Beispiel* (do the first one as an example).

 Wo wohnst du?

1 – Wo wohnst du?
  – In Pinneberg.
  – Was gibt's da für junge Leute?
  – Nicht viel. Pinneberg ist eine kleine Stadt. Es gibt zwei Discos, ein Jugendzentrum, ein Stadion und ein Schwimmbad.

2 – Wo wohnst du?
  – Ich wohne in Tornesch.
  – Was gibt's da für junge Leute?
  – Es gibt eine Sporthalle im Schulzentrum und zwei Tennisplätze. Wir haben kein Jugendzentrum, aber wir haben eine Disco.

3 – Wo wohnst du?
  – In Uetersen.
  – Was gibt's da für junge Leute?
  – Wir haben fünf Sporthallen, ein Schwimmbad und Tennisplätze.

4 – Und du?
  – Ich wohne in Quickborn. Es gibt da nicht viel für junge Leute. Es gibt ein Schwimmbad, zwei Sporthallen, eine Disco, ein Jugendzentrum und ein Kino.

5 – Wo wohnst du?
  – In Norderstedt.
  – Was gibt's da für junge Leute?
  – Absolut nichts. Es ist stinklangweilig! Keine Disco, kein Jugendzentrum ... gar nichts.

6 – Und wo wohnst du?
  – Ich wohne in Elmshorn. Das ist eine Stadt in Norddeutschland.
  – Was gibt's da für junge Leute?
  – Ein schönes Jugendzentrum und ein paar Kinos. Es gibt auch ein Schwimmbad, eine Sporthalle und ein Stadion. Es gibt viel für junge Leute, finde ich.

Solution:

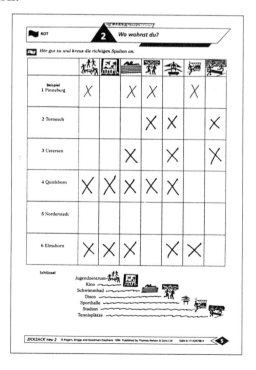

Wo ist das, bitte?

  ROT GOLD

Listening
Writing

Further dialogues in which places in town are mentioned, and directions first introduced, albeit passively at this stage. Ask students to listen to the dialogues and write down the places mentioned. Alternatively, for a *GOLD* exploitation, ask students to put the visuals from copymaster 1 (*In meiner Stadt*) in the correct order.

Teacher: *Hört gut zu. Diese Leute sind in der Stadt. Was suchen sie? Schreibt die Antworten auf. Zum Beispiel* (play the first dialogue and write up the answer).

(GOLD:) Wie ist die richtige Reihenfolge? (Play the first two examples and show students the matching visuals.)

Wo ist das, bitte?

1 – Entschuldigung. Wo ist die Stadthalle, bitte?
   – Hier links.
2 – Entschuldigung. Ich suche das Verkehrsamt. Wo ist das, bitte?
   – Hinter der Kirche.
   – Danke.
3 – Ist hier ein Stadion in der Nähe?
   – Ein Stadion? Ja, da drüben.
   – Danke sehr.
   – Bitte sehr.
4 – Wo ist der Dom, bitte?
   – Da hinten.
   – Danke schön.
5 – Entschuldigung. Wo ist der Bahnhof?
   – Der Bahnhof? Das ist ganz einfach. Da drüben, sehen Sie?
   – Ach klar. Danke.
   – Nichts zu danken.
6 – Ich möchte das Schloß besichtigen. Wo ist das, bitte?
   – Es ist hinter dem Park.

Solution:

1 Stadthalle **2** Verkehrsamt **3** Stadion
4 Dom **5** Bahnhof **6** Schloß

Stadtrundfahrt

Listening
Speaking
Reading

The next two activities centre on the town of Osnabrück, and provide more detail about places of interest in a town. The first is a guided bus tour of Osnabrück, incorporating basic directions and setting the town vocabulary in a real context.

Present and practise *links, rechts* and *geradeaus* using arrows on the board/OHP and/or directing students around the classroom. For further consolidation, call out the directions quickly in rapid succession and require students to make the appropriate arm movements. Then ask students to look at the visual and the photos and listen to the recording, and to note the location of each of the places mentioned.

Teacher: *Hier ist ein Bus. Die Leute im Bus sind Touristen. Sie besuchen Osnabrück und machen eine Stadtrundfahrt. Wie heißt das auf englisch – Stadtrundfahrt? Der Mann mit dem Mikrofon erklärt alles. Er sagt: ‚Hier links ist der Dom', usw. Seht euch die Fotos an. Wo ist hier der Dom? Links, rechts oder geradeaus?*

Finally, some students may be able to take on the role of the tour guide and direct the rest of the class around town. If they can be seated as if in a coach, you could ask them to roleplay tourists and turn their heads to look in the appropriate direction each time. Write up some apposite comments such as *Ach, wie schön!, Toll!, Oh, fantastisch!, Das ist aber schön!, Ach, wie häßlich!*

Teacher: *Wer möchte jetzt das Mikrofon haben?* (to the rest:) *Ihr seid Touristen im Bus. Seht euch jetzt die Stadt an* ('sit' with them in the bus and encourage them to look and comment). If your cassette recorder has a public address facility, it would add authenticity to this activity.

Stadtrundfahrt

– Guten Morgen, meine Damen und Herren. Mein Name ist Weismann. Herzlich willkommen in Osnabrück. Wir machen jetzt eine Stadtrundfahrt. Können Sie alle gut hören, oder soll ich das Mikrofon ein bißchen lauter stellen? OK? Gut … Hier links ist der Dom. Der Dom ist aus dem elften Jahrhundert. Hier rechts ist die Stadthalle. Hier gibt es viele Popkonzerte.
– Wo ist das Schloß, bitte?
– Das Schloß? Das ist hier geradeaus … Dort links

ist das Rathaus. Das Rathaus ist aus dem Jahr 1512 ... Hier vorne geradeaus sehen Sie die Stadtmauer. Die Stadtmauer ist aus dem fünfzehnten Jahrhundert ... Hier rechts ist die Altstadt ... Dort links ist die Stadtmitte. Hier steigen wir aus. Die Stadtrundfahrt ist zu Ende. Auf Wiedersehen. Ich wünsche Ihnen einen schönen Aufenthalt in Osnabrück.

Solution:

der Dom – links; die Stadthalle – rechts;
das Schloß – geradeaus; das Rathaus – links;
die Stadtmauer – geradeaus; die Altstadt – rechts;
die Stadtmitte – links

Stadtrundgang

*Listening
Speaking
Reading*

A 'guided tour' on foot round the centre of Osnabrück. Tell students they are going to be taken on a more detailed guided tour of the town. They should look at the visuals and note the order in which the places shown are visited. Complete the first one or two with the whole class. Briefly practise pronunciation of new places, where appropriate.

Teacher: *Seht euch diese Bilder an. Sie sind von der Stadtmitte von Osnabrück. Hier ist der Dom, das Haus Walhalla, usw. Wiederholt. Jetzt hört gut zu. Wir machen einen Stadtrundgang – wie heißt das auf englisch? Was sehen die Touristen zuerst? Und dann?*

Stadtrundgang

– Herzlich willkommen zu unserem Stadtrundgang! Wir stehen hier vor dem Domhof. Der Dom ist aus dem 11. bis 13. Jahrhundert. Hier vor dem Dom ist jede Woche einmal Markt. Kommen Sie jetzt bitte mit!

Hier rechts ist das Verkehrsamt. Hier bekommen Sie Informationen über die Stadt, einen Stadtplan, Hotellisten, Broschüren usw.

Diese Kirche ist die Marienkirche aus dem 13. Jahrhundert. Wir gehen jetzt ein paar Schritte weiter über den alten Markt zum Rathaus.

So, hier ist also das Rathaus. Es ist über 450 Jahre alt. Folgen Sie mir jetzt bitte in die Bierstraße – hier gleich um die Ecke.

Hier in der Bierstraße stehen einige schöne alte Häuser. Dies ist das Haus Walhalla, heute ein Restaurant. Wir gehen jetzt weiter die Bierstraße hinauf.

Hier sehen Sie das Jugendzentrum.

Sehen Sie, wie eng die Straßen hier sind? Dies ist die Altstadt. Hier fahren keine Autos. Es ist eine Fußgängerzone mit ein paar schönen Cafés und Restaurants.

Das hier ist die zweite Fußgängerzone, die Große Straße. Hier finden Sie Geschäfte, Straßencafés und Kinos.

Unser Stadtrundgang geht jetzt noch zum Schloß. Das sind noch gut zehn Minuten zu Fuß. Wer nicht mit will, kann hier vielleicht in ein Café gehen. Guten Appetit und auf Wiedersehen. Die anderen folgen mir bitte zum Schloß.

As a follow up, you could ask students to use their notes to reconstruct the tour. An OHP copy of the town plan would be helpful here. Some students will probably be able to incorporate some of the incidental comments made by the guide.

Teacher: *Jetzt seid ihr dran. Macht den Kommentar für den Stadtrundgang.*

Solution:

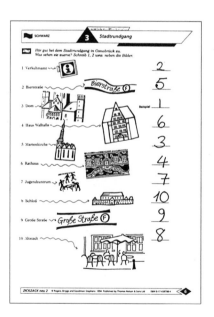

Im Verkehrsamt

*Listening
Speaking
Reading*

Play the recording of a dialogue in a tourist information office, without referring students to the visuals, and ask them where it takes place. Some students might be able to say who is speaking. Then ask students to listen to the recording a second time whilst looking at the visuals.

Teacher: *Hört gut zu. Wo sind diese Leute? Sind sie am Bahnhof? Im Stadion? Wo? Seht euch jetzt den Text und die Bilder an.*

 Im Verkehrsamt

– Guten Tag. Was für Informationsmaterial haben Sie über die Stadt?
– Wir haben einen Stadtplan. Wir haben aber auch Broschüren, Poster, Hotellisten, und sogar auch Bücher.
– Also, ich möchte einen Stadtplan, eine Broschüre und eine Hotelliste.
– Ja, hier, bitte schön.
– Haben Sie auch Prospekte?
– Ja, über Restaurants, Konzerte und Ausflüge. Hier, bitte schön.
– Danke. Was kostet das, bitte?
– Gar nichts. Das ist alles kostenlos.
– Oh, schön. Vielen Dank.
– Bitte schön. Auf Wiedersehen.
– Auf Wiedersehen.

Focus attention on the use of the accusative case by asking students to reiterate what materials the receptionist in the tourist office says she has. Students could also compare this with the materials the customer actually requests.

Teacher: *Was hat die Frau im Verkehrsamt? Seht euch die Bilder an. Sie hat ...*
Student: *Einen Stadtplan.*
Teacher: *Gut. Sie hat einen Stadtplan und ...*
Student: *Broschüren.*
Teacher: *Und jetzt ... Was bekommt die Touristin? Sie bekommt ...?*
Student: *Einen Stadtplan.*
Teacher: *Gut. Sie bekommt einen Stadtplan und ...*
Student: *Eine Broschüre.*

You could also revise *kein, keine* by asking students what the tourist did not request.

Teacher: *Bekommt die Touristin ein Poster?*
Student: *Nein.*
Teacher: *Nein, sie bekommt kein Poster.*
Teacher: *Bekommt sie ein Buch?*

Students could prepare their own recorded version of a guided tour, accompanied by a brochure, using a desktop publishing package to incorporate visuals and a variety of text styles. They could produce the whole package using CD-ROM and base it either on Osnabrück or on their own home area.

Partnerarbeit

Listening
Speaking
Reading

Finally, students can act out the model dialogue and/or invent their own, drawing on the model dialogue and the visuals of the materials available.

Teacher: *Jetzt seid ihr dran. Wiederholt den Dialog (und/oder erfindet Dialoge. Zum Beispiel ...).*

Ich kenne die Stadt nicht

Listening
Speaking
Reading
Writing

   ROT

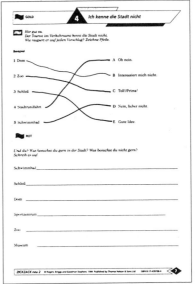

Another dialogue at the tourist office. This time the customer has asked for suggestions for things to do. Ask students to listen to the conversation and join up the suggested outing and the corresponding tourist's reaction.

Teacher: *Hört zu. Dieser Tourist im Verkehrsamt kennt die Stadt nicht. Was sagt die Frau? Und wie reagiert er? Positiv oder negativ? Mach Linien.*

 Ich kenne die Stadt nicht

– Guten Tag. Ich kenne die Stadt nicht. Was gibt es hier zu sehen?
– Es gibt den Dom. Man kann den Dom besichtigen.
– Ach, der Dom interessiert mich nicht.
– Es gibt ein modernes Schwimmbad in der Stadt. Man kann schwimmen gehen.
– Nein, lieber nicht. Es ist zu kalt. Was kann man hier noch machen?

– Oder das Schloß. Man kann das Schloß
  besichtigen.
– Ja, gute Idee. Was noch?
– Es gibt Stadtrundfahrten.
– Oh nein. Ich fahre nicht gern mit dem Bus.
– Oder der Zoo. Es gibt einen Zoo hier.
– Toll! Ich kann den Zoo besuchen. Prima.

Solution:

1B **2**C **3**E **4**A **5**D

As a *ROT* follow up, students can write their own
reactions to places of interest on the bottom section
of the copymaster.

Also follow up the activity by asking students in pairs
to produce their own versions of the dialogue, using
the language provided in the *Tip des Tages*. Some of
the dialogues could then be performed in front of the
rest of the class.

Teacher: *Partnerarbeit. Partner(in) A sagt: ‚Ich
kenne die Stadt nicht. Was gibt es hier zu sehen?‘
Partner(in) B macht Vorschläge.*

Was gibt es hier (in ...) zu sehen?

*Speaking
Writing*

 For the final activity in this *Lernziel*, ask
students what there is to see either in their
own or the nearest sizeable town. They could
then either produce a written leaflet using word
processing or desktop publishing software,
identifying the places of interest in their town,
or alternatively record their work. More able
students could give more detail about each place
of interest, whilst the activity can still be done at
a simpler level as a list.

Students may now attempt the *Lernziel 1*
activities in the *Selbstbedienung* section on
pages 12-13 of the students' book. See page 26 of
this book for more details.

Lernziel 2
Wie findest du deine Stadt?

Presentation of language (adjectives to describe towns)

*Listening
Speaking*

Before embarking on descriptions and opinions of
towns and villages, introduce the following
adjectives: *ruhig, schmutzig, sauber, zuviel/zu viele
(Rauch, Autos, Touristen), nicht genug (Kinos/
Jugendzentren/Geschäfte)*, using mime and gesture
and by relating them to places known to students.

Teacher: *Sch!!* (Then when it's quiet say:) *Es ist
ruhig hier. Wie heißt das auf englisch? Klar – nicht
laut.* (Draw a smoking chimney and cough and
splutter:) *Ach, zuviel Rauch.* (Then wipe your finger
across the board/a dusty surface) *... und schmutzig.*
(Clean the surface and say:) *Das ist jetzt sauber,
nicht schmutzig. In ...* (a local town or industrial
area) *gibt es zuviel Rauch/Autos ... In ...* (another
popular tourist town) *gibt es zu viele Touristen. Wie
heißt ‚zuviel‘ auf englisch? Gut. In ...* (a large town)
gibt es viele Kinos – das ist gut, aber in ... (smaller
local town) *gibt es nicht genug Kinos.*

Wie findest du Osnabrück?

*Listening
Speaking
Reading
Writing*

A number of comments by young people who live in
some of the towns and villages introduced in
Lernziel 1. Ask students to listen and follow the texts
in their books. They can then answer your questions
on what is said about each place. Finally, they can
classify the comments as either positive or negative,
using the written text.

Teacher: *Hört gut zu. Diese Jugendlichen sprechen
über ihre Wohnorte. Seht euch die Texte an – was
sagen sie über Osnabrück? Und über Krempe?
Jetzt macht ihr eine Tabelle so:* (draw students'
attention to the table in the students' book and the
examples given there).

Wie findest du Osnabrück?

– Wie findest du Osnabrück?
– Osnabrück? Naja, die Stadt ist ganz schön.
– Und du?
– Es gibt zu viele Autos.
– Es ist ganz ruhig in der Fußgängerzone.
– Ich finde Osnabrück schmutzig. Es gibt zuviel Rauch.
– Es gibt nicht genug Jobs für junge Leute hier in Osnabrück.
– Wie findest du Krempe?
– Ach, Krempe ist viel zu klein.
– Krempe? Ich wohne gern hier. Die Stadt ist sehr sauber.
– Wohnst du gern hier in Krempe?
– Nein. Es gibt keine Discos und kein Jugendzentrum.
– Ich auch nicht. Hier ist gar nichts los!

– Wie findest du Braunau?
– Braunau ist fantastisch!
– Ja, das stimmt. Braunau ist schön, ruhig und sauber.
– Und du?
– Ich wohne ganz gern in Braunau.
– Ja, ich auch. Braunau gefällt mir gut.
– Und du? Was meinst du?
– Es gibt viel zu viele Touristen.

Solution:

	positiv	**negativ**
Osnabrück	Die Stadt ist ganz. schön. Es ist ruhig.	Es gibt zu viele Autos. Schmutzig – zuviel Rauch. Es gibt nicht genug Jobs für junge Leute.
Krempe	Sehr sauber.	Viel zu klein. Keine Disco, kein Jugendzentrum. Hier ist gar nichts los.
Braunau	Fantastisch. Schön, ruhig und sauber. Ich wohne ganz gern hier. Gefällt mir gut.	Es gibt zu viele Touristen.

Wie denn?

Reading
Writing

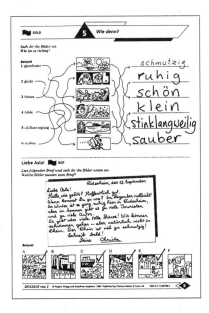

Consolidation of adjectives and adjectival phrases. Ask students to look at the visuals and unjumble the accompanying words.

Teacher: *Seht euch die Bilder an. Wie ist es richtig? Zum Beispiel* (talk them through the example on the copymaster.)

Solution:

1 schmutzig **2** ruhig **3** schön

4 klein **5** stinklangweilig **6** sauber

Schön, oder ...?

Listening
Speaking
Reading
Writing

A number of pictures of imaginary towns and villages. Ask students to comment on each of them, using the language introduced.

Teacher: *Seht euch diese Bilder an. Wie findet ihr diese Städte und Dörfer? Schön? Schmutzig? Ruhig?*

Follow up the activity by asking students to comment on their own town or village or any place they choose. Some may wish to illustrate their comments with photographs or magazine cutouts.

Teacher: *Wie findet ihr* (town/village/district they live in), *oder* (other places possible)? *Schreibt eure Bemerkungen auf, und macht eine Collage,* (wenn ihr wollt).

Liebe Asla!

Reading
Writing

The second part of the copymaster contains a penfriend letter from a girl in Rüdesheim. Ask students to read the letter and decide which of the drawings beneath it are referred to in it.

Teacher: *Lest den Brief und seht euch die Bilder an. Welche Bilder passen zum Brief?*

Solution:

A, C, D and **E** are all referred to in the letter.

Some students could use the letter as a stimulus for their own penfriend letters on the same subject.

Teacher: *Jetzt seid ihr dran. Schreibt an einen Brieffreund/eine Brieffreundin über eure Stadt/ euer Dorf.*

Students may now attempt the *Lernziel 2* activities in the *Selbstbedienung* section on page 13 of the students' book. See below for more details.

Lernziel 1
Straßenschilder

 GOLD

A true/false activity based on street signs.

Solution:

1 richtig **2** richtig **3** richtig **4** falsch **5** falsch

Und deine Stadt?

SCHWARZ

Comprehension questions based on a letter.

Solution:

1 Was gibt es in Deiner Stadt zu sehen?

2 Es gibt den Dom, das Rathaus und die Stadthalle.

3 Popkonzerte.

4 Ganz modern.

5 Das Stadion und den Fluß.

Lieber Andreas!

ROT

In this activity, students are asked to copy the text of a letter, substituting the correct words for the pictures.

Solution:

ein Rathaus; eine Stadthalle; ein Sportzentrum; einen Dom; ein Schwimmbad; einen Campingplatz; zwei Kinos; das Verkehrsamt; (kein) Jugendzentrum

---

Using a word processor, students could produce the letter, loading a prepared skeleton letter and editing it, or merging a file of names with a computer-generated letter. They could obtain pictures from national database over a telephone line and use desktop publishing to produce a leaflet about their home area, combining text and graphics.

Finally, they could consider designing a map for an overlay on the concept keyboard to simulate a tour of the area.

Was kann man hier machen?

 ROT

Students should complete the tourist's questions in a tourist office, using the visuals.

Solution:

1 Haben Sie ein Poster?

2 Haben Sie eine Broschüre?

3 Haben Sie eine Hotelliste?

4 Ich möchte einen Propekt über Konzerte.

5 Ich möchte einen Stadtplan.

6 Ich möchte einen Prospekt über Ausflüge.

Lernziel 2
Halb und halb

 ROT

A matching activity in which students must spot the correct ending for each sentence.

Solution:

1C 2A 3B 4F 5D 6E 7G

Meine Stadt

 GOLD

Students are asked to design a poster advertising their town.

Bildvokabeln. In der Stadt

Reading

This illustration about other places in a town is not intended for detailed exploitation, but provides students with the opportunity to expand their vocabulary.

A version of the artwork is provided on copymaster for students to label themselves and to colour.

Grammar exercises 1-5 on copymaster 75 are based on the material in this chapter.

75 +82

The students' personal profile for this chapter is on copymaster 84.

84

After completing work on this chapter, check whether any further reinforcement is appropriate from the video material, Activity Box cards and Assessment Support Pack tasks.

Main teaching points

Lernziel 1: Asking the way

Lernziel 2: Saying whereabouts and how far away something is

Language presented:

- *Wo ist hier ...?*
- *Erste, zweite, dritte*
- Prepositions with dative (*in, an, hinter, vor*)
- *Auf der linken/rechten Seite*
- *In der -straße*
- *Ich suche* (+ accusative)
- *Mit dem Bus, zu Fuß*
- Giving and understanding directions

Before beginning work on this chapter, check where the video material, Activity Box cards and Assessment Support Pack tasks will be most appropriate.

Lernziel 1

Wo ist hier die Post?

Wo ist hier die nächste Post?

Listening
Speaking

Tell students that you are going to play some dialogues and ask them to guess what they are about. Also ask them for any vocabulary they can recall from the previous chapter. Collate their answers before playing the cassette a second time and asking students to repeat the questions and the answers. Illustrate the meaning of *da drüben* and *da hinten* by drawing the following diagram on the board/OHP:

Teacher: *Ihr hört jetzt Dialoge. Worum geht es hier? Was sagen die Leute? Wiederholt jetzt. Ich spiele das noch einmal. Seht auf das Bild. Ich bin hier vorne* (point to the front of the classroom and the drawing). *Du* (to a student at the back:) *bist da hinten. Wo ist das Poster? Ach ja, da drüben.* (Point at students in various parts of the classroom, e.g.): *Du da hinten, steh auf. Du da drüben, heb die Hand. Du hier vorn, mach dein Buch zu.*

 Wo ist hier die nächste Post?

1 – Entschuldigung. Wo ist hier die nächste Post, bitte?
  – Hier um die Ecke.
  – Danke schön.

2 – Entschuldigung. Wo ist hier das nächste Kino?
  – Da drüben.
  – Ach ja, danke.

3 – Entschuldigung. Wo ist der Bahnhof, bitte?
  – Da hinten.
  – Ach ja, danke.

4 – Entschuldigung. Wo ist hier der nächste Parkplatz?
  – Hier links.
  – Danke.

5 – Entschuldigung. Wo ist das Krankenhaus, bitte?
  – Da drüben.
  – Vielen Dank.

6 – Entschuldigung. Wo ist das Rathaus, bitte?
  – Hier rechts, um die Ecke.
  – Danke schön.

Presentation of language (Wo ist ...?)

Listening
Speaking
Reading

Revise the places in town in groups of two or three at a time. Ask students to repeat chorally and individually.

Teacher: *Was ist das?*
Student: *Das ist der Bahnhof.*

Play some of the games listed on page 10 of the Introduction and encourage students to assume the role of teacher/questioner as soon as they feel confident. Then hold up the flashcards one at a time and encourage students to ask where various places are. Write up the question forms once one or two students have produced answers/questions. Draw students' attention also to the fact that *nächste* is used frequently, but only when there is more than one of the places concerned in the same town, e.g. if there is only one station, use: ,*Wo ist der Bahnhof?'* If there is more than one: ,*Wo ist der nächste Bahnhof?'*

Teacher: (To a student:) *Du willst zur Post gehen. Was sagst du?*
Student: *Wo ist die Post, bitte?*
Teacher: *Prima. Entschuldigung, wo ist die Post, bitte?* (Write up:) *die Post? Da drüben* (point).

Continue similarly until *da drüben, da hinten* and *hier vorne* have been consolidated. Then ask students to complete similar dialogues in pairs.

Stadtplan

Listening
Speaking
Reading

Ask students to study the town map of Osnabrück and decide whether the grid references and street names they hear correspond to the places being sought. Support students' comprehension by drawing a simple grid to start with, thus:

	A	B	C	D	E
1					
2					
3					
4					
5					

Write in some of the boxes the initial letter of a place in town, e.g. R *(Rathaus)*, D *(Dom)*, etc. Circle the letters to avoid confusion with the lettering for the axis. Make sure students realise what the letters stand for. Then ask them to give you the correct grid references for the places you ask about.

Teacher: *Hier seht ihr einen Plan. Auf dieser Seite sind die Buchstaben A bis E, und hier die Zahlen 1 bis 5. Das hier (write in D) ist der ...?*
Student: *Dom?*
Teacher: *Richtig. Wo ist das? 1A? 2B? usw.*

Students can practise this in pairs afterwards. Prepare students for the fuller answers required in the activity relating to Osnabrück by introducing *In der -straße.*

Refer to *Stadtplan* and ask questions about the places, making sure students can pronounce the street names.

Teacher: *Wo ist das Krankenhaus? In der Martinistraße oder in der Natruperstraße?*
Student: *In der Natruperstraße.*
Teacher: *Richtig. Nummer eins sagt: ,Vier A, in der Martinistraße'. Das ist also falsch. Hört jetzt gut zu. Ist das richtig oder falsch? Schreibt es auf.*

Stadtplan

1 – Wo ist hier das Krankenhaus?
 – Hier, vier A, in der Martinistraße.

2 – Wo ist der Dom?
 – Hier, zwei C – am Domhof.

3 – Wo ist das Schloß?
 – Hier, vier E – am Goethering.

4 – Wo ist das Museum?
 – Hier, drei A – am Heger-Tor-Wall.

5 – Wo ist die Fußgängerzone?
 – Hier, drei C – in der Großen Straße.

6 – Wo ist das Verkehrsamt?
 – Hier, eins B – in der Natruperstraße.

7 – Wo ist der Parkplatz?
 – Hier, zwei B – in der Bierstraße.

Solution:

1 falsch 2 richtig 3 falsch
4 richtig 5 richtig 6 falsch 7 falsch

Once these have been corrected, you may invite students to give the correct answers for numbers **1, 3, 6** and **7**.

Teacher: *Nummer eins ist falsch. Wie ist es richtig? Nicht vier A, in der Martinistraße, sondern ...?*
Student: *Eins B – in der Natruperstraße.*

Partnerarbeit. Was ist das?

Listening
Speaking
Reading

Ask students to take it in turns to refer to the *Stadtplan* and choose a place marked on the map Then ask them to work out which place their partner has chosen.

Teacher: (To student:) *Ich bin Partner(in) A, du bist Partner(in) B. Also, drei D – in der Wittekindstraße. Was ist das?*
Student: *(Das ist) der Parkplatz.*
Teacher: *Richtig. Jetzt bist du dran.*

Wer spricht?

Listening
Speaking
Reading
Writing

Ask students to work out which picture belongs with which question. When they have finished writing, check their answers orally.

Teacher: *Wer spricht? Zum Beispiel, Bild eins, wer sagt das? Welche Sprechblase ist das?*
Student: *G.*
Teacher: *Richtig. Also, macht weiter.*

Solution:

1G **2**D **3**E **4**H **5**F **6**B **7**A **8**C

Follow up by asking students to produce their own ideas for people or animals or imaginary figures asking the way to various places.

Teacher: *Jetzt seid ihr dran. Zeichnet andere Bilder mit Text, wie im Buch. Wer sagt was? Lest vor.*

Wie ist es richtig?

Listening
Speaking
Reading

Four cartoons to illustrate the differences between *Eingang/Einfahrt* and *Ausgang/Ausfahrt*. Only one of the pictures shows the correct use being made of the different types of entrance and exit.

Teacher: *Seht euch die Bilder an. Wie heißt Eingang auf englisch? Und Einfahrt? Schlagt in der Wörterliste nach. Ja, richtig – Eingang ist für Leute zu Fuß und Einfahrt ist nur für Autos, Mofas und so weiter. Und Ausgang/Ausfahrt?*

Point out afterwards the use of *Einfahrt/Ausfahrt* on motorway signs. Students could label entrances and exits in the school with the appropriate signs.

Solution:

Bild 2 ist richtig.

Partnerarbeit. Ist hier ein Kino in der Nähe?

Listening
Speaking
Reading

An activity designed to draw a contrast between the use of the definite article in *Wer spricht?*, and the indefinite article as used in expressions for asking the way. Ask students to follow the model printed in the students' book, substituting the words in green each time with another place in town and the correct street name. Work through the model dialogue with students to demonstrate. If necessary, revise the *der/ein, die/eine* and *das/ein* connections before starting students on the pairwork.

Teacher: *Partnerarbeit. Stellt einander Fragen. Zum Beispiel: ,Ist hier ein Kino in der Nähe?'*
Student: *Ja. In der Krahnstraße, hier.*
Teacher: *Gut. An die Arbeit.*

Wegbeschreibungen

Listening
Speaking
Reading

A gap-filling activity relating to asking the way in town. Ask students to listen to the dialogues. Talk them through the first two examples, filling in the gaps in the printed text. If necessary, revise *geradeaus, links* and *rechts*.

Teacher: *Seht euch die Bilder an und hört gut zu. Füllt die Lücken aus.*

 Wegbeschreibungen

1 – Entschuldigung. Wo ist die nächste Post?
  – Die nächste Post? Hier links.
  – Danke schön.
2 – Entschuldigung. Wo ist das Schwimmbad?
  – Das Schwimmbad ist da rechts.
  – Danke schön.
3 – Entschuldigung. Wo ist der Bahnhof?
  – Der Bahnhof? Hier geradeaus.
  – Danke schön.

4 – Entschuldigung. Wo ist die nächste Disco?
– Hier bis zur Ampel und dann rechts.
– Danke schön.
– Bitte schön.

5 – Entschuldigung. Wo ist das Rathaus, bitte?
– Hier bis zur Kreuzung und dann links.
– Danke schön.
– Bitte schön.

6 – Entschuldigung. Wo ist das Krankenhaus, bitte?
– Hier bis zur Ampel und dann rechts.
– Danke schön.
– Bitte schön.

7 – Entschuldigung. Wo ist das Jugendzentrum, bitte?
– Hier links.
– Danke.
– Bitte.

8 – Entschuldigung. Wo ist die Stadthalle, bitte?
– Hier rechts.
– Danke.
– Bitte.

9 – Entschuldigung. Wo ist die Fußgängerzone, bitte?
– Hier bis zur Ampel und dann rechts.
– Danke schön.
– Bitte schön.

10 – Entschuldigung. Wo ist der Dom, bitte?
– Hier links.
– Danke.
– Bitte.

Solution:

1 links

2 rechts

3 geradeaus

4 die nächste Disco; rechts

5 das Rathaus; links

6 das Krankenhaus; rechts

7 das Jugendzentrum; links

8 Entschuldigung; die Stadthalle

9 ist die Fußgängerzone bitte; rechts

10 Entschuldigung; der Dom; Hier links

Students could practise the dialogues in pairs and consolidate in writing, if required.

Partnerarbeit. Erste Straße links

Listening
Speaking
Reading

Teach *erste/zweite/dritte Straße links/rechts* by using the visual in the students' book. Also demonstrate using the board/OHP.

Teacher: *Ich bin hier bei X* (hold up book, and point to X). *Wo ist der Bahnhof? Die erste Straße links? Die zweite Straße links? Die dritte Straße rechts?*
Student: *Die erste Straße rechts.*
Teacher: *Gut. Macht weiter. Partnerarbeit.*

Die Post? Das ist ganz einfach

Listening
Speaking
Reading

    GOLD

Tell students that they are going to hear dialogues in which people ask the way to various places and that they should mark where each place is on the appropriate street map.

For a *GOLD* approach, use only the first three or four examples, where the instructions are generally more staightforward.

Teacher: *Seht euch den Arbeitsbogen an. Das sind Ausschnitte aus einem Stadtplan. Ihr hört jetzt Dialoge. Jemand fragt: ‚Wo ist hier die Post?' Dann kommt die Antwort: ‚Nehmen Sie die dritte Straße links', und so weiter. Wo ist die Post? Macht ein Kreuz an die richtige Stelle.* (Demonstrate on the board/OHP.)

Results are best checked by using an OHP copy of the copymaster, plus a blank overlay for locations. This can be done either by the teacher, or by calling on individual students to mark a location on the overlay. Ask the rest of the class whether they agree or not.

Teacher: *Du, komm nach vorn. Mach ein Kreuz an die richtige Stelle.* (To the rest of the class:) *Ist das richtig?/Stimmt das?/Ist das die Post?*

Die Post? Das ist ganz einfach

1 – Entschuldigung. Wo ist hier die Post?
  – Tja, das ist ganz einfach, nehmen Sie die dritte Straße links.
  – Danke.
  – Bitte.

2 – Entschuldigung. Wo ist das Krankenhaus?
  – Das Krankenhaus? Ja, hier geradeaus, dann die erste Straße links.
  – Also – geradeaus, dann die erste Straße links. Danke schön.
  – Bitte sehr.

3 – Entschuldigung. Wo ist hier die nächste Bank, bitte?
  – Eine Bank? Ja, gehen Sie hier links, dann geradeaus. Dann rechts. Das heißt, die erste Straße rechts. Dann sehen Sie die Bank.
  – Also, hier links, dann die erste Straße rechts. Schönen Dank.
  – Nichts zu danken.

4 – Entschuldigung. Können Sie mir sagen, wo das Sportzentrum ist?
  – Das Sportzentrum?
  – Ja.
  – Das Sportzentrum ist die dritte Straße links.
  – Also geradeaus, und die dritte Straße links.
  – Genau.
  – Danke schön.
  – Gern geschehen.

5 – Entschuldigung. Wo ist denn hier eine Bushaltestelle?
  – Da drüben. Sehen Sie?
  – Ach ja. Danke.
  – Bitte.

6 – Entschuldigung. Geht's hier zum Dom?
  – Zum Dom? Hier geradeaus, die dritte Straße links. Dann kommen Sie direkt zum Dom. Alles klar?
  – Ja, danke. Auf Wiedersehen.
  – Auf Wiedersehen.

7 – Entschuldigung. Wo ist das Rathaus, bitte?
  – Das Rathaus? Gehen Sie hier geradeaus bis zum Dom, dann rechts, dann etwa 500 Meter geradeaus.
  – Danke.
  – Bitte schön.

Solution:

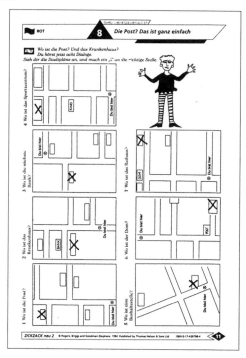

Wo ist das Jugendzentrum?
Listening
Speaking
Reading

An information-gap pairwork activity practising giving directions. Tell students that they must work out in turn what is located in the blank boxes on their maps. Refer students to the cue questions on their sheets and teach *auf der linken/rechten Seite*. When partner B has discovered the location of the six places (s)he needs to find, they should swap roles and B direct A to the six places (s)he is looking for. They can compare their sheets at the end of the activity, which should have all 12 places correctly marked.

Teacher: *Jetzt Partnerarbeit.* (Demonstrate with one pair:) *Partner(in) B, du bist hier* (point to the cross). *Du fragst* (point to the first question on the sheet:) *‚Wo ist das Jugendzentrum?‘* (To the second student:) *Partner(in) A, du antwortest: ‚Das ist die dritte Straße links auf der rechten Seite.‘ Partner(in) B, du schreibst hier: Jugendzentrum* (point to the appropriate box on the copymaster). *Jetzt seid ihr alle dran.*

Solution:

Using desktop-publishing students could produce a town map for visitors, incorporating grid references for places and streets. They could also produce a concept keyboard overlay of the town centre to make access to the information even more straightforward.

Students may now attempt the *Lernziel 1* activities in the *Selbstbedienung* section on page 22 of the students' book. See page 37 of this book for more details.

Presentation of language (prepositions followed by the dative case)

Listening
Speaking
Reading

Although some expressions using the dative case have been encountered during Stage 1 of the course (e.g. *im Winter; mit dem Computer; in einer Jugendherberge* etc.), the concept has not yet been formally introduced. Explain that *der/die/das* and *ein/eine/ein* change to the dative case after certain words (some prepositions), and demonstrate how they change (i.e. *dem/der/dem* and *einem/einer/ einem*). Concentrate first of all on the use of *in* plus the dative. Point out the contracted form of *in dem* (i.e. *im*). Ask students where you and they are at the moment, then write up the following:

> *in dem   in der*
>
> *im*

Blutack the flashcards for *Dom* and *Rathaus* below *in dem/im*, and *Stadthalle* below *in der*.

Teacher: *Wo sind wir? Im Park? Im Rathaus? Im Klassenraum? Ja, gut, im Klassenraum. Seht auf die Karten: wo bin ich jetzt?* (point to cathedral card).
Student: *Im Dom.*
Teacher: *Prima, und jetzt?*
Student: *In der Stadthalle.*

Continue similarly for *hinter* and *vor*, using a visual of a car or a person. Then illustrate the meaning of *an dem/am* and *an der* using a table or desk and the board.

Teacher: *Wo ist das Auto? Hinter dem Dom oder vor dem Dom? Ich sitze am Tisch.* (Write up *an dem/ am*, then say to a number of individual students:) *du auch, du sitzt am Tisch … wo sitzt du?*
Student: *Am Tisch.*
Teacher: *Fein. Ich stehe jetzt an der Tafel* (stand to the side rather than immediately in front). *Wie heißt das auf englisch: hinter, vor, an?* (Consolidate, if necessary, using other flashcards, such as the bus stop and the station.)

Wo ist das, bitte?

Listening
Speaking
Reading

Tell students they are going to hear a number of dialogues in which places are mentioned, and should identify the picture which matches each dialogue. Complete the first one, which appears as a model dialogue in the students' book, with the whole class to demonstrate.

Teacher: *Hört gut zu.* (Play the first dialogue.) *Seht euch die Bilder an. Nummer eins – welches Bild ist das, A? B? C? Richtig, Bild B. Und Nummer zwei? Hört zu.*

Wo ist das, bitte?

1 – Entschuldigung. Ich suche das Haus Walhalla. Wo ist das, bitte?
  – In der Bierstraße.

2 – Du, Walter. Wo ist nur das Auto?
  – Es ist im Parkhaus.
    Ach ja, im Parkhaus, natürlich.

3 – Entschuldigung. Ich such' das Verkehrsamt. Wo ist das, bitte?
  – Hinter der Kirche.
  – Danke.

4 – Ist hier ein Stadion in der Nähe?
  – Ein Stadion? Ja, hinter dem Schwimmbad.
  – Ach ja. Da drüben. Danke sehr.
  – Bitte sehr.

5 – Wo ist der Parkplatz?
  – Da hinten – hinter dem Dom.

6 – Wo hast du geparkt?
  – Vor der Stadthalle.
  – Wo?
  – Vor der Stadthalle.
  – Ach so!

7 – Entschuldigung. Wo ist die nächste Bushaltestelle, bitte?
  – Da drüben, sehen Sie? Vor dem Bahnhof.
  – Danke.

8 – Ich möchte das Schloß besichtigen. Wo ist das, bitte?
  – Es ist hinter dem Park.

9 – Du, hör mal. Ich bin in fünf Minuten da.
  – OK. Ich warte an der Bushaltestelle.
  – An der Haltestelle?
  – Ja.
  – Alles klar. Tschüs.
  – Tschüs.

10 – Sie können den Dom besichtigen.
  – Wo ist das, bitte?
  – Am Marktplatz.
  – Am Marktplatz. Ist das weit von hier?
  – Nein – zwei Minuten.
  – Vielen Dank.
  – Nichts zu danken.

Solution:

1B 2J 3H 4D **5**A 6I **7**C 8F 9G **10**E

Partnerarbeit

Listening
Speaking
Reading

Follow up the previous activity by asking students to say where the places are that you nominate. Hand over to students in pairs.

Teacher: *Bild A – wo ist der Parkplatz?*
Student: *Hinter dem Dom.*

Finally, they might like to play a guessing game in pairs, for example *Wo bin ich?* Students could take it in turns to try and guess the places chosen. The element of competition is heightened if students keep a record of the number of questions asked.

Teacher: *Wir spielen jetzt ,Wo bin ich?' Wählt ein Bild und stellt einander Fragen. Wo bin ich?* (Write up some sample questions, such as *,Bist du hinter dem Dom?' ,Bist du vor der Stadthalle?'*)

Vor dem Museum

Listening
Speaking
Reading

A series of illustrations providing further practice of the prepositions introduced. They can be used in a number of ways, including matching text to drawings, Pelmanism, labelling without the support of the written text and whole class communicative games, such as *Treffen wir uns?* In this game, each student is given an illustration card and they must find the other people in the class who will meet them at the same place.

Teacher: (For *Treffen wir uns?*:) *Jeder bekommt ein Bild – das ist der Treffpunkt. Wie heißt das auf englisch? Stellt einander die Frage: ,Treffen wir uns ...?' und findet eure Partner. Zum Beispiel* (question a few students until you find a match:) *,Treffen wir uns vor dem Museum?'*
Student: *Nein – (hinter dem Dom).*

Teacher: (To another student:) *Treffen wir uns vor dem Museum?*
Student: *Ja.*

Ist das weit von hier?

Listening
Speaking
Reading
Writing

Introduce the idea of distance by referring to places locally.

Teacher: *Ich gehe zur Post. Ist es weit von hier? Hundert Meter?* (Write up 100 m.) *Zweihundert Meter? Ein Kilometer? Ja, gut. Ist das fünf Minuten zu Fuß oder fünf Minuten mit dem Bus? Und der Sportplatz? Ist er weit von hier?*

Once students are aware of the possible variables (*Meter, Kilometer, Minuten zu Fuß/mit dem Bus*) play the cassette and ask them to say where the people want to go and what the distance is.

Teacher: *Hört gut zu. Wohin gehen die Leute? Zum Bahnhof? Zur Post?* (Play the first dialogue.) *Und wie weit ist das? Schreibt die Antworten auf.*

 Ist das weit von hier?

1 – Ich suche die Post. Ist das weit von hier?
   – Ja, ziemlich weit. Am besten fahren Sie mit dem Bus. Es ist zehn Minuten mit dem Bus.
   – Danke.
2 – Ich suche das Schwimmbad. Ist es weit von hier?

   – Nein, nur zehn Minuten zu Fuß. Hier immer geradeaus.
   – Danke.
   – Bitte.
3 – Entschuldigung. Wo bitte ist das Krankenhaus? Ist es weit von hier?
   – Das Krankenhaus? Moment mal. Ja, das ist hier geradeaus. Vielleicht fünf Minuten zu Fuß.
   – Danke schön.
   – Bitte schön, gern geschehen.
4 – Entschuldigung. Ich suche den Bahnhof.
   – Ja, der Bahnhof ist zwei Kilometer von hier.
5 – Ich suche das Stadion. Ist es weit von hier?
   – Nein, nicht so weit. So zweihundert Meter oder so.
6 – Entschuldigung. Ist der Dom weit von hier?
   – Den Dom suchen Sie? Das ist nicht weit. Vielleicht fünfhundert Meter. Hier geradeaus und dann gleich rechts.
   – Danke.
   – Bitte.
7 – Wo ist die Stadthalle, bitte? Ist das weit von hier?
   – Nein, nicht weit. Vielleicht ein Kilometer.
   – Danke.
   – Bitte.
8 – Entschuldigung. Wo ist der Park? Ist er weit von hier?
   – Nein, überhaupt nicht. Er ist gleich hinter dem Dom. So hundert Meter entfernt.
   – Ach, danke schön.
   – Bitte schön.

Solution:

1 Post (10 Minuten mit dem Bus)
2 Schwimmbad (10 Minuten zu Fuß)
3 Krankenhaus (5 Minuten zu Fuß)
4 Bahnhof (2 km)
5 Stadion (200 m)
6 Dom (500 m)
7 Stadthalle (1 km)
8 Park (100 m)

Partnerarbeit

Listening
Speaking
Reading

Students in pairs reconstruct the recorded dialogues.

Ein Kilometer

Listening
Speaking
Reading

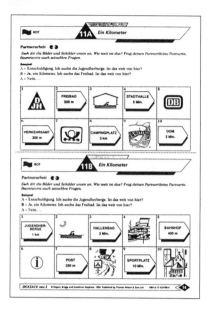

An information-gap activity practising asking how far away somewhere is and understanding distances. Complete a model dialogue in front of the class with a student.

Teacher: *Also, Partnerarbeit. Wie weit ist das? Stellt einander Fragen* (point to the first question on the copymaster:) *‚Entschuldigung. Ich suche die Jugendherberge. Ist das weit von hier?'*
Student: *Ja, ein Kilometer.*
Teacher: *Jetzt macht weiter.*

Students could then make up their own dialogues about distances, and produce an information sheet for tourists about their own or an imaginary town, giving details of the distances away of places of interest. Ask them to use as their starting point the Tourist Information Office or town centre. Write up one or two examples to illustrate. Students could also word-process these details and attach illustrations/photographs. The really ambitious could use desktop-publishing software to produce a professional-looking document.

Wo ist das Schwimmbad?

Listening
Speaking
Reading

A recorded photo story practising various forms of asking the way. This could be performed by students as a playlet, possibly introducing different instructions/directions. Some students might like to record their own versions onto cassette.

Teacher: *Hört zu und lest den Text. Wie heißt ‚geschlossen' auf englisch? Schlagt in der Wörterliste nach.* (Playlets:) *Gruppenarbeit. Wiederholt die Szenen oder macht andere Dialoge. Ihr geht vielleicht zum Sportzentrum oder zum Schloß.*

 Wo ist das Schwimmbad?

– Entschuldigung. Wo ist hier das Schwimmbad?
– Ich kann dir leider nicht helfen, ich bin hier fremd.

– Entschuldigen Sie, bitte. Ich suche das Schwimmbad. Ist es weit von hier?
– Keine Ahnung. Ich wohne nicht hier.

– Entschuldigung. Wo geht's denn hier zum Schwimmbad?
– Das Schwimmbad? Ich weiß nicht.

– Zum Schwimmbad, bitte?
– Du gehst hier geradeaus und dann links, nein rechts, und dann ist das Schwimmbad auf der rechten Seite. Nein, das stimmt nicht, du gehst hier links …
– Danke …

… Das Schwimmbad?
– Das ist weit. Am besten fährst du mit dem Bus, Nummer 12 oder 40.

– Zum Schwimmbad?
– Ja.

– Ach nein!

Ein Brief an David

Reading

A letter to an English penfriend describing the exact location of a house. This provides written consolidation of directions. Students are required to check the instructions with the map of the town in order to find the house. Note that the date of the letter is 1st April!

Using a word-processor or a desktop-publishing package, students could design labels for the school/college complete with distances and visual information.

Students may now attempt the *Lernziel 2* activities in the *Selbstbedienung* section on page 23 of the students' book. See below for more details.

Selbstbedienung ◀ sb

Lernziel 1
Spiegelbilder

 GOLD

Mirror images of the names of places in town.
Solution:
1 die POST
2 der BAHNHOF
3 das KINO
4 das RATHAUS
5 der PARKPLATZ
6 der DOM
7 das SCHLOSS
8 das MUSEUM

Wo ist das Museum?

 ROT

Jumbled texts and visuals on asking the way and giving directions.
Solution:
1 – Wo ist das Museum?
  – Hier rechts.
2 – Entschuldigung. Wo ist die nächste Disco?
  – Hier geradeaus.
3 – Entschuldigung. Wo ist das Krankenhaus, bitte?
  – Hier links.
4 – Wo ist die Stadthalle, bitte?
  – Hier geradeaus und dann rechts.

Wo ist hier das nächste Kino?

 SCHWARZ

A fairly complex map with directions for students to follow.
Solution:
H

Lernziel 2
Im Restaurant

 ROT

A problem-solving activity in which students have to work out where people are sitting in a restaurant.

Solution:

1H 2E 3I 4A **5F** 6B 7G 8J

Wie weit ist das Krankenhaus von hier?

 GOLD

A spaghetti diagram linking places and distances away.

Solution:

Das Krankenhaus ist ein Kilometer von hier.

Der Bahnhof ist zwei Minuten zu Fuß von hier.

Der Dom ist fünf Kilometer von hier.

Die Stadthalle ist 100 Meter von hier.

Das Schwimmbad ist fünf Minuten mit dem Bus von hier.

Die Post ist 500 Meter von hier.

Touristen

Listening
Speaking
Reading

This humorous song contains the expressions needed when giving or understanding directions. Play the song to the class, and then get students to sing it together.

 Touristen

Überall Touristen
In dieser feinen Stadt.
Leider scheint's, daß keiner
Einen Stadtplan hat.
Alle hundert Meter
Hält mich einer an.
Es gibt nur eine Antwort,
Die ich geben kann:

Erste links, zweite rechts,
Dann geradeaus.
Wenn ich das nicht sage,
Komm' ich nie nach Haus'!

Im Winter wie im Sommer,
Touristen überall.
Wohin sie gehen wollen,
Das ist mir egal.
‚Wo ist das Museum?'
‚Ist hier eine Bank?'
Ich gebe meine Antwort,
Sie sagen: ‚Vielen Dank!'

Refrain

Sie fragen: ‚Welche Straße?'
Sie fragen: ‚Ist es weit?'
Ich könnt' es ihnen sagen,
Doch hab' ich keine Zeit.
‚Ist es in der Nähe?'
‚Nehme ich den Bus?'
Du kennst ja schon die Antwort,
Die ich geben muß:

Refrain

Steffi

Reading

Further adventures of Steffi – not intended for detailed exploitation.

Grammar exercises 6-8 on copymaster 76 are based on the material in this chapter.

The students' personal profile for this chapter is on copymaster 84.

After completing work on this chapter, check whether any further reinforcement is appropriate from the video material, Activity Box cards and Assessment Support Pack tasks.

Main teaching points

Lernziel 1: **Shops and what they sell**

Lernziel 2: **Shopping for food and drink**

Language presented:

- *Man*
- Shops
- *In* + accusative/dative (with shops)

- Further items of food and drink
- Weights, quantities and containers

> Before beginning work on this chapter, check where the video material, Activity Box cards and Assessment Support Pack tasks will be most appropriate.

Lernziel 1
Wo kauft man das?

Presentation of language (shops)

Listening Speaking

84 – 95

Present the shops using the flashcards. Begin with the feminine shops (*Bäckerei, Metzgerei, Drogerie, Buchhandlung, Konditorei* and *Apotheke*). Ask students to repeat individually then chorally before writing up the names on the board.

Teacher: *Welches Geschäft ist das? Das ist die Bäckerei. Wiederholt.*

When all the feminine nouns have been presented and their names written on one side of the board, write *die* above them. Then follow the same procedure with the neuter shops (*Sportgeschäft, Kleidergeschäft, Kaufhaus*), and finally the masculine ones (*Supermarkt* and *Markt*), displaying them and writing *das* and *der*. Practise the names of the shops by concealing a card and inviting students to win it by guessing correctly the answer to the question: ,*Welches Geschäft ist das?*'

Partnerarbeit. Welches Geschäft ist das?

Listening Speaking

26

Reinforce students' grasp of the shop names in this activity, in which one partner chooses a shop, and the other must give its name.

Teacher: *Also, jetzt Partnerarbeit. Partner(in) A wählt ein Geschäft. Partner(in) B muß den Namen sagen. Zum Beispiel, Bild 5 – welches Geschäft ist das?*

Student: *(Das ist) die Metzgerei.*

Teacher: *Richtig! Macht weiter.*

Die Geschäfte

Listening Speaking Reading Writing

13 GOLD

Copymaster versions of the shops with the names jumbled. First of all students should unjumble the shop names, and then label the pictures with the correct name. The copymaster can also be used in conjunction with the visuals on copymaster 14 in a game of Happy Families/Rummy.

Was kann man hier kaufen?

Listening
Speaking
Reading

Now you can focus on what is sold in the shops which have been introduced. Ask students to listen to the cassette and pick the correct picture each time.

Teacher: *Seht euch die Bilder an und hört zu. Was kann man hier kaufen? Nummer eins – die Bäckerei. Was kann man hier kaufen?*
Student: *Brot und Brötchen.*

Was kann man hier kaufen?

1 – Das ist die Bäckerei. Hier kann man Brot und Brötchen kaufen.

2 – Das ist das Sportgeschäft. Hier kann man Fußbälle, Turnschuhe und so weiter kaufen.

3 – Das ist die Drogerie. Hier kann man Zahnpasta, Filme, Seife und so weiter kaufen.

4 – Das ist die Buchhandlung. Hier kann man Bücher und Zeitschriften kaufen.

5 – Das ist die Metzgerei. Hier kann man Fleisch, Wurst, Schinken und so weiter kaufen.

6 – Das ist der Markt. Hier kann man Obst kaufen, zum Beispiel, Bananen, Äpfel und so weiter.

7 – Das ist die Apotheke. Hier kann man Medikamente, Tabletten, Hustenbonbons und so weiter kaufen.

8 – Das ist das Kleidergeschäft. Hier kann man Kleider, Jeans, Pullover, T-Shirts und so weiter kaufen.

9 – Das ist die Konditorei. Hier kann man Kuchen und Kekse kaufen.

10 – Das ist das Schuhgeschäft. Hier kann man Schuhe und Sandalen kaufen.

Solution:

1C 2F 3A 4B 5E 6D 7I 8J 9G 10H

Then repeat some of the items in groups and see how many of the shops students can identify. Provide multiple choice alternatives, if necessary.

Teacher: *Welches Geschäft ist das: Brot und Brötchen? (Ist das die Buchhandlung? Oder das Sportgeschäft? Oder die Bäckerei?)*

Das kann man alles kaufen

Listening
Speaking
Reading

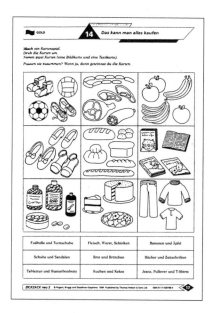

Copymaster versions of the goods available in the shops listed. The copymaster can be used for Pelmanism, Lotto, or pictures can be stuck into exercise books and labelled. Additionally, students could play Happy Families in groups of three or four. Make one copy of each of copymasters 13 and 14 for for each group. Students should cut out, shuffle and divide up the cards between them. The aim is to collect as many pairs of shops/goods as possible. This is done by asking someone else in the group: ‚*Hast du die Karte mit Fleisch darauf?*' or ‚*Hast du die Metzgerei?*' etc. If that person does have the card, (s)he must pass it over to the person asking, who then makes a pair, and can then have another turn. If not, the turn passes to the next player.

Teacher: *Gruppenspiel. Ihr müßt Paare sammeln, zum Beispiel die Bäckerei und das Brot (die Brötchen). Zum Beispiel, ich habe die Bäckerei. Ich frage jemanden in der Gruppe: ‚Hast du die Karte mit Brot und Brötchen darauf?' Wenn ja, dann bekomme ich die Karte und habe ein Paar. Wenn nein, so ist der Nächste dran.*

Kann ich Ihnen helfen?

   SCHWARZ

Listening
Speaking
Reading
Writing

A number of transactional dialogues in shops, in which the items students are expected to identify are embedded. List the shops concerned, if necessary, and ask students to note the items requested and then name the shop.

Teacher: *Hört gut zu. Einige Leute gehen einkaufen. Was kaufen sie? Welches Geschäft ist das? Schreibt die Antworten so* (complete the first one and write it up).

 Kann ich Ihnen helfen?

1 – Guten Tag.
  – Guten Tag. Kann ich Ihnen helfen?
  – Ja, eine Tube Zahnpasta, bitte.
  – Und sonst noch etwas?
  – Einen Film.
  – So. Das macht sieben Mark, bitte.

2 – Tag.
  – Guten Tag.
  – Ich möchte ein Landbrot, bitte.
  – Ein Kilo?
  – Ja, bitte.
  – Bitte schön. Sonst noch etwas?
  – Nein, danke.
  – Also, vier Mark und fünfzig, bitte. Danke schön. Wiedersehen.

3 – Was kostet diese Zeitschrift?
  – Drei Mark, bitte.
  – Danke.
  – Bitte schön.

4 – Ich möchte 200 Gramm Leberwurst.
  – Die grobe?
  – Ja, bitte.
  – Fünf Mark. Sonst noch etwas?
  – 200 Gramm Schinken, bitte.
  – So. Das macht zusammen zehn Mark, bitte.

5 – Guten Tag. Kann ich Ihnen helfen?
  – Guten Tag. Was kostet dieser Fußball, bitte?
  – Dieser hier? 40 Mark.

  – Oh … Na gut, ich nehme ihn.
  – Vielen Dank. Auf Wiedersehen.

6 – Bitte schön?
  – Ein Pfund Bananen, bitte.
  – Eine Mark 80. Sonst noch etwas?
  – Nein, das ist alles, danke.
  – Also, eine Mark achtzig, bitte.

Solution:

1 Zahnpasta, Film + Drogerie
2 Brot + Bäckerei
3 Zeitschrift + Buchhandlung
4 Wurst, Schinken + Metzgerei
5 Fußball + Sportgeschäft
6 Bananen + Markt

Partnerarbeit. Am Markt, oder?

 27

Listening
Speaking
Reading

Present *im, in der* and *am* by showing the flashcards of items to be purchased in the shops. Ask and answer the question: ‚*Wo kauft man das?*' Present items which may be purchased in the 'feminine shops' initially.

Teacher: (Show flashcard of bread:) *Wo kauft man Brot? In der Bäckerei.* (Write up.) *Und Bücher? In der Buchhandlung …*

Follow the same procedure for masculine and neuter shops, starting with *im* and the shops and ending with *am Markt*. By referring to the title *Am Markt, oder?* you can also bring out the fact that *am* is the exception here. Consolidate by asking students to complete the pairwork activity in the students' book. These dialogues provide practice of both the items to be purchased and the shops in which you can find them.

Ralf der Räuber

 28 15 ROT

Listening
Speaking
Reading
Writing

A cartoon about a robber on a 'shopping spree', illustrating the difference between the use of the preposition *in* with the accusative and the dative cases. In the story the police surveillance unit tracks Ralf's every move and provides a commentary on his shopping trip. Ask students to look at the text and listen to the cassette. Once they have understood what has happened, ask them to point out the difference between the statements describing Ralf's entry into the various shops and the police officers' commentary about where Ralf is. Write up *in den/in die/ins* on the board, and *im/in der/im* alongside, perhaps with arrows to indicate movement, and dots to indicate the idea of already being in a place. If you wish, you can also refer students to *Grammatik: Überblick* on page 121 of the students' book.

Teacher: *Hört zu und lest den Text. Ralf der Räuber geht einkaufen. Er hat kein Geld, aber eine Pistole. Im text steht: ,Ralf geht in den Supermarkt', aber was sagen die Polizisten? Ralf ist ...?*

 Ralf der Räuber

1 – Ralf der Räuber geht in die Bank.
– Hände hoch, oder ich schieße!

2 – Wo ist der Räuber?
– Er ist in der Bank.

3 – Zehntausend Mark in die Tasche. Schnell!

4 – Danke. Auf Wiedersehen.

5 – Dann geht Ralf in den Supermarkt.
– 500 Gramm Käse und 300 Gramm Wurst!

6 – Wo ist er jetzt?
– Im Supermarkt.

7 – Jetzt geht Ralf ins Sportgeschäft.
– Ich möchte ein Paar Turnschuhe. Größe 40. Sofort!

8 – Ist er immer noch im Supermarkt?
– Nein. Im Sportgeschäft.
– Könnt ihr ihn da schnappen?
– Ja.

9 – Die Polizisten gehen auch ins Sportgeschäft.
– Beine auseinander! Hände gegen die Wand!

10 – Ralf, wir haben ein Sonderangebot für dich: Kleider, Essen, Getränke ... alles kostenlos!
– Kostenlos?! Toll!

11 – Ralf geht ins Gefängnis.

12 – Jetzt sitzt Ralf im Gefängnis.
– Alles kostenlos!!

Then use the copymaster version to reinforce the point. Students should fill in the commentary on each picture using either the accusative or the dative form, as shown in the menu box.

Finally, some students may wish to act out the scenes themselves, possibly adding their own variants.

Wo gehst du hin?

Listening
Speaking

Hand four or five shop flashcards to students standing in different parts of the room. Then tell them where you are going on your shopping trip.

Teacher: *Ich gehe in die Bäckerei ...* (stop before you reach the student with the card) ... *nein, ich gehe ins Schuhgeschäft ... ach nein, ich gehe in den ...*

Encourage students to join in the activity individually, and stop and question them before they arrive.

Teacher: *Wo gehst du hin?*
Student: *(Ich gehe) in die Metzgerei.* (Stop him/her and direct him/her towards another place.)
Teacher: *Und jetzt?*
Student: *Ich gehe ins Sportgeschäft.*

In den? In die? Ins?

Listening
Speaking

Ask students which shop they would go to for the various items. If necessary, display the flashcards of shops beneath the labels *in den, in die, ins*.

Teacher: *Ihr geht einkaufen. Wohin geht ihr für einen Film? Brot? Turnschuhe? usw.*

Jörgs Einkaufsliste

Listening
Reading
Writing

A text describing a shopping trip and incorporating the use of prepositions followed by the accusative. Ask students to read the text, and supply the missing shop names and correct use of *in* or *an* with the accusative each time.

Teacher: *Lest den Text „Jörgs Einkaufsliste", und füllt die Lücken mit ‚in die', ‚in den' oder ‚auf den' und den richtigen Geschäftsnamen aus. Schreibt die Antworten auf.*

Solution:

in die Bäckerei

in die Metzgerei

auf den Markt

in den Supermarkt

in die Apotheke

Wo treffen sie sich vielleicht?

Listening
Speaking
Reading

A problem-solving activity requiring students first to listen to the recording and identify which shopping list belongs to which person. They are then asked to study the lists again and find out the only shop in which the three people might meet.

Teacher: *Seht euch die drei Einkaufslisten an und hört zu. Wem gehört jede Liste?* (For the problem-solving activity:) *Lest die Einkaufslisten noch einmal. Findet heraus, in welchem Geschäft die drei Leute sich treffen könnten.*

 Wo treffen sie sich vielleicht?

1 – Also, Mutti, ich gehe jetzt einkaufen. Hast du eine Liste geschrieben?

– Ja, hier. Ich brauche Bananen, Käse und Butter, sowie auch einen Film und Aspirintabletten – Vati hat nämlich Kopfschmerzen. Und du kannst dir auch ein paar neue Sandalen für deinen Urlaub kaufen, Karin. Geh jetzt! Mach schnell.

2 – Nun ... was kaufe ich? Äpfel ... Seife ... Hustenbonbons ... eine Zeitschrift für mich ... und ... Jörg?

– Ja?

– Hast du alles, was du für die Schule brauchst?

– Ich brauche neue Fußballschuhe, Mutti. Meine sind mir zu klein.

– Gut. Sonst noch etwas? Ich gehe nämlich in die Stadt.

– Kaufst du mir auch einen neuen Pulli?

– Ja, wenn du unbedingt einen neuen brauchst.

3 – Wofür gibst du das Geld aus, das du zum Geburtstag bekommen hast, Uschi?

– Oh ... ich kaufe vielleicht ein paar Sachen für die Schule, so Bücher, Schuhe, ein T-Shirt ... Tennisbälle.

– Uschi! Kaufst du mir bitte eine Fernsehzeitung und eine Tube Zahnpasta?

– Ja, Mutti.

Solution:

1b 2a 3c   In der Drogerie

Mastermind

Listening
Speaking
Reading
Writing

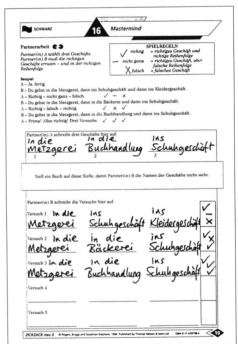

A game of logic based on the well-known game by the same name. Tell students they must take it in turns to choose any three shops and the order in which they intend to visit them. Their partner must try to work out both the shops chosen and the order. First, Partner A must choose and Partner B guess. Partner A answers in this way: *richtig* = correct shop + correct order; *nicht ganz* = correct shop + wrong order; *falsch* = wrong shop.

Make an OHP copy of the copymaster and fill in the answers as on the reduction above on an overlay. Then talk students through the model dialogue on the copymaster to demonstrate. Students then share the copymaster, standing an object such as a book in the middle so that the guessing partner cannot be tempted to look at the answer. Each guess is marked, until the partner guessing has had up to five guesses to solve the puzzle. Students then swap roles.

Teacher: *Wir spielen jetzt Mastermind. Partner A wählt drei Geschäfte und schreibt die Namen auf. Zum Beispiel* (work through the example on the copymaster).

🖥 Using a word-processor or desktop-publishing package, students could produce an alternative town plan labelled only with shops and businesses. They could adapt the town plan they produced for the previous chapter. A shopper's guide of shops and businesses could be attached, including opening and closing times. Again, a concept keyboard overlay version would make access even easier.

Students may now attempt the *Lernziel 1* activities in the *Selbstbedienung* section on page 32 of the students' book. See page 51 of this book for more details.

Revision of food and drink and presentation of language (quantities)

Listening
Speaking

Present the flashcards dealing with weights, measures and containers in groups of three or four, starting with the smaller weights and working upwards, before moving onto different measures.

Teacher: (Showing card for *Wurst 100g*, but covering the individual weight:) *Was ist das?*
Student: *Wurst.*
Teacher: *Gut.* (Uncovering:) *Wieviel Wurst? Hundert Gramm. Hundert Gramm Wurst.* (To student:) *Wieviel Wurst? usw.*

Use the same approach for *Liter*, then use the bottle of wine to switch to containers:

Teacher: *Das ist ein Liter Wein. Oder eine Flasche Wein ... usw.*

Wieviel?

Listening
Speaking
Reading

Read through the language with the students and reinforce with your own examples. Illustrate how much these weights and measures amount to in practical terms by using the expression *Das reicht x Personen/für x belegte Brote*. Note that a German *Pfund* is exactly 500g, and is, therefore, slightly different from an English pound (454g).

Teacher: *Seht euch die Bilder an. Wieviel Gläser Milch sind in einem Liter? Vier? Fünf? Sechs? Ja, so ungefähr vier. Für wie viele belegte Brote reichen 100 Gramm Wurst? Ja, ungefähr fünf. Und 500 Gramm Käse? Das reicht für zehn belegte Brote, oder?*

Students might practise the concepts further by drawing other quantities of food and drink in their exercise books and analysing them in terms of portions, measures per person, etc.

Alternatively, they could use the cartoons of the mouse and the camel as a stimulus for a more creative/humorous approach. If necessary you could suggest other animals and quantities/foods, e.g. *Erdnüsse* and *Schimpansen*, *Heu* and *Pferde*, *Fische* and *Pinguine*, etc.

Teacher: Seht euch die Bilder an. Das Kamel braucht viel Wasser, aber die Maus braucht nicht viel Käse. Zeichnet ähnliche Bilder, zum Beispiel …

Was wiegt das?

Listening
Speaking

An auctioneer game in which students must make intelligent guesses as to the weight either of food on the flashcards, or of items you have brought into the classroom. The use of a set of weighing scales makes such an activity come to life. Display the object and allow students to discuss, in pairs or in groups, what the weight might be.

Teacher: (Showing loaf of bread or bag of apples:) *Was wiegt das?* (Mime weighing with your hand.) *Hundert Gramm? Ein Kilo?*
Student: *Fünfhundert Gramm.*
Teacher: *Fünfhundert Gramm.* (To class:) *Stimmt das?*
Student: *Nein.*
Teacher: *Ist es mehr oder weniger? Mehr? Ein Kilo, zwei Kilo? Oder weniger? Dreihundert Gramm?*

Allow students to take over the bidding before finally weighing the item to discover the most accurate assessment.

Das Einkaufslied

Listening
Speaking
Reading

Quantities and containers vocabulary are embedded into this humorous song. Students could join in, when the tune becomes familiar. The song can be used now, or after the group of activities about containers and quantities.

 Das Einkaufslied

1 Ich gehe gern einkaufen
Im Supermarkt.
Ich muß alles kaufen,
Was Mutti mir sagt:

Zahnpasta, Apfelsaft,
Käse und Tee,
Und wenn du noch Geld hast,
Dann eine CD.

2 Ich gehe gern einkaufen
Im Supermarkt.
Ich muß alles kaufen,
Was Mutti mir sagt:

Eine Flasche Cola,
Ein Becher Joghurt,
'ne Schachtel Pralinen,
Kartoffeln und Brot.
Zahnpasta, Apfelsaft,
Käse und Tee,
Und wenn du noch Geld hast,
Dann eine CD.

3 Ich gehe gern einkaufen
Im Supermarkt.
Ich muß alles kaufen,
Was Mutti mir sagt:

Hundert Gramm Bierwurst,
Ein Pfund Bananen,
Ein Glas Konfitüre,
Ein Pfund Tomaten.
Eine Flasche Cola,
Ein Becher Joghurt,
'ne Schachtel Pralinen,
Kartoffeln und Brot.
Zahnpasta, Apfelsaft,
Käse und Tee,
Und wenn du noch Geld hast,
Dann eine CD.

Was kaufen die Leute im Geschäft?

Listening
Reading

Use the photos to teach the names of the various containers. Ask students first to listen and give the letter of the items you nominate randomly. Ask them to repeat chorally and individually.

Teacher: *Seht euch die Fotos an. Kartoffeln – welches Foto ist das?*

Now ask students to look at the photos again and listen to the cassette in order to decide which customer buys which items in the shop. Play the first two examples and complete them with the class.

Teacher: *Hier gibt es keinen Supermarkt. Die Leute kaufen in kleinen Geschäften ein. Aber was kaufen sie? Schreibt eins bis vierzehn in euer Heft. Hört gut zu. Welches Foto ist Nummer eins?*

Note that some of the recorded items relate to more than one photo.

Was kaufen die Leute im Geschäft?

1 – Bitte schön?
– Ein Kilo Tomaten, bitte.

2 – Bitte schön?
– Einen Becher Margarine, bitte.

3 – Bitte schön?
– Ich möchte eine Dose Tomatensuppe, bitte.

4 – Was darf es sein?
– Eine Dose Cola.

5 – Bitte schön?
– Fünf Kilo Kartoffeln, bitte.
– Sonst noch etwas?
– Nein danke. Das ist alles.

6 – Was darf's sein?
– Dreihundert Gramm Käse, bitte.
– Bitte schön.

7 – Bitte schön?
– Einen Liter Milch, bitte.

8 – Was darf es sein?
– Eine Tube Zahnpasta und einen Marsriegel, bitte.
– Sonst noch etwas?
– Ja, eine Tüte Gummibärchen für meine Schwester.

9 – Ja bitte?
– Eine Flasche Apfelsaft.
– So, bitte schön. Sonst noch etwas?
– Ja. Ich möchte auch ein Glas Erdbeermarmelade.

10 – Was darf es sein?
– Ich möchte eine Packung Kaffee.
– Jacobs oder Melitta?
– Jacobs, bitte.

11 – Bitte schön?
– Ähm … ein Glas Honig, bitte.

12 – Sie wünschen?
– Eine Packung Kekse, bitte.
– So, bitte schön. Wünschen Sie noch etwas anderes?
– Ja, ich möchte auch ein Stück Seife, bitte.

13 – Ja, bitte?
– Ich möchte eine Schachtel Pralinen, bitte.
– Bitte schön.

14 – Guten Tag. Was darf es sein?
– Anderthalb Kilo Käse.
– Anderthalb Kilo Käse? So viel? Darf es sonst noch etwas sein?
– Nein danke.

Solution:

1H **2**O **3**G **4**D **5**B **6**C **7**N **8**Q, K, R
9M, E **10**I **11**L **12**F, P **13**J **14**A

Follow up by focusing students' attention on the weights, measures and containers relating to the photos. Nominate one of the items and see who is first to identify the weight, measure or container.

Teacher: *Seht euch die Fotos nochmal an. Hört gut zu. Ich sage: ‚Kekse'. Ist das eine Tüte Kekse?*
Student: *Nein. Das ist eine Packung.*
Teacher: *Gut. Also, hört gut zu. Hebt die Hand. Kaffee? usw.*

Hand the activity over to students to continue in pairs as soon as possible.

Partnerarbeit. Einkaufslisten

Listening
Speaking
Reading
Writing

Ask students to take it in turns to dictate a shopping list to their partner. Only the student dictating may refer to the text. When they have dictated at least five items they may check to see if the right list has been produced. Perform the first dialogue with a student and write the answers up.

Teacher: *Partnerarbeit. (To student:) Mach dein Buch zu. Hier ist deine Einkaufsliste: eine Dose Tomatensuppe, eine Packung Kaffee … schreib alles in dein Heft auf.*

Was kauft ihr für das Picknick?

Listening
Speaking
Reading
Writing

Divide the class into groups of four and distribute one copy of each copymaster to each group. Ask students to study the price list of food and drink items on copymaster 18 and decide in their groups how they would like to spend the 30 marks they have between them to pay for their proposed picnic. They must decide how much of each item they will need to buy to cater for their own group. Ask them to write down in the appropriate column on copymaster 17 the quantities required of each item, its total cost, and then to work out how much they will spend overall.

Teacher: *Ihr macht ein Picknick. Ihr habt 30 Mark für die ganze Gruppe, und ihr seid sehr hungrig. Was kauft ihr für das Mittagessen? Schreibt alles auf. Zum Beispiel, ihr seid vier, ja? Also, drei Wurstbrote pro Person (zwölf Wurstbrote). Zweihundert Gramm Wurst reicht für fünf Wurstbrote, also zwölf Wurstbrote, das macht ungefähr fünfhundert Gramm Wurst. Das kostet zehn Mark. Alles klar? Gut. An die Arbeit!*

After each group has finished the task, one nominee from each group should read out that group's list and the results could be collated on the board/OHP.

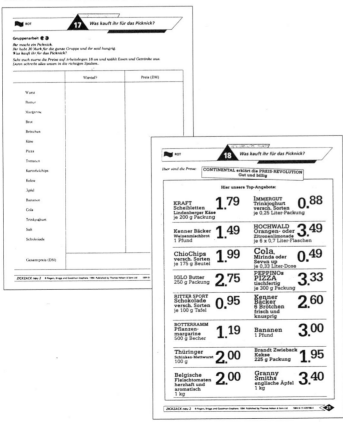

Follow up by asking students to analyse the results before them, to establish which foods and drinks were most popular.

Teacher: *Welche Getränke sind am populärsten? Und zum Essen? Wurst, oder Käse, oder …?*

 Details could be word-processed and displayed with accompanying visuals.

Einkaufszettel

Listening
Speaking
Reading
Writing

Ask students to work in pairs in order to piece together the torn shopping list. As they agree on each item on the list, they should each write it out in full on the copymaster.

Teacher: (Tear a piece of paper:) *Das Blatt Papier ist durchgerissen. Ihr habt einen durchgerissenen Einkaufszettel. Was ist darauf?* (Speaking to Partner B while pointing to Partner A's page:) *zweihundert Gramm S …?*
Student: *Schinken.*
Teacher: *Danke. Also, ich schreibe es hier auf und du hier, zweihundert Gramm Schinken.* (Write the answer up:) *zweihundert Gramm, so, nicht 200g. Alles klar? Gut. Jetzt Partnerarbeit.*

Collate the results afterwards to check that each list has been reconstructed correctly.

Ich habe den Zettel verloren. Was war darauf?

 ROT GOLD

Listening
Speaking
Reading
Writing

A type of Kim's Game. Write up a shopping list with, say, ten items. Ask students to study the list for one or two minutes before you rub it out/cover it up. Students then work in pairs to reconstruct it. As an alternative *GOLD* approach, you could just remove certain elements on the list, e.g. weight/container or the item itself, and ask students in pairs or as a whole class to fill in the gaps.

Teacher: *Lest die Einkaufsliste. Ihr habt nur zwei Minuten. Jetzt wische ich alles ab/decke ich alles. Partnerarbeit. Was war auf meiner Liste? Schreibt die Liste auf.*

Obst- und Gemüsespiele

Listening
Speaking
Reading

Visuals of fruits and vegetables labelled both in the singular and the plural. Use them to play a number of games, such as bingo. Ask students to place nine of the visuals on their grid. Say the names of the items in any order. The student to turn over all nine wins. Encourage students to take over the role of caller as soon as possible.

You could also play a variation of noughts and crosses. Students work in pairs: one has all the singular items of food, the other has the plurals. They take it in turns to place a card on the grid, saying what it is. The winner is the first one with three singulars or three plurals in a row.

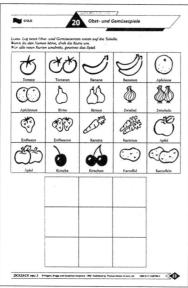

Radiorezepte

 SCHWARZ

Listening
Reading
Writing

Provide students with a list of the ingredients for making *Risotto* and *Eintopf,* but don't tell them the quantities. Ask them to listen to the *Radiorezepte* and note the quantities for each ingredient. Explain *Zutaten* if necessary, e.g. *Die Zutaten für Risotto sind Champignons, Tomaten, Margarine ...*

Teacher: *Hört zu. Radiorezepte. Hier sind die Zutaten für Risotto und Eintopf.* (Write up and ask:) *Wie heißt Zutaten auf englisch? Und Eintopf? Wieviel Gramm Champignons und so weiter braucht man?*

🔲 Radiorezepte

– Guten Tag, meine Damen und Herren. Es ist 16 Uhr. Wir bringen Ihnen ,Radiorezepte für heute'. Heute kochen wir Risotto und Eintopf. Der Risotto ist für vier Personen und der Eintopf für sechs. Haben Sie alle Bleistift und Papier zur Hand? Ja, dann fangen wir mit den Zutaten an. Zuerst für den Risotto für vier Personen. Sie brauchen folgendes:

100g Champignons
8 Tomaten
30g Margarine (das sind 3 Löffel)
4 Scheiben Schinken
300g Reis
Bouillonwürfel für einen Liter Wasser
200g Hähnchen
100g Karotten
100g Bohnen
150g Krabben
Salz, Pfeffer und Gewürze.

Und für den Eintopf für sechs Personen brauchen Sie:
30g Mehl
15g Pfeffer
15g Salz
1,5 Kilo Fleisch
2 Kilo Kartoffeln
500g Karotten
500ml Wasser
1 große Zwiebel

Ich wünsche Ihnen guten Appetit!

Solution:

As on tapescript.

Ladendieb!

Listening
Reading
Writing

Tell students they are to play the part of assistant store detectives. Four customers are being questioned about their purchases, and their answers are being checked against their till receipts and the contents of their shopping bags. Students must identify who is not telling the whole truth and write his or her name and the stolen article at the bottom of the copymaster, after the questions: *Wer ist der (die) Ladendieb(in)? Was hat er (sie) gestohlen?* To help them eliminate suspects, they should cross off purchases on the till receipts, as they are mentioned by the four customers in turn. This is a long and detailed recording, so pause the tape where indicated and check comprehension so far.

Teacher: *'Ladendieb'. Was ist denn das?*
Student: Shoplifter?
Teacher: *Richtig. Gut. Also, hier seht ihr vier Kassenbons und vier Kunden: Frau Fromm, Herr Ehrlich, Herr Klau und Frau Ernst. Wer ist ein Ladendieb? Ihr seid Ladendetektive. Ihr müßt herausfinden, wer was gestohlen hat. Seht euch die Bons an, hört gut zu und streicht die Artikel durch, so.* (Play the first item, and point to the example, in which *2kg Schweineschnitzel* has been crossed out.)

 Ladendieb!

Det.:	Guten Tag, meine Damen und Herren. Ich bin Ladendetektiv, und ich muß Ihnen leider ein paar Fragen stellen. Wie heißen Sie, bitte?
Frau F.:	Fromm. Frau Fromm heiße ich.
Det.:	Also, was für Fleisch haben Sie gekauft?
Frau F.:	Zwei Kilo Schweineschnitzel.
Det.:	Danke. Und Sie, wie ist Ihr Name?
Frau E.:	Frau Ernst, junger Mann.
Det.:	Also, Frau Ernst. Was für Fleisch haben Sie gekauft?
Frau E.:	Ich? Ich habe kein Fleisch gekauft. Nur Wurst.
Det.:	Und Sie ...? Wie heißen Sie, bitte?
Herr K.:	Egon. Egon Klau. Anderthalb Kilo Rouladen.
Det.:	Danke. Und Sie? Wie ist Ihr Name, bitte?
Herr E.:	Ja, ich heiße Herr Ehrlich. Und ich habe ein Kilo Schweinebraten und ein Kilo Rinderleber gekauft.

(Pause tape)

Det.:	Und Käse?
Herr E.:	Ja. Dreihundert Gramm. Das heißt, zweihundert Gramm Wilstermarschkäse und hundert Gramm französischen Weichkäse.
Det.:	Und Sie, Frau Fromm? Was für Käse haben Sie gekauft?
Frau F.:	Ich habe keinen Käse gekauft.
Det.:	Frau Ernst?
Frau E.:	Tja, Gouda habe ich gekauft – zweihundert Gramm, glaube ich.
Det.:	Zweihundert Gramm, danke. Und Sie, Herr Klau?
Herr K.:	Nein, ich habe keinen Käse gekauft.
Det.:	Also, kein Käse für Herrn Klau. Und Wurst?
Herr K.:	Ja, dreihundert Gramm Salami.
Det.:	Frau Ernst?
Frau E.:	Hundert Gramm Jagdwurst.
Det.:	Herr Ehrlich?
Herr E.:	Wurst haben Sie gesagt? Nein, ich habe keine Wurst gekauft.
Det.:	Frau Fromm?
Frau F.:	Ja, ich habe zweihundert Gramm Leberwurst gekauft.

(Pause tape)

Det.:	Und haben Sie Fisch oder Fischgerichte gekauft?
Frau F.:	Fisch? Nein. Keinen Fisch.
Det.:	Frau Ernst – Sie haben auch keinen Fisch gekauft?
Frau E.:	Doch. Ich habe eine Dose Sardinen gekauft.
Det.:	Und Sie, Herr Ehrlich?
Herr E.:	Ja, ich habe einen Becher Heringssalat gekauft.
Det.:	Einen Becher Heringssalat. Danke. Herr Klau?
Herr K.:	Nein. Ich habe keinen Fisch gekauft.

(Pause tape)

Det.:	Haben Sie Butter oder Margarine gekauft, Herr Klau?
Herr K.:	Nein – keins von beiden.
Det.:	Frau Ernst?
Frau E.:	Butter oder Margarine? Ja, zwei Becher Margarine.
Det.:	Herr Ehrlich?
Herr E.:	Ja – ein Stück Butter.
Det.:	Und Sie, Frau Fromm? Was für Butter oder Margarine haben Sie gekauft?

Frau F.:	Fünfhundert Gramm Butter und einen Becher Margarine.
Det.:	Also, Butter und Margarine.

(Pause tape)

	Haben Sie auch Kekse gekauft?
Frau F.:	Ja.
Det.:	Wieviel?
Frau F.:	Eine Packung.
Det.:	Und Sie, Herr Klau?
Herr K.:	Ja, ich auch. Eine Packung Kekse.
Det.:	Herr Ehrlich?
Herr E.:	Nein – keine Kekse.
Det.:	Frau Ernst?
Frau E.:	Auch keine Kekse.

(Pause tape)

Det.:	Na, Frau Ernst, was für Getränke haben Sie gekauft?
Frau E.:	Getränke? Ja, einen Liter Milch, sechs Flaschen Pils und eine Packung Tee.
Det.:	Frau Fromm?
Frau F.:	Drei Flaschen Wein.
Det.:	Herr Ehrlich?
Herr E.:	Nein. Keine Getränke.
Det.:	Herr Klau?
Herr K.:	Ja, ich habe eine Flasche Sherry und eine Packung Kaffee gekauft.

(Pause tape)

Det.:	Aha, und haben Sie Waschmittel oder Seife gekauft?
Herr K.:	Ja, eine Packung Conlei und ein Stück Seife.
Det.:	Herr Ehrlich?
Herr E.:	Ich habe eine Packung Persil gekauft.
Det.:	Frau Fromm?
Frau F.:	Hm, ja, ich habe ein Stück Seife gekauft.
Det.:	Frau Ernst?
Frau E.:	Nein – kein Waschmittel und keine Seife.

(Pause tape)

Det.:	Ist das alles, Frau Ernst?
Frau E.:	Ja, ich glaube schon.
Det.:	In Ihrer Tasche war auch eine Tafel Schokolade.
Frau E.:	Oh, Entschuldigung. Das ist richtig. Ich habe auch Schokolade gekauft.
Det.:	Danke. Frau Fromm?
Frau F.:	Ja, das ist alles, glaube ich.
Det.:	In Ihrer Tasche war auch ein Liter Milch.
Frau F.:	Ach, ja, Milch. Das habe ich vergessen.
Det.:	Herr Klau – ist das alles?

Herr K.:	Ja.
Det.:	In Ihrer Tasche war auch eine Flasche Whisky.
Herr K.:	Ach ja, genau.
Det.:	Herr Ehrlich, ist das alles?
Herr E.:	Ja, sicher.
Det.:	Danke.

Solution:

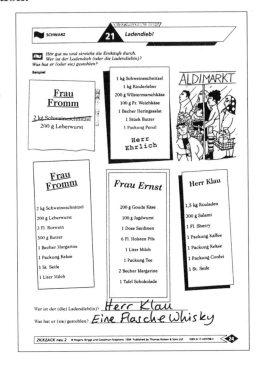

Using word-processing or desktop-publishing students, could produce a supermarket store guide, incorporating visuals and a variety of text styles. Using CD-ROM they could generate their own multi-media guide, with intercom messages to shoppers related directly to the pictures of goods which appear on the screen.

Students may now attempt the *Lernziel 2* activities in the *Selbstbedienung* section on page 33 of the students' book. See below for more details.

Selbstbedienung sb

Lernziel 1
Welches Geschäft ist das?

 GOLD

Photographs of shop windows. Students must write down the name of each shop.

Solution :

1 Das ist die Bäckerei.

2 Das ist das Sportgeschäft.

3 Das ist die Metzgerei.

4 Das ist die Drogerie.

5 Das ist die Apotheke.

6 Das ist das Schuhgeschäft.

Wo sind die Sachen?

 SCHWARZ

A problem-solving activity, in which students must identify where the named articles are concealed.

Solution:

Der Käse ist in Tasche 1.

Die Schokolade ist in Tasche 2.

Die Cola ist in Tasche 3.

Die Gummibärchen sind in Tasche 4.

Die Wurst ist in Tasche 5.

Purzelwörter

 SCHWARZ

Jumbled items of shopping. Students must unjumble them and write the name of the shop where they could buy them.

Solution

1 Buch – in der Buchhandlung

2 Zahnpasta – in der Drogerie

3 Hustenbonbons – in der Apotheke

4 Sandalen – im Schuhgeschäft

5 Pullover – im Kleidergeschäft

Lernziel 2
Wieviel?

 SCHWARZ

Students must match containers/weights to the named items.

Solution:

Eine Tube Zahnpasta

Zweihundert Gramm Käse

Ein Liter Milch

Ein Becher Margarine

Fünf Kilo Kartoffeln

Eine Tüte Gummibärchen

Eine Packung Kaffee

Eine Dose Cola

Im Doofimarkt!

 GOLD

Students must draw and label items of shopping with silly containers/packaging, as in the example.

Meine Einkaufsliste

 GOLD

Students should put together a shopping list using the quantities given and the visuals.

Solution:

ein Kilo Bananen

zwei Flaschen Bier

300 Gramm Wurst

eine Flasche Limonade

ein Liter Milch

eine Packung Kaffee

ein Pfund Äpfel

ein Stück Seife

ein Becher Margarine

ein Glas Honig

Bildvokabeln. Im Supermarkt *Reading*

This illustration about different items for sale in a supermarket is not intended for detailed exploitation, but provides students with the opportunity to expand their vocabulary.

A version of the artwork is provided on copymaster for students to label themselves and to colour.

Grammar exercises 9-11 on copymasters 76 and 77 are based on the material in this chapter.

76-77 +82

The students' personal profile for this chapter is on copymaster 84.

84

After completing work on this chapter, check whether any further reinforcement is appropriate from the video material, Activity Box cards and Assessment Support Pack tasks.

Main teaching points

Lernziel 1: **Modes of transport**

Lernziel 2: **Travel by bus and train**

Language presented:

- *Mit dem/der*
- Modes of transport
- *Wie kommst du zum/zur/nach ...?*
- *Einfach/hin und zurück*

- *Von welchem Gleis?*
- *Abfahren/ankommen*
- *Welche Linie ist das?*
- Language for bus and railway travel

> Before beginning work on this chapter, check where the video material, Activity Box cards and Assessment Support Pack tasks will be most appropriate.

Lernziel 1
Verkehrsmittel

Presentation of language (modes of transport)

Listening
Speaking

103–112

Display the transport flashcards and ask students how they travel to various places.

Teacher: *Du willst zum Schwimmbad. Wie kommst du dahin?* (Point to flashcards in turn and say:) *Mit dem Zug? Mit dem Wagen? Mit der Straßenbahn? Zu Fuß?*

Student: *Zu Fuß.*

Teacher: (Continue similarly with other places, e.g.:) *Du willst zur Disco/zum Kino/nach* (+ nearby place name). *Wie kommst du dahin?*

Write up the expressions for travelling by different modes of transport on the board, and repeat the list of means of transport until students are confident to reproduce them without direct prompting. Play some of the flashcard games with the class and hand over the activities to them as soon as they are confident.

Wie kommst du dahin?

Listening
Speaking
Reading
Writing

36 | 23 ROT

Ask students to look at the pictures and listen to the recording and say which picture fits which conversation.

Teacher: *Seht euch die Bilder an und hört gut zu. Welches Bild ist das?* (Play the first one.)

Student: *Bild C.*

Teacher: *Richtig. Jetzt machen wir weiter.*

Wie kommst du dahin?

1 – Wie kommst du zur Schule?
 – Ich gehe zu Fuß. Es sind nur zehn Minuten.

2 – Wie kommst du zum Sportplatz?
 – Zum Sportplatz fahre ich immer mit dem Rad.

3 – Und wo wohnt deine Freundin?
 – In Gütersloh. Das sind zehn Kilometer von hier.
 – So weit? Fährst du immer mit dem Bus?
 – Nein, mit dem Mofa.

4 – Ich muß morgen nach Köln.
 – Und wie kommst du dahin?
 – Mit dem Zug. Mein Mofa ist kaputt.

5 – Kommst du heute nachmittag mit zum Hallenbad?
 – Ja, gern.

53

– Fahren wir mit der Straßenbahn?
– Ja, von mir aus.

6 – Du kommst doch heute abend zur Disco, oder? Sie beginnt um acht Uhr.
– Acht Uhr? Oh, dann muß ich mit dem Bus fahren.

7 – Kommst du morgen mit dem Moped zu Ullas Party?
– Nein, mein Vater bringt mich mit dem Wagen hin.

8 – Du fährst nächste Woche nach England?
– Nein, ich fahre nicht, ich fliege.

9 – Was machst du in den Sommerferien?
– Wir fahren nach England.
– Fahrt ihr mit dem Auto? In England muß man links fahren!
– Nein, wir fahren mit dem Zug und mit der Fähre.

Solution:

1C **2**A **3**B **4**D **5**E **6**I **7**G **8**H **9**F

Follow up with the copymaster, in which students choose the correct options to fill in the gaps.

Solution:

1 zu	**5** mit der	**8** fliege
2 mit dem	**6** mit dem	**9** mit dem
3 mit dem	**7** mit dem	mit dem
4 mit dem	mit dem	mit der

Wie fahren sie dahin?

Listening
Speaking
Reading
Writing

A gap-filling exercise giving written practice of the means of transport.

Teacher: *Schreibt die Sätze in euer Heft und füllt die Lücken aus. Zum Beispiel* (talk students through an example).

Solution:

1 mit dem Rad

2 fliege

3 mit der Straßenbahn

4 mit dem Mofa

5 mit dem Bus

6 mit dem Zug/mit der Fähre

7 zu Fuß

8 mit dem Auto

> 🖥 Using a word-processor, students could produce labels for the means of transport and display them in the classroom and/or corridors and stick them in their books. They could also produce a concept keyboard overlay version.

Partnerarbeit. Wie kommst du zum Sportplatz?

Listening
Speaking

Tell students to take it in turns to pick a destination from the visuals, and ask each other the question: *‚Wie kommst du zum/zur/nach ...?'*

Teacher: *Partnerarbeit. Stellt und beantwortet Fragen.* (To one student:) *Wie kommst du zum Sportplatz?*
Student: *Mit dem Rad.*
Teacher: *Richtig. Jetzt bist du dran.*

Follow up by conducting a class survey relating to means of travel. Revise if necessary *zum/zur* and *nach*. Then ask students to tell you how they travel to different places and record the results on the board/OHP. You could ask them to conduct the survey themselves in groups, following an agreed number of questions/destinations which you write up. Groups could then report back to the rest of the class and you could collate their findings.

Some students may wish to take the process one stage further and produce bargraphs for display or enter the details in a data-base. The results could be merged with the data from other classes.

Teacher: *Wir machen jetzt eine Umfrage. Wie kommt man dahin? Zum Beispiel* (to one student:) *Wie kommst du zur Schule?*
Student: *Zu Fuß.*
Teacher: (To the rest:) *Und ihr? Wer kommt zu Fuß? Hebt die Hand.* (Identify destinations with the class and write them up.) *Gruppenarbeit. Stellt einander die Frage: ,Wie kommst du ..?' Macht Notizen, so* (write up columns to demonstrate).

Sonntags bin ich immer müde! *Listening Speaking Reading Writing*

A written description of a long journey undertaken each week by a teenager to visit her grandma. Ask students to read the text, listen to the recording and look at the four sets of symbols depicting journeys. They must decide which set of symbols fits the description.

Teacher: *Lest den Text und hört gut zu. Asla beschreibt, wie sie jeden Sonntag zu ihrer Großmutter kommt. Das ist eine lange, komplizierte Reise. Wie kommt sie dahin? Wählt die passende Antwort: A, B, C oder D.*

Sonntags bin ich immer müde!
– Jeden Sonntag gehe ich zu meiner Großmutter. Sie wohnt in einem Dorf auf dem Land. Ich stehe früh auf und fahre mit dem Rad zum Bahnhof. Dann fahre ich mit dem Zug nach Hamburg. In Hamburg fahre ich mit der Straßenbahn zum Busbahnhof. Dann fahre ich zwanzig Minuten mit dem Bus zu dem Dorf, wo meine Großmutter wohnt. Von der Bushaltestelle gehe ich dann fünf Minuten zu Fuß. Es ist nicht sehr weit, aber es dauert immer mehr als zwei Stunden.

Solution:
C
Students working individually, in pairs or in groups could use the other sets of symbols to put together their own tiring journeys. Encourage them to re-use as much of the original text as possible. They could then read aloud or give to other students their texts

and challenge them to work out which set of symbols represents their chosen journey.

Teacher: *Jetzt macht ihr eine solche Reise. Wählt Symbole (A, B oder D) und schreibt euren eigenen Text mit Hilfe des Texts von Asla. (Lest euren Text vor. Welche Symbole sind das?)*

Wie fährst du? *Reading Writing*

This final activity in *Lernziel 1* draws together the language already presented and practised relating to modes of transport, and extends it to include some language of views and opinions, which will make more demands on abler students.

Tell students to read the texts, in which young people give their views on different modes of transport, and their reasons for using them, and when any new language has been clarified, get students to pick out from the text the advantages and disadvantages of the modes of transport and to produce their findings in chart form.

Teacher: *Lest den Text. Was sagen die Jugendlichen? Was sind die Vorteile und Nachteile von den verschiedenen Verkehrsmitteln? Schreibt die Tabelle in euer Heft und füllt sie aus.*

Follow up by asking students how they prefer to travel and why. To help get them started, students should call out any reasons they can think of for using various means of transport and you assemble a list on the board. Examples could include: *Das ist billig; das fährt schnell; das ist praktisch; das macht fit,* etc.

Teacher: *Fahrt ihr am liebsten mit dem Rad, oder mit dem Bus, oder ...?* (To one student:) *Fährst du am liebsten mit dem Rad?*
Student: *Nein, ich fahre am liebsten mit dem Auto.*
Teacher: *Warum?*
Student: *Das fährt schnell.*

Students may now attempt the *Lernziel 1* activities in the *Selbstbedienung* section on page 42 of the students' book. See page 61 of this book for more details.

Lernziel 2
Wie komme ich dahin?

Entschuldigung ... Ich suche den Bahnhof

Listening
Speaking
Reading

A straightforward matching exercise as a lead-in to the language needed when using the public transport system. It follows logically the process of getting to stations, bus stops, etc. before considering how to use the transport system.

Teacher: *Seite 39. Seht euch die Bilder an und hört gut zu. Was paßt wozu?* (Play the first one.)
Student: *1E.*
Teacher: *Gut. Ihr schreibt 1E in euer Heft.*

 Entschuldigung ... Ich suche den Bahnhof

1 – Entschuldigung. Gibt es hier in der Nähe eine U-Bahnstation?
– Die U-Bahn ist da drüben, sehen Sie?
2 – Entschuldigung, wo ist hier der Busbahnhof? Ist das weit von hier?
– Den Busbahnhof finden Sie hier gleich um die Ecke.
3 – Entschuldigung ... ich suche den Bahnhof.
– Den Bahnhof suchen Sie? Hier geradeaus etwa fünfhundert Meter auf der linken Seite.
– Danke schön.
4 – Entschuldigung. Ich muß nach Thesdorf. Wie komme ich am besten dahin?
– Nach Thesdorf – am besten fahren Sie mit der S-Bahn.
5 – Wo ist die nächste Straßenbahnhaltestelle, bitte?
– Da drüben, sehen Sie? Vor der Post.

Solution:

1E **2**A **3**B **4**D **5**C

Partnerarbeit. Der Bus nach Schenefeld kommt

Listening
Speaking
Reading

A pairwork activity focusing on bus routes and providing practice of numbers in a useful context. Revise numbers up to the nineties, if necessary, before expecting students to ask and answer the questions relating to the bus routes. Talk students through the model dialogue in the students' book, to demonstrate.

Teacher: *Hier ist eine Bushaltestelle, und hier kommt der Bus nach Schenefeld. Das ist die Linie 37. Und der Bus nach Pinneberg? Das ist die Linie ...? Partnerarbeit. Stellt einander die Frage: ,Welche Linie ist das?' Zum Beispiel ...*

Welche Linie ist das?

Listening
Speaking
Reading

A plan of the railway network around Munich, showing the *S-Bahn* lines and several underground lines. Talk students through the details on the plan, making sure they have the opportunity to hear and pronounce (some of) the station names. First, play the recording of station announcements, and students should locate the place names on the map and say which line it is each time.

Teacher: *Seht euch den Plan an. Das hier ist München in Süddeutschland. Und das sind Bahnhöfe – wiederholt: Münchener Hauptbahnhof, Marienplatz ... Hört zu und findet die Bahnhöfe. Welche Linie ist das? Nummer eins? Petershausen?*
Student: *Das ist die Linie S2.*
Teacher: *Richtig.*

 Welche Linie ist das?

1 – Petershausen. Petershausen.
2 – Olympiazentrum. Olympiazentrum.
3 – Wolfratshausen. Wolfratshausen.
4 – Geltendorf. Geltendorf.
5 – Herrsching. Herrsching.
6 – Ebersberg. Ebersberg.

Solution:

1S2 **2**U2 **3**S7 **4**S4 **5**S5 **6**S5

Partnerarbeit

Listening
Speaking
Reading

Use the model dialogue in the students' book to prepare students for the pairwork task. Focus their attention on: *Ich muß nach ...; Welche Linie ist das?*; and *Das ist die Linie ...* Then ask students to perform the model dialogue in pairs before producing their own variants.

Teacher: *Seht euch den Plan an. Ihr seid am Münchener Hauptbahnhof. Was sagt man, wenn man Auskunft über die Linien braucht?* (To the first cued student:) *Stell deine Frage: ‚Entschuldigung. Ich muß nach ...'*
Student: *Entschuldigung. Ich muß nach Ebersberg. Welche Linie ist das?*
Teacher: *Ebersberg ist die Linie S5.*
Student: *Vielen Dank.*
Teacher: *Nichts zu danken.* (To the rest of the class, after completing two or three further examples:) *Macht weitere Dialoge.*

München Hauptbahnhof

   SCHWARZ

Listening
Reading

As a *SCHWARZ* extension, you can play students the dialogues in which the information being sought is embedded in more demanding language. Tell students they are going to hear a series of short dialogues involving people in and around Munich wanting to go out on day trips to various tourist attractions. Students must consult the map and write down which line the tourists must take in order to reach their destinations. Draw their attention to the word *umsteigen* and see if they can say what it means.

Teacher: *Hört gut zu. Wohin fahren die Passagiere? Fahren die Passagiere mit der S-Bahn oder mit der U-Bahn? Welche Linie ist das? Müssen sie umsteigen? Wie heißt ,umsteigen' auf englisch? Zum Beispiel, ich bin in Petershausen, und ich will nach Freiheit. Das ist die S2 bis zum Marienplatz. Am Marienplatz muß ich umsteigen, dann ist es die U6 bis Freiheit. Toll, 'change trains'.*
Hört gut zu und schreibt die Antworten in euer Heft. (Complete the first one with students.)

München Hauptbahnhof

1 – München Hauptbahnhof. München Hauptbahnhof.
– Entschuldigung. Ich möchte den Aussichtsturm in Ebersberg besuchen. Fährt dieser Zug nach Ebersberg?
– Ja, der Zug fährt nach Ebersberg.
– Schön. Vielen Dank.

2 – Ebersberg. Ebersberg.
– Entschuldigung. Ich muß zum Olympiazentrum. Welche Linie ist das, bitte?
– Sie fahren mit der S5 bis München Hauptbahnhof, dann müssen Sie umsteigen und mit der U-Bahn weiterfahren.
– Vielen Dank.
– Nichts zu danken.

3 – München Hauptbahnhof. München Hauptbahnhof.
– Ich möchte St. Alto besuchen.
– Dann müssen Sie nach Altomünster fahren.
– Muß ich umsteigen?
– Ja, in Dachau. Dort fahren Sie mit dem Bus nach Altomünster weiter.

4 – München Hauptbahnhof. München Hauptbahnhof.
– Wie komme ich am besten zum Ammersee, bitte?
– Am besten fahren Sie mit der S-Bahn nach Herrsching.

5 – Pasing. Pasing.
– Entschuldigung. Fährt dieser Zug nach Tutzing? Ich will nämlich den Starnberger See sehen.
– Nach Tutzing? Ja.
– Gut. Danke schön.
– Bitte schön.

Solution:

1 S5 2 S5/U2 3 S2 + Bus 4 S5 5 S6

Einmal nach Pfarrkirchen, bitte

Listening
Speaking
Reading

Tell students they are going to hear two dialogues, in which railway tickets are purchased. See if they can work out each time if a single or return ticket is required, before following the text in their books.

Teacher: *Hört zu – wir sind auf dem Bahnhof.* (Play the two dialogues.) *Also, wie war das: einmal, zweimal ...?*

Student: *Einmal.*
Teacher: *Nach Kiel?*
Student: *Nach Pfarrkirchen.*
Teacher: *Einfach oder hin und zurück?*
Student: *Einfach.*
Teacher: *Wie heißt ,einfach' auf englisch?* etc.

Einmal nach Pfarrkirchen, bitte

1 – Einmal nach Pfarrkirchen, bitte.
  – Einfach oder hin und zurück?
  – Einfach.
  – Einmal einfach nach Pfarrkirchen ... 27 Mark.
  – Bitte schön.
  – Danke.

2 – Einmal nach Pfarrkirchen, bitte.
  – Einfach oder hin und zurück?
  – Hin und zurück.
  – Eine Rückfahrkarte nach Pfarrkirchen ... 54 Mark.
  – Bitte schön.

Einfach oder hin und zurück? *Listening Speaking Reading Writing*

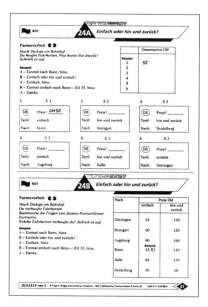

This copymaster practises the language introduced relating to purchasing rail tickets. Students should complete the information-gap activity in pairs. Partner A has information about his/her destination, and the type and number of tickets required, and must find out the cost of each ticket (s)he wants to buy, and also fill in on the grid the total cost of tickets purchased. Partner B works at the station ticket office and has the prices of single and return tickets to each destination. (S)he should make a

note of how many tickets are bought each time. Work through the model dialogue.

Teacher: *Partnerarbeit. Partner(in) A – wohin willst du fahren? Wie viele Fahrkarten kaufst du? Ist das einfach oder hin und zurück? Was kostet das? Frag deinen Partner/deine Partnerin, und schreib es auf. Was kostet das zusammen? Schreib es hier auf (pointing to the grid). Partner(in) B – du arbeitest am Schalter. Wohin fährt dein(e) Partner(in)? Was kostet das? Schreib auf, wie viele Fahrkarten du verkaufst.*

Partnerarbeit. Abfahrt *Listening Speaking Reading*

A section from a departures timetable at a railway station and a model dialogue to cue pairwork dealing with understanding information about train departure and arrival times. Talk students through the information and help them to work out the meaning of *Gleis*. Explain how the verb *ankommen* works, i.e. it is a separable verb, and although students have encountered similar constructions in Stage 1, you may like to refer them to the *auf einen Blick* section, and abler students to the explanation of separable verbs in the *Grammatik: Überblick* (students' book page 116). Revise also and practise the 24-hour times with them, until they are happy about the dialogues they must produce themselves.

Teacher: *Seht euch die Tabelle an. Das sind die Abfahrtszeiten der Züge, und hier sind auch die Ankunftszeiten. Hier steht auch, welcher Gleis das ist. Wann fährt der nächste Zug nach Bielefeld? usw.*

Auskunft *Listening Reading Writing*

Before doing this activity, check that students understand *HBF (Hauptbahnhof)*, *abfahren* and *Verspätung*. Then ask students to listen to the dialogues and decide whether the details on the copymaster are correct each time. Bring out the meaning of *Zuschlag* and that it is usually to be paid on *Intercity* and *Eurocity* trains. If students note that a piece of information is false, they should write the correct details alongside. Note that some of the details, for example train numbers, are not always specified on the recording.

Teacher: *Seht euch die Auskunft für die Züge an.
Nummer eins. D-Zug – das heißt direkt. Dieser Zug
fährt nach Hamburg. Er fährt um 15 Uhr 30 und
hat fünf Minuten Verspätung. Wie heißt das auf
englisch ‚Verspätung'? Gut. Und ‚Zuschlag'
bedeutet, daß man bei bestimmten Zügen extra
bezahlt. Hört zu. Sind die Informationen richtig
oder falsch? Schreibt es hier auf. Wenn falsch, wie
ist es richtig?*

Auskunft

1 – Guten Tag. Wann fährt der nächste Zug nach
   Hamburg?
   – Um 15.30 Uhr. Aber der Zug hat fünf Minuten
   Verspätung.
   – Ist das ein Intercity?
   – Nein, das ist ein D-Zug: D dreißig
   einundsechzig.
   – Muß man da Zuschlag bezahlen?
   – Nein.
   – Von welchem Gleis fährt der Zug ab?
   – Von Gleis drei.

2 – Wann fährt der nächste Zug nach Verl, bitte?
   – Das ist ein Eilzug, und er fährt planmäßig um
   16.17 Uhr von Gleis sieben ab. Er hat aber
   leider dreizehn Minuten Verspätung.

3 – Wann fährt der nächste Zug nach Kiel, bitte?
   – Um 16.25 Uhr von Gleis zwei.
   – Muß man da Zuschlag bezahlen?
   – Ja, sieben Mark. Das ist ein Intercity.

4 – Fährt der nächste Zug nach Emden um 17.00
   Uhr?
   – Ja, ein D-Zug von Gleis vier.
   – Muß man da Zuschlag bezahlen?
   – Nein.

5 – Guten Tag. Ich muß nach Bonn. Wann fährt da
   der nächste Zug, bitte?
   – Um 17.09 Uhr haben Sie einen Intercity nach
   Bonn Hauptbahnhof.
   – Muß man da Zuschlag bezahlen?
   – Ja, fünf Mark 50.
   – Von welchem Gleis fährt der Zug ab?
   – Von Gleis acht.

6 – Wann fährt der nächste Zug nach Köln, bitte?
   – Der nächste Zug fährt planmäßig um 17.51 Uhr
   von Gleis vier ab, hat aber vier Minuten
   Verspätung.
   – Was für ein Zug ist das – ein Eilzug, oder?
   – Das ist ein D-Zug.
   – Muß man da Zuschlag bezahlen?
   – Nein.

7 – Wann fährt der Intercity nach München, bitte?
   – Um 18.02 Uhr von Gleis eins. Haben Sie schon
   Ihre Fahrkarte gekauft?
   – Nein, noch nicht.
   – Man muß nämlich sieben Mark Zuschlag
   bezahlen.
   – Ach so, danke.

8 – Von welchem Gleis fährt der Zug nach
   Tübingen ab, bitte?
   – Der D-Zug, um 19.25 Uhr?
   – Ja, ich glaube.
   – Gleis eins. Aber machen Sie schnell. Der Zug
   hat keine Verspätung, und es ist schon 19.20
   Uhr.
   – Ja, sicher. Danke.
   – Bitte. Gute Reise.

9 – Wann fährt der nächste Intercity nach
   Osnabrück?
   – Morgen vormittag.
   – Morgen?
   – Ja, der nächste Zug nach Osnabrück ist der
   letzte heute – das ist ein Eilzug. Der fährt erst
   um 21.00 Uhr von Gleis sechs ab.
   – Aber da muß man keinen Zuschlag bezahlen,
   oder.
   – Nein – gar keinen.
   – Danke schön.

Solution:

Follow up by asking students to work in pairs, using
the now completed copymaster, to practise the
various question forms.

Teacher: *Partnerarbeit. Stellt und beantwortet
Fragen. Zum Beispiel* (complete one dialogue with a
student in front of the class).

Abfahrt-Ankunft

Listening
Speaking
Reading

A reading comprehension and pairwork exercise continuing the theme of understanding information in railway stations. Ask students to take it in turns to ask and answer the questions they have on their respective sheets.

Teacher: *Partnerarbeit. Seht euch die Tabellen an. Stellt oder beantwortet die Fragen. Zum Beispiel, Partner(in) B stellt die erste Frage: ‚Wann fährt der erste Zug nach Elmshorn?' usw.*

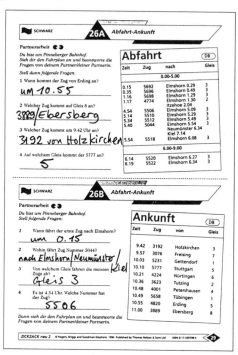

Using a word-processing package, students could customise local bus and railway timetables for German-speaking visitors.

Zurückbleiben, bitte

 SCHWARZ

Listening
Speaking

These recordings are intended to plunge students into the reality of coping with railway announcements. Gist comprehension only is required. Ask students to listen to the recordings two or three times in order to pick out where possible, destinations, times and other information.

Zurückbleiben, bitte

1 – Zurückbleiben, bitte.

2 – In Richtung Bergedorf, bitte zurückbleiben.

3 – Gleis 14 bitte Vorsicht.

4 – Auf Gleis 12, bitte einsteigen und Türen schließen. Vorsicht bei der Abfahrt.

5 – Auf Gleis 13, bitte einsteigen. Türen schließen selbsttätig. Vorsicht bei der Abfahrt.

6 – Andere Seite aussteigen.

7 – Ein Ausruf. Frau Dorothee Grabo aus Leipzig. Ich wiederhole, Frau Dorothee Grabo aus Leipzig, bitte kommen Sie zur Aufsicht auf Gleis 7.

8 – Hauptbahnhof. Bitte alle aussteigen, alle aussteigen bitte. Dieser Zug endet hier. Alle aussteigen, bitte.

9 – Frau Paech wird dringend gebeten, zur Aufsicht zwischen den Gleisen 11 und 12 zu kommen.

10 – Auf Gleis 13 steht bereit der IC 79 ‚Enzian' nach Zürich, planmäßige Abfahrt 13.02 Uhr. Der Zug fährt über Hannover, Göttingen, Fulda, Frankfurt, Mannheim, Karlsruhe, Offenburg, Freiburg und Basel. Für diesen Zug ist ein IC-Zuschlag erforderlich. Die Wagen in der 1. Klasse stehen im Abschnitt A außerhalb der Halle. Die Wagen der 2. Klasse in den Abschnitten B, C, D and E.

Einige Informationen

Reading

Two fairly demanding texts focusing on buying tickets – purchasing tickets from a machine, and date stamping one's ticket before travelling. Ask students to read the texts and answer the *richtig/falsch* questions alongside them. Refer them to the word list, where necessary.

Solution:

Am Automaten

1 richtig **2** falsch **3** richtig

Vergessen Sie nicht, Ihre Fahrkarte zu entwerten

1 richtig **2** richtig **3** falsch

Students may now attempt the *Lernziel 2* activites in the *Selbstbedienung* section on page 43 of the students' book. See below for more details.

Selbstbedienung **sb**

Lernziel 1
Gespräche

 GOLD

Two dialogues, in which various means of transport are mentioned. These are exploited by multiple-choice exercises. Ask students to choose the correct answer each time. Consolidate in written form.

Solution:

1 a Samstag **b** Evi Bamm **c** München
 d Wagen **e** Bahn

2 a London **b** der Bahn **c** der Fähre
 d der Bahn **e** DM 1 200; 14

Ein Brief aus Perpignan

 SCHWARZ

A letter followed by comprehension questions.

Solution:

1 Er macht Ferien da.

2 Am 10. August.

3 Mit der Fähre und mit dem Zug.

4 In Hannover.

Lernziel 2
Was ist das?

 GOLD

Photographs taken from unusual angles. Students should give the name for each one.

Solution:

1 eine Bushaltestelle

2 ein Fahrrad

3 eine Fahrkarte

4 ein Zug

5 eine Straßenbahn

Zweimal nach Hamburg, bitte

 ROT

Students should write mini-dialogues based on the information given.

Solution:

1 – Zweimal nach Hamburg, bitte. Hin und zurück.
   – Fünfundsechzig Mark, bitte.

2 – Einmal einfach nach Kiel, bitte.
   – Dreiunddreißig Mark fünfzig, bitte.

3 – Dreimal nach Bonn, bitte. Hin und zurück.
   – Dreiundneunzig Mark, bitte.

4 – Einmal einfach nach Osnabrück, bitte.
   – Neunzehn Mark fünfzig, bitte.

5 – Zweimal einfach nach München, bitte.
   – Zweiundachtzig Mark, bitte.

6 – Einmal nach Köln, bitte. Hin und zurück.
   – Siebenundvierzig Mark, bitte.

Wann fährt der nächste Zug?

 SCHWARZ

Students should consult the section of a train departures timetable and answer the questions following it.

1 Um 19.02 Uhr.

2 Um 19.56 Uhr.

3 Von Gleis 3.

4 Vier Züge.

5 Eine Stunde und 51 Minuten.

Bildvokabeln. Am Bahnhof

Reading
Writing

This illustration of the inside of a railway station is not intended for detailed exploitation, but provides students with the opportunity to expand their vocabulary.

A version of the artwork is provided on copymaster for students to label themselves and to colour.

> Students could provide a concept keyboard overlay version of the *Bildvokabeln.*

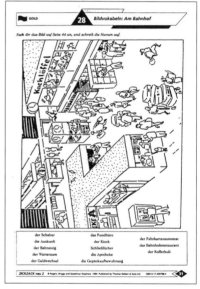

Steffi

Reading

Another tale of the indomitable Steffi, intended for entertainment.

> Grammar exercises 12-14 on copymaster 77 are based on the material in this chapter.
>
>
> 77 +82

> The students' personal profile for this chapter is on copymaster 84.
>
>
> 84

> After completing work on this chapter, check whether any further reinforcement is appropriate from the video material, Activity Box cards and Assessment Support Pack tasks.

Main teaching points

Lernziel 1: Describing people

Lernziel 2: Opinions about people

Language presented:

- *Aussehen/tragen*
- Colours
- Clothing vocabulary

- Adjectives of appearance and character
- Adjectival agreement with the accusative case
- Accusative pronouns *ihn/sie*

Before beginning work on this chapter, check where the video material, Activity Box cards and Assessment Support Pack tasks will be most appropriate.

Lernziel 1

Sieht schön aus!

Presentation of language (adjectives describing appearance)

*Listening
Speaking
Reading*

Present the following language by using students as models, writing the phrases on the board/OHP as they occur:

Er/Sie ist groß, mittelgroß, klein, ziemlich groß/klein, ganz groß/klein.

Er/Sie hat lange, mittellange, kurze, glatte, lockige, braune, blonde, rote, schwarze Haare.

Er/Sie hat braune, blaue, grüne, graue Augen.

When the majority of this language has been used, test students' understanding of it by referring to other members of the class.

Teacher: *Nun, Simon. Er ist mittelgroß und hat kurze, blonde Haare. Stimmt das oder nicht?*

Ask students to try and correct the part that is wrong. Do the same for other members of the class, but include a few correct descriptions as well. Make sure students are familiar, at least receptively, with this new language before going on to the next activity.

Wer ist das?

*Listening
Speaking
Reading*

   **SCHWARZ**

Written descriptions of eight teenagers, focusing on physical features, including height, hair length and colour and colour of eyes. Ask students to read the descriptions in the speech bubbles and match them to the pictures.

Teacher: *Seht euch diese Bilder an und lest die Texte. Welches Bild paßt zu welchem Text?* (Complete one or two with the class.) *Zum Beispiel, wer ist A? Sie ist mittelgroß. Sie hat lange, blonde Haare und blaue Augen.*

Student: *Anja.*

Teacher: *Prima. Jetzt macht weiter.*

Solution:

A Anja **B** Asaf **C** Wiebke **D** Pepe
E Petra **F** Gianni **G** Oliver **H** Maren

Students could follow up this activity by taking it in turns in pairs to choose either a text or a picture at random and challenge their partner to find the correct match – name or full text – as quickly as possible.

Teacher: *Partnerarbeit. Wählt jeweils ein Bild oder einen Text. Euer Partner/eure Partnerin muß den passenden Text, beziehungsweise das passende Bild, so schnell wie möglich finden. Zum Beispiel* (perform a model dialogue with a student to demonstrate:) *Text A – wer ist das?*
Student: *Das ist Anja.*
Teacher: *Petra – welches Text ist das?*
Student: *Text E.*

As a *SCHWARZ* follow up, you could also ask students to convert the texts from third to first person and play *Wer bin ich?* in pairs.

Teacher: *Partnerarbeit. Wer bin ich? Wählt einen Text und lest so vor: ,Ich bin mittelgroß. Ich habe ...' usw. Wer bin ich?*

Partnerarbeit.
Haarige Probleme

Listening
Speaking
Reading
Writing

In this activity one student pretends to be one of the people in the photos and the partner has to work out who (s)he is by asking questions. Demonstrate with one student, writing up the details as they are revealed by your questions. Introduce the question: *Trägst du eine Brille?* at this stage. Finally, list the number of questions it takes you to discover the student's chosen identity.

Teacher: (To a student:) *Komm nach vorn. Hier sind viele Leute. Such dir eine Person aus. OK? Du bist jetzt diese Person. So, bist du ein Junge?* (Continue using the model dialogue in the students' book.)
Teacher: *Also, das waren sieben Fragen. Jetzt bist du dran. Ich wähle eine Person ...*

Follow up by asking students to write down descriptions of themselves with the help of the *Tip des Tages* on page 46. Then ask five students to come to the front with their written descriptions. Collect the descriptions and read them out in random order. Ask the class to identify each person.

Teacher: (To the five students:) *Kommt nach vorne. Bringt eure Hefte mit. Stellt euch hier in einer Reihe auf. So, ihr anderen, hört gut zu. Wer ist das?*

Using a word-processor or a desktop-publishing package, students could produce descriptions of themselves and friends to feature in posters, teenage magazines and wanted advertisements. Photographs and spoken descriptions could be merged in a CD-ROM version.

Paßt das?

Listening
Speaking
Reading

Jumbled texts and drawings for students to use for matching activities such as Pelmanism. Ask them to jumble the text and picture cards and turn them face down. They must then take it in turns to turn over two cards and see how many matches they can make. Each matched pair is retained by the student who turns them up. Students can complete this activity in pairs or groups of three or four.

Teacher: *Dreht die Bilder und Texte so um. Jetzt müßt ihr die passenden Texte und Bilder finden. Zum Beispiel* (try to find two matching cards and encourage other students to watch and build on the information they gain from seeing the cards you have turned over).

Wie heißen die Mädchen?

Listening
Speaking
Reading

An information-gap activity, in which students must pool the details they have been given and work out the names of the four girls pictured. Check comprehension by using an OHP version to go through students' findings.

Teacher: *Partnerarbeit. Seht euch das Bild und die Sätze an. Findet heraus, wer Steffi ist, usw. Zum Beispiel* (get one student to read out one of the statements). *Also, Steffi hat kurze, lockige Haare, ... und?* (Continue until Steffi has been identified.)

Solution:

1 Asla 2 Steffi 3 Petra 4 Moni

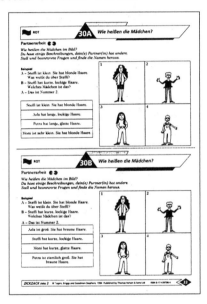

As a follow-up to the section on describing people, use appropriate illustrations such as drawings on the board, or use references to members of staff or well-known people to help students use similar descriptive vocabulary. A selection of home-made flashcards will make this more fun. These can be further exploited by asking a student to come and choose one, then describe it to the class, who have to guess which one it is. You could also ask students to write their own description of a member of staff. Then ask one student at a time to read out his/her description and get the rest of the class to guess who it is.

Kleider

Listening
Speaking
Reading
Writing

First, present items of clothing using the copymaster as an OHP master. Then reinforce the names by playing games such as bingo with the cards, or by issuing copies of the copymaster for students to label the pictures themselves.

Move on to point out the use of *tragen* with items of clothing by commenting on what students in your class are wearing. Show students how the accusative case must be used after *tragen*.

Teacher: *Mark trägt einen Pullover, eine Hose, ein Hemd, Socken und Schuhe. Alison trägt einen Rock, eine Bluse usw. Was trägt Karen?*

Gruppenfoto

Listening
Speaking
Reading

First, talk students through the colours as shown next to the *Tip des Tages*. Then tell them that they are going to hear and read descriptions of the ten people in the photograph and that they must decide who is being talked about each time. This item combines clothing vocabulary with adjectives of colour. Look through the text before you play the recording to make sure that students have enough understanding of the new clothing items to identify the young people from the descriptions given of them. At this stage the adjectival agreements used with adjectives of colour are for receptive understanding only.

Teacher: *Seht euch die Personen an und hört gut zu. Welcher Text paßt zu welcher Person? Schreibt zuerst die Zahlen 1 bis 10 von oben nach unten in euer Heft, so* (write up, then play the first recording as an example). *Also, Nummer 1 – wer ist das? A? B? C?*

Write up the correct answer. Then play the other recordings.

 Gruppenfoto

1 – Max hat eine Mütze und trägt eine schwarze Lederjacke und eine schwarze Hose. Er hat auch eine Schultasche in der Hand.

2 – Vanessa hat blonde Haare und trägt einen blauen Pullover und einen roten Anorak.

3 – Marie hat blonde Haare und trägt eine grüne Hose und einen bunten Pullover.

4 – Henrike trägt eine blaue Hose zu einem blau-weiß gestreiften Pulli. Sie trägt auch einen Schal und hat kurze, braune Haare.

5 – Tobias trägt eine schwarze Hose, schwarze Schuhe und einen grünen Pullover zu einer blauen Jacke. Er hat kurze, blonde Haare.

6 – Patrick trägt eine schwarze Jacke und ein blau-weißes Hemd. Er hat rote Haare.

7 – Kerstin hat kurze, braune Haare und trägt eine grüne Jacke, eine hellblaue Hose und braune Schuhe. Sie trägt auch eine Brille.

8 – Sebastian hat kurze, braune Haare und trägt eine blau-weiß-rote Jacke.

9 – Elisabeth hat dunkelbraune Haare. Sie trägt einen Anorak, eine schwarze Wolljacke und schwarze Schuhe.

10 – Carlos trägt Jeans, einen blauen Pullover und eine blau-grüne Jacke. Er hat schwarze Haare.

Solution:

1 (Max) A	5 (Tobias) D	9 (Elisabeth) H
2 (Vanessa) E	6 (Patrick) I	10 (Carlos) = B
3 (Marie) F	7 (Kerstin) J	
4 (Henrike) G	8 (Sebastian) C	

Ausgeflippte Kleider

Listening
Speaking
Reading

[32 ROT]

Students must work out the colours relating to the girl's and boy's clothes by completing the simple sums shown and relating them to the numerical key. They can then colour in the pictures.

Teacher: *Seht euch dieses Mädchen und diesen Jungen an. Wie sind die Farben richtig? Zum Beispiel, die Haare von dem Mädchen. Sechs plus sechs?*
Student: *Zwölf.*
Teacher: *Gut. Seht euch den Schlüssel an. Welche Farbe ist zwölf?*
Student: *Rot.*
Teacher: *Prima. Das Mädchen hat also rote Haare. Macht weiter, und malt die Kleidungsstücke richtig an.*

Solution:

Girl: red hair, yellow scarf, brown pullover, blue skirt, green tights, blue shoes

Boy: yellow hair, blue shirt, red shorts, grey socks, yellow shoes, green bag on the ground

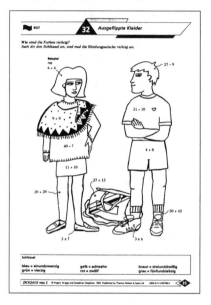

Bunte Kleider

Listening
Speaking
Reading
Writing

[49]

As a lead-in to the next activity, comment again on students' clothes, but this time describe the colours as well as the items, for example: *Das ist eine weiße Bluse. Peters Hemd ist blau. Monica trägt einen roten Pullover.* Explain that some of these words are adjectives, and then write the following sentences on the board/OHP and ask the students to point to the adjectives:

Sandras Bluse ist weiß. Jörgs Pullover is groß. Sandra trägt eine weiße Bluse. Jörg trägt einen großen Pullover.

Once students have identified the adjectives, ask them if they notice how the endings change.

Ask students to look at the clothes the young people are wearing, and to compile a description of each item. Ask students firstly to produce statements using *ist/sind* and the simple form of the adjective.

Teacher: *Seht euch die Bilder an. Fünf junge Leute – Marga, Nicola, Jochen, Gisela und Ralf – gehen aus. Welche Farbe haben ihre Kleider? Zum Beispiel, Margas Bluse ist weiß. Und ihr Rock? usw.*

The second stage involves the use of *trägt* plus the accusative form of the adjectives. First, show that adjectival agreement occurs only when the adjective precedes the noun, and not if the adjective is placed after *ist/sind*, as has just been practised. Direct students' attention to the *Tip des Tages* on page 48 and the *auf einen Blick* page at the end of the chapter.

Teacher: *Seht euch diese Sätze an. Was ist der Unterschied?* (Write up: *Margas Bluse ist weiß./Marga trägt eine weiße Bluse.*)

Solution:

Marga trägt: eine weiße Bluse, graue Schuhe, einen schwarzen Rock

Nicola trägt: weiße Schuhe, eine gelbe Hose, eine grüne Jacke, ein graues T-Shirt

Ralf trägt: ein weißes T-Shirt, eine blaue Hose, blaue Schuhe

Jochen trägt: ein gelbes Hemd, eine rote Jacke, eine schwarze Hose, braune Schuhe

Gisela trägt: ein rotes Hemd, rote Schuhe, einen grünen Pullover, eine graue Hose

Steffi   *Reading*

More adventures of Steffi, intended for fun rather than detailed exploitation.

> 🖥 Using CD-ROM, students could generate their own fashion show on video, complete with commentary text summarising the garments worn by each model.

> Students may now attempt the *Lernziel 1* activities in the *Selbstbedienung* section on page 52 of the students' book. See page 72 of this book for more details.

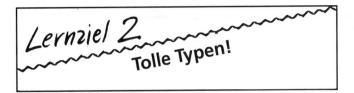

Lernziel 2
Tolle Typen!

Was hältst du von Asla?   *Listening*
                                     Reading
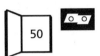   *Writing*

A series of statements about the same person, Asla, made by various people. You can ask students to read the texts without the support of the cassette, in order to find out who, if anybody, does not get on well with Asla. Using the cassette version helps students in so far as they can tell by the speakers' intonation whether or not the comments are positive.

Teacher: *(Hört gut zu und) lest die Texte. Die Leute sprechen über Asla. Wie finden sie Asla? Wer mag sie? Wie heißt ‚mag' auf englisch? Wer kommt mit Asla nicht gut aus? Wer mag sie nicht?*

The *Meinungsmeter* should also help students to understand the expressions relating to liking and disliking. Talk students through the adjectives, emphasising meanings through facial expressions and mime and gesture.

Teacher: *Seht euch den Meinungsmeter an. Fies – ist das gut oder schlecht? Und sympathisch?*

Was hältst du von Asla?

– Mit Asla bin ich ganz zufrieden. Sie ist fleißig und immer pünktlich. Ich finde sie sehr sympathisch.

– Die ist ziemlich OK.

– Asla ist meine beste Freundin. Ich finde sie toll.

– Die ist eine gute Tochter, aber manchmal ein bißchen unordentlich.

– Sie ist ganz lieb. Sie hilft auch viel zu Hause.

– Ich kann sie nicht leiden. Die ist blöd.

– Ich finde sie unheimlich nett.

Extend students' understanding by asking them to list the positive and negative statements made about Asla. Refer them to the word list and ask them to say what they think *unheimlich* means.

Teacher: *Die Mitschülerin von Asla mag sie, oder? Warum? Was sagt sie? Ja, nett – unheimlich nett. Wie heißt das auf englisch? Und was sagt ihr Vater? Ist das positiv oder negativ? Macht eine*

Tabelle von positiven und negativen Bemerkungen, so: (draw up a starter list, thus:)

positiv	negativ
Sie ist fleißig.	Die ist blöd.

Graffitimauer

Reading
Writing

Refer students to the visual of the graffiti wall with the names and adjectives which begin with the same letter. Ask students to invent their own slogans, using the German names shown or names they choose themselves (preferably NOT those of classmates!). Some may be able to incorporate other adjectives (*fantastisch, faul, normal, schlecht, nicht schlecht*) to add to the variety.

Teacher: *Seht euch die Graffitimauer an. Nicole ist nett, aber Frank ist fies. Schreibt andere reimende Paare. Zum Beispiel, Susi ist …?*
Student: *Sympathisch.*
Teacher: *Gut, oder schlecht. Macht weiter.*

Teenager

Listening
Reading

Tell students that they are going to hear six conversations involving invitations and discussion about people's qualities. The task is to decide which of the words and phrases listed on the copymaster occur in each conversation. Ask students to underline a word or phrase as they hear it. The words and phrases are in the order in which they appear on tape, but the number varies from one conversation to another. Play the first conversation as an example, then check the results.

Teacher: *Gleich hört ihr sechs Gespräche. Auf dem Arbeitsbogen habt ihr sechs Listen. Seht euch Liste eins an. Das ist für Gespräch Nummer eins. Welche Wörter hört ihr im Gespräch? Hört ihr das Wort ‚Disco‘? Hört ihr das Wort ‚Party‘? Hört gut zu!* (Play the first line of conversation 1.) *Also, sagt sie das Wort ‚Disco‘?*
Student: *Nein.*
Teacher: *Sagt sie das Wort ‚Party‘?*
Student: *Ja!*
Teacher: *Dann unterstreicht das Wort ‚Party‘ auf der Liste.* (Demonstrate.) *Und jetzt hört zu.*

 Teenager

1 Petra: Kommst du heute abend zur Party?
Gerd: Ja, ich bringe meinen englischen Brieffreund mit.
Petra: Oh, ist er nett?
Gerd: Ja, sehr. Er spricht auch gut Deutsch.

2 Rolf: Kommst du am Sonnabend schwimmen?
Werner: Wer kommt denn alles?
Rolf: Torsten, Christoph.
Werner: Ach Christoph?
Rolf: Ja, wieso?
Werner: Ach, den finde ich nicht so toll.
Rolf: Also, kommst du oder nicht?
Werner: Doch, doch, ich komme.

3 Franz: He, Uwe. Was machst du morgen abend?
Uwe: Nichts Besonderes. Wieso?
Franz: Da ist 'ne Party in Kirchheim.
Uwe: Bei wem?
Franz: Sie heißt Andrea, glaube ich.
Uwe: Moment mal. Kennst du die etwa gar nicht?
Franz: Doch, doch. Sie ist nett. Ich glaube, du kennst sie auch. Glatte, schwarze Haare, schlank.
Uwe: Ach ja, ich glaube schon. Aber geht das, wenn ich auch mitkomme?
Franz: Ganz bestimmt. Kein Problem.

4 Ruth: He, Inge! Wir fahren Dienstag zum Hansaland. Kommst du mit?
Inge: Gern. Wer kommt denn noch?
Ruth: Die Sabine, Jutta, Karola.
Inge: Wer?
Ruth: Karola. Sabines Freundin.
Inge: Kenne ich die? Wie sieht sie aus?
Ruth: Sie hat kurze Haare: blond. Sie ist ziemlich klein.
Inge: Nee, kenne ich nicht.
Ruth: Sie ist recht nett.
Inge: Also Dienstag. Und wann?
Ruth: Wir treffen uns um halb zehn am Bahnhof.
Inge: Prima! Ich komme mit.

5 Hans: Du, wer ist das Mädchen da drüben, bei Regina?
Peter: Wer, die große blonde?
Hans: Nein, die links, mit dem schwarzen Rock.
Peter: Das ist Daniela.
Hans: Sie sieht nett aus.

Peter:	Naja, ganz OK. Ich find' sie aber blöd.
Hans:	Mal sehen … Willst du tanzen?
6 Simone:	Sag mal, Karin, was hältst du eigentlich von Martin?
Karin:	Ganz sympathisch.
Simone:	Findest du, er sieht gut aus?
Karin:	Mmm, nicht schlecht. Warum fragst du?
Simone:	Sein langes Haar finde ich schön. Und er hat tolle dunkelbraune Augen!
Karin:	Und er tanzt mit Anja.

Solution:

The words and phrases spoken in each list are:

1 Party, Brieffreund, nett, gut
2 schwimmen, nicht so toll, ich komme
3 nichts Besonderes, doch, schwarze, geht das, kein Problem
4 klein, treffen
5 da drüben, Rock, blöd, tanzen
6 sympathisch, gut, warum, schön, tolle

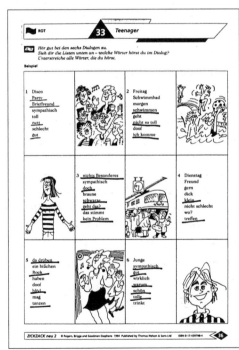

Was hältst du von Elke? *Listening*

Ask students to copy the chart below. Tell them that they are going to hear three people saying what they think of Elke, Hanno, Iris, Pamela and Viktor. They should decide whether the comments are favourable, neutral or unfavourable and indicate this by putting a cross in the appropriate box.

Teacher: *Übertragt diese Tabelle in euer Heft.*

	😀	😐	🙁
Elke			
Hanno			
Iris			
Pamela			
Viktor			

Teacher: *Gleich hört ihr drei junge Leute. Sie sagen etwas über Elke, über Hanno und so weiter. Ist das gut? Oder ist das schlecht? Oder so in der Mitte? Macht Kreuze in den richtigen Kasten. Und jetzt hört gut zu.* (Do the first one as an example.)

You may also wish to draw students' attention to some of the variants and new ways of commenting on people which occur in these interviews.

🔊 Was hältst du von Elke?

1 – Sag mal, was hältst du von Elke?
– Sie ist nett.
– Und Hanno?
– Hanno? Naja, er ist nicht schlecht.
– Und Iris. Wie findest du Iris?
– Die mag ich nicht.
– Und wie findest du Pamela?
– Ach, die ist toll.
– Und Viktor?
– Ja, der ist auch sehr nett.

2 – Du, findest du Elke nett?
– Nicht besonders. Naja, ziemlich OK.
– Und Hanno?
– Ach, der Idiot!
– Ja, und Iris. Was hältst du von ihr?
– Iris finde ich sehr sympathisch.
– Pamela?
– Ja, die auch. Die ist wirklich sehr nett.
– Und Viktor?
– Ja, das ist ein toller Typ.

3 – Wie findest du Elke?
– Ach, ich finde sie unheimlich nett.
– Und Hanno?
– Hanno kann ich nicht leiden. Der ist blöd.
– Iris?
– Na also, Iris ist ein bißchen egoistisch, nicht? Aber sie kann auch ganz nett sein.
– Und Pamela?
– Die ist prima.
– Und Viktor?
– Der nervt mich. Der ist richtig fies.

Solution:

Elke	xx	x	
Hanno		x	xx
Iris	x	x	x
Pamela	xxx		
Viktor	xx		x

Students can now practise the language themselves. Draw their attention to the questions: *,Was hältst du von ...?'; ,Wie findest du ...?'*; and *,Wie ist ...?'* Begin by asking a student about a well-known personality (actor, singer, politician), not a fellow student. Then encourage them to take over your role and ask questions round the class.

Teacher: *Jetzt seid ihr dran.* (To a student:) *Was hältst du von (Michael Jackson? Arnold Schwarzenegger? etc)?*

Student: *Er ist toll/fies ...*

Teacher: *Fein. Partnerarbeit. Stellt einander Fragen.* (Write up the questions and some of the possible answers or refer students to the *Tip des Tages*.)

Interviews

Listening
Speaking
Reading
Writing

Ask students to produce another chart like *Was hältst du von Elke?*, putting in five names of well-known people of their own choice. Then ask them to interview their fellow students and record their opinions about all five on the chart. Some students may wish to produce a popularity chart.

> Some could record the information in a data-base for computer printouts and for exchange with penfriends or paired/exchange classes.

Teacher: *Macht noch eine Tabelle wie bei ,Was hältst du von Elke?' Schreibt jetzt fünf neue Namen in die Tabelle, zum Beispiel* (give some examples of television personalities, pop or sport stars etc.). *Jetzt geht zu den anderen in der Klasse und fragt sie: ,Was hältst du von ...?', oder ,Wie findest du ...?' Macht Kreuze in den richtigen Kasten.*

Conclude the activity by asking individuals: *,Wer ist der Star auf deiner Liste?'*

Partnerarbeit. Wer spricht?

 SCHWARZ

Listening
Speaking
Reading
Writing

A pairwork activity in which students must look at the information contained in the spaghetti diagram and take it in turns to choose to be one of the people depicted on the left. Their partner must work out from statements and/or questions their partner's chosen identity. Talk students through the model dialogue to demonstrate.

Teacher: *Partnerarbeit. Wählt eine Person auf der linken Seite, und seht euch den Schlüssel an. Sagt etwas über die Personen auf der rechten Seite. Zum Beispiel, wer bin ich? Ich finde Markus doof, aber ich finde Petra nett.*

Student: *Gabi?*

Teacher: (To the rest of the group:) *Stimmt das? Ja, gut.*

Although it is important for students to avoid making unfavourable comments about each other in front of the class, many will wish to express their opinions in a genuine context. As a *SCHWARZ* follow up, you could ask students to write penpal letters, incorporating their views of people in their family and friends and/or others in their class whom they like or find irritating. To make the activity less challenging, you could provide a skeletal letter with gaps for students to complete.

> There may be a student prepared to word-process a model letter with variants/gaps for other students to use as a framework for their own efforts.

Teacher: *Schreibt einen Brief an euren Briefpartner/eure Briefpartnerin. Schreibt über eure Familie, Freunde und Klassenkameraden. Wie findet ihr zum Beispiel eure Cousins/Kusinen? Und Onkel (Michael)/Tante (Elisabeth)?*

Sag mir jemand, wer sie war

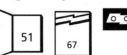

Listening
Speaking
Reading

A song based on the same theme as the rest of the material in the chapter, for students to listen to and then sing along to.

Sag mir jemand, wer sie war

Ich habe sie zuerst im Park gesehen,
Hat sie mich gesehen? Das weiß ich nicht.
Ich weiß nicht, wie sie heißt,
   ich weiß nicht, wo sie wohnt.
Ich denke aber noch an ihr Gesicht.

Dunkle Augen, lockiges Haar,
Sag mir jemand, wer sie war.

Das zweite Mal war mitten in der Stadt.
Hat sie mich gesehen? Es könnte sein.
Ich habe ihr nichts gesagt, ich hab' es nicht gewagt.
Dann war sie wieder weg, und ich allein.

Dunkle Augen, lockiges Haar,
Sag mir jemand, wer sie war.

Das letzte Mal, das war schon lange her.
Es war ein Nachmittag – ich weiß nicht wann.
Sie ging mit einem Jungen, der älter war als sie.
Er hatte eine Lederjacke an.

Dunkle Augen, lockiges Haar,
Sag mir jemand, wer sie war.

Austauschpartner

Listening
Speaking
Reading

Details of ten British and ten German exchange partners. Students must work in pairs and work out from the details they have on their cards, who has been paired with whom. Talk students through the model dialogue, then ask them to complete the remaining nine themselves.

Teacher: *Partnerarbeit. Partner(in) A hat Informationen über zehn Mädchen und Jungen aus Großbritannien. Partner(in) B hat Informationen über zehn Mädchen und Jungen aus Deutschland. Alle zehn sind Austauschpartner. Aber wer ist Jamies Partner? Wer ist Christianes Partnerin? Stellt und beantwortet Fragen und schreibt die Namen auf die Tabelle.*

Solution:

Jamie + Holger

Sharon + Anne

Andrew + Rainer

Catherine + Hedwig

Darren + Stefan

Joanna + Kerstin

Lisa + Christiane

Greg + Thomas

Linda + Sabine

Robin + Bruno

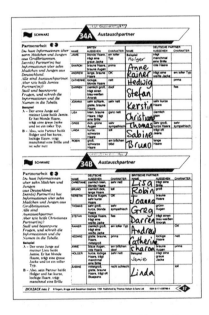

Using a word-processor, students could compile a class letter to send to their potential exchange partners in Germany. Using desktop-publishing they could incorporate illustrations and photographs.

Students may now attempt the *Lernziel 2* activities in the *Selbstbedienung* section on page 53 of the students' book. See below for further details.

52–53   72

Lernziel 1
So ein Durcheinander!

 SCHWARZ

Four jumbled photographs and factfiles. Students must read the factfiles and match them to the photographs. They are then asked to describe the four girls, using the information given in the factfiles.

Solution:

Bärbel 4   Jutta 2   Anne 1   Bettina 3

Im Umkleideraum

 GOLD

Students must work out the owners of items of clothing illustrated by reading the statements.

Solution:

A Karins Hose
B Marias Pullover
C Monis Socken

D Juttas Pullover
E Steffis Hose
F Sabines Socken

Lernziel 2
Popstar

 SCHWARZ

Students are asked to describe a favourite personality/rockstar, in terms of appearance, clothing and personal appeal.

Quatsch!

 ROT

Five statements about people. Students must decide whether the statements are reasonable or contradictory.

Solution:

1 Das stimmt nicht.
2 Das stimmt nicht.
3 Das stimmt.

4 Das stimmt nicht.
5 Das stimmt.

Unheimlich bunt

 SCHWARZ

A mini wordsearch grid with the letters of five adjectives jumbled, but matched by colour. Students are asked to make up their own grids, too.

Solution:

sympathisch; fies; doof; blöd; nett

Bildvokabeln. Im Freibad

Reading
Writing

54   35 GOLD

A swimming pool setting to provide the opportunity for students to learn new items of vocabulary relating to clothing. A version of the artwork is provided on copymaster for students to label and colour themselves.

Grammar exercises 15-17 on copymaster 78 are based on the material in this chapter.

 78 + 83

The students' personal profile for this chapter is on copymaster 84.

 84

After completing work on this chapter, check whether any further reinforcement is appropriate from the video material, Activity Box cards and Assessment Support Pack tasks.

Main teaching points

Lernziel 1: **Making and declining invitations and suggestions about what to do**
Lernziel 2: **Arranging when and where to meet**

Language presented:

* *Mitkommen*
* *Hast du Lust, ... zu ...?* + infinitive
* Further activities language
* Prepositions with the dative case (*hinter, neben, vor, an*)

> Before beginning work on this chapter, check where the video material, Activity Box cards and Assessment Support Pack tasks will be most appropriate.

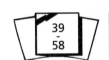

Lernziel 1
Kommst du mit?

Revision (days of the week/ leisure pursuits)

Listening Speaking

Revise the days of the week and leisure activities as a prelude to the idea of going out and inviting friends to accompany you. Use the activities flashcards for support.

Teacher: *Was machst du am Samstag?* (Showing flashcard.)
Student: *Ich gehe ins Kino.*

Kommst du?

Listening Speaking Reading

Ask students to listen to the recordings and say what they think each one is about. After each one, ask students to produce the words used in the invitation itself: (*Kommst du?/Kommst du mit?*). You can use the flashcards to support students' comprehension and, later as a springboard to their own pairwork activities. Now refer students to the visuals in the students' book and ask them to match them to the recordings.

Teacher: *Hört zu. Worum geht es hier? Was machen die Leute? Was sagen die Leute?* (Showing flashcards:) *Ich gehe am Samstag schwimmen. Kommst du mit?*
Student: *Ja, gerne.*
Teacher: (To another student:) *Ich gebe morgen eine Party. Kommst du?*
Student: *Nein danke.*
Teacher: *Schade. Seht euch die Bilder an, und hört nochmal zu. Was paßt wozu?*

Kommst du?

1 – Wir gehen heute schwimmen. Kommst du mit?
– Ja, gerne.

2 – Morgen nachmittag gehen wir Rollschuhlaufen. Kommst du mit?
– Nein, danke.

3 – Ich gehe am Samstag ins Kino. Kommst du mit?
– Oh, ja, toll!

4 – Werner gibt nächsten Mittwoch eine Party. Kommst du mit?
– Ja, gerne.

5 – Anja und ich gehen heute abend in die Disco. Kommst du mit?
– Nein, danke. Heute nicht.

Solution:

1B **2**D **3**E **4**C **5**A

Follow up the activity by asking students to work in threes and take it in turns to choose what two of them want to do and invite the third person to join them. Perform a model dialogue with two students to demonstrate.

Teacher: (Pointing to a student:) *Wir (das heißt Anne und ich) gehen in die Disco.* (Ponting to another student:) *Und Peter? Peter, wir gehen in die Disco. Kommst du mit?*
Student: *Nein, danke.*
Teacher: *Arbeitet jetzt in Dreiergruppen. Zwei Personen machen eine Aktivität zusammen und laden die dritte Person ein. Macht Dialoge mit Hilfe dieser Bilder* (point to the visuals in the book).

Students can also use the *Tip des Tages* for language support.

Partnerarbeit. Hast du Lust?

Listening
Speaking
Reading

Four short dialogues, in which invitations are issued, to cue students' own dialogues. Draw students' attention to the two possible ways given of asking someone if they wish to do something, i.e. a statement plus *Kommst du mit?*, and *Hast du Lust ...?* with *zu* and the infinitive, emphasising the use of *zu* in the latter. Finally, ask students to practise the dialogues or invent their own. Not all students will be able to cope with both constructions.

Teacher: *Lest die Dialoge. Die Leute gehen aus. Was sagen sie? Hast du ...?*
Student: *Lust.*
Teacher: *Genau. Und im zweiten Dialog: Hast du Lust, Tischtennis ...?*
Student: *Zu spielen.*
Teacher: *Gut. (Write up Lust, ... zu spielen.) Macht weitere Dialoge jetzt mit ,Hast du Lust?' oder ,Kommst du mit?' Seht euch auch den Tip des Tages an.*

Wer hat Lust?

Reading
Writing

Language presented so far in this chapter is consolidated on this copymaster, which requires students to work out responses to invitations in three stages. Firstly, they unjumble the sentences; secondly, they fill in gaps; and finally they should write their own responses, according to whether the invitation is accepted or declined (shown by a tick or a cross).

Solution:

Kommt: Boris
Kommt nicht: Dorit und Barbara

Nina: Nein/habe/Lust.
Frank: Ja/Ich/mit.
Christiane: habe

Wer kommt mit zur Party?

Reading

A photo story drawing together some of the language relating to making (and declining!) invitations. Students might well enjoy re-enacting the scenes for themselves and/or recording them on cassette.

Solche Freunde!

Reading
Writing

 **SCHWARZ**

The crossword on the copymaster could be used to check comprehension of the previous reading activity.

For a *ROT* approach, simply use the crossword as it stands. For a more demanding *SCHWARZ* activity, you could give students the solution and ask them to work in pairs or groups and compile the matching clues.

Teacher: *Der arme Jens. Er will zur Party, aber niemand kommt mit. Füllt das Kreuzworträtsel aus. Schreibt die passenden Wörter in die Kästchen. SCHWARZ: Hier ist die Lösung eines Kreuzworträtsels. Schreibt die Schlüssel!*

Solution:

Tut mir leid

Listening
Speaking
Reading
Writing

 **SCHWARZ**

Five conversations, in which invitations are turned down. Play the first two and ask students to decide what they have in common, i.e. that the invitations are declined. Then ask students to note down the reasons for the invitations not being accepted. Check orally after each one.

Teacher: *Hört zu. Sie sagen alle ‚nein'. Warum? Welche Gründe haben sie? Schreibt soviel wie möglich über jede Antwort. Zum Beispiel* (complete the first one, as follows:)

	Aktivität/ Einladung	Sagt ‚nein'	Warum?
1 Jens	gibt eine Party	Uschi	hat Familienbesuch Tante aus Goslar essen zusammen

🔊 **Tut mir leid**

1 – Mehde.
– Uschi!
– Ja. Ist das Jens?
– Ja. Hör mal. Morgen geb' ich eine Party bei uns im Keller. Kannst du kommen?
– Ja, gern. Oh – aber Moment mal. Morgen haben wir Familienbesuch.
– Ach nein.
– Doch. Ich kann nicht weg. Meine Tante aus Goslar kommt.
– Kannst du nicht später kommen?
– Das geht auch nicht. Wir essen zusammen. Zu schade.
– Also nein?
– Tja. Tut mir wirklich leid. Aber viel Spaß.
– Danke. Naja – tschüs.
– Tschüs.

2 – Hallo Holger. Am Freitag habe ich Geburtstag und gebe eine Party. Kannst du kommen?
– Danke, Wolf, aber du, es geht mir momentan nicht so gut.
– Oh – was hast du denn?
– Tja, ich habe Grippe.
– Oh, das tut mir aber leid. Mußt du im Bett liegen?
– Ja.
– Ja, dann gute Besserung.
– Danke, tschüs.
– Tschüs, Holger.

3 – Hier bei Schäfer.
 – Wer ist da?
 – Christine.
 – Ach so. Hier Asla. Ist Jürgen da?
 – Nein, er ist weg.
 – Also, paß auf. Morgen gehen wir schwimmen. Kommt ihr mit?
 – Nein, morgen können wir nicht. Wir gehen aus.
 – OK, ein anderes Mal, vielleicht.
 – Ja gut.
 – Tschüs dann.
 – Tschüs.

4 – Krämer.
 – Katrin?
 – Ja. Birgit?
 – Ja, wie geht's?
 – Gut.
 – Ich gehe heute abend ins Kino. Kommst du mit?
 – Ich kann leider nicht.
 – Was machst du denn? Gehst du aus?
 – Nein … aber ich kann nicht. Ich hab' kein Geld, du.
 – Oh, schade.
 – Ja, tut mir leid.
 – Naja – also bis bald.
 – Tschüs.

5 – Bernd, du? Warte mal!
 – Ja? Hallo Ulrich.
 – Du, hast du morgen Zeit?
 – Morgen? Wann denn?
 – Abends. Silke gibt 'ne Party.
 – Ach nee.
 – Komm doch!
 – Nee, wirklich du, ich hab' keine Lust.
 – Schade. Na denn …
 – Ja, tschüs.

Solution:

	Aktivität/ Einladung	**Sagt ‚nein'**	**Warum?**
1 Jens	gibt eine Party	Uschi	hat Familienbesuch Tante aus Goslar essen zusammen
2 Wolf	gibt am Freitag eine Party	Holger	krank: Grippe
3 Asla	geht schwimmen	Christine & Jürgen	gehen aus
4 Birgit	geht ins Kino	Katrin	hat kein Geld
5 Ulrich	Party bei Silke morgen	Bernd	hat keine Lust

Leider nicht

Listening
Speaking
Reading
Writing

In this activity students have to match up the speech bubbles with the explanations in the box by filling in the appropriate names. Through doing this activity students will see the written forms of some of the phrases they have heard in the previous recording. You could encourage students to speculate first as to the excuses the people are likely to give. Write up students' suggestions and see how close their guesses were once they have completed the activity.

Teacher: *Der arme Rolf. Er gibt eine Party, aber niemand kommt. Wißt ihr warum? Was sagen sie vielleicht?* (To a student:) *Ich bin Rolf. Ich gebe eine Party. Kommst du?*
Student: *Leider nicht.*
Teacher: *Schade. Warum nicht?*
Student: *Ich bin krank./Ich habe keine Lust.*
Teacher: (Writing up the answer given:) *Gut, oder ich …?*

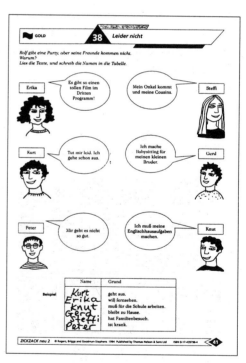

Students could enter a range of excuses into a data-base. This could provide opportunities for creativity and humour.

Hallo Inge!

*Reading
Writing*

Ask students to assume the role of Inge and read the invitations she receives from seven of her friends. They must consult her diary and decide how she answers each time by choosing suitable responses from the menu box. Allow students to support each other by working in pairs, if necessary.

Teacher: *(Partnerarbeit.) Seht euch Inges Terminkalender an. Ihr seid Inge. Ihr bekommt viele Einladung von euren Freunden. Wie antwortet ihr? Zum Beispiel* (complete the first one with the class).

Solution:

1 Ja, gerne.
2 Tut mir leid, da kann ich nicht. Ich gehe schon aus.
3 Da bin ich leider nicht frei – ich muß ins Krankenhaus gehen.
4 Ja, ich habe Lust.
5 Leider nicht, ich will fernsehen.
6 Ja, ich komme mit.
7 Nein, ich muß zu Hause bleiben.

Wann denn?

*Listening
Speaking
Reading*

A communicative activity focusing on invitations and arrangements to go out together. Tell students they must work out when they are all free to go and see a film together. Divide the class into groups of four or (preferably) five. Cut up the copymaster and give a different week's diary page to each member of the group. Give students the following information on the board or OHP: *Der Film* (or give a topical title) *beginnt um 15.00 Uhr, 17.30 Uhr und 20.00 Uhr.*

Students should not only tell each other when they are and are not free, but should give their reasons if a date is unacceptable. Emphasise that they must not see each other's diaries. Each group should tell you when they have found a suitable date and time. Selected groups could be asked to re-enact the discussion in front of the class.

Teacher: *Gruppenarbeit. Ihr wollt den neuen Film im Kino zusammen sehen. Der Film beginnt um 15.00 Uhr, 17.30 Uhr und 20.00 Uhr. Aber an welchem Tag und um wieviel Uhr habt ihr alle Zeit? Seht euch euren Terminkalender an, und stellt und beantwortet Fragen. Vergeßt nicht, eure Gründe dafür zu geben, wenn ihr ,nein' sagt. Zum Beispiel* (talk students through the model dialogue).

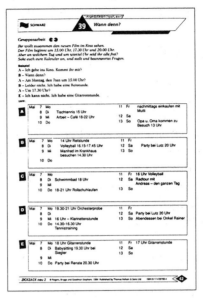

Solution:

For groups of five the only possible solution is **Freitag, um 20 Uhr.** More solutions will be possible with groups of fewer than five.

Die Clique am Samstagabend

*Listening
Speaking
Reading*

A number of telephone conversations about going out on a Saturday evening. In some cases the invitation is accepted, in others it is turned down. Ask students to listen and complete the multiple-choice activity.

Teacher: *Es ist Samstagabend. Was macht die Clique (das heißt auf englisch 'the gang')? Hört zu und seht euch die Texte an. Wählt die passenden Antworten.*

Die Clique am Samstagabend

1 – Uwe Bäcker.
– Hallo, Uwe! Hier ist Peter. Was machst du heute abend?
– Ich bin Babysitter bei meiner Schwester.
– Oh, das ist Pech! Lutz gibt nämlich eine Party.
– Naja, viel Spaß. Tschüs!

2 – Christina Bauer.
  – Hallo, Christina! Hier ist Annette. Hör mal, was machst du heute abend?
  – Weiß nicht. Vielleicht sehe ich 'was im Fernsehen an. Wieso?
  – Tja, einige aus der Clique gehen zum Jugendclub. Hast du auch Lust?
  – Oh ja, prima! Wann?
  – Wir kommen um sieben bei dir vorbei. OK?
  – Ja, gut.

3 – Thomas Schön.
  – Hallo Thomas!
  – Hallo Renate.
  – Wohin gehst du heute abend?
  – Zum *Evi Bamm* Konzert. Gehst du auch hin?
  – Ich weiß nicht. Ich hab' keine Karte.
  – Ach, kein Problem. Karten gibt's sicher noch. Komm doch mit.
  – Ja gut. Bis heute abend.

4 – Doris Seifert.
  – Hallo, Doris! Hier Lars.
  – Ach du! Wie geht's?
  – Gut. Und dir?
  – Nicht so gut.
  – Was? Aber du kommst doch zu Werners Party?
  – Nein, ich gehe ins Bett.
  – Schade. Hoffentlich geht's dir morgen besser.
  – Danke.

5 – Inge Reis.
  – Inge? Hier ist Marianne. Kommst du heute mit in die Stadt?
  – Leider nicht. Ich arbeite.
  – Was machst du denn?
  – Ich arbeite im Supermarkt. Das mache ich jeden Samstag.
  – Schade. Aber wir sehen uns bald. Tschüs!
  – Tschüs!

6 – Frauke Meyer.
  – Hallo, Frauke, hier ist Barbara. Kommst du heute abend zum Jugendclub?
  – Ich weiß noch nicht. Warum?
  – Ich bringe einen Freund aus Frankreich mit, und du lernst doch Französisch, also …
  – Ist er nett?
  – Ich finde, ja.
  – Dann komme ich vielleicht doch. Gegen neun?
  – Fein. Bis dann. Tschüs.

7 – Stefan Fuhrmann.
  – Hier ist Jörg. Hast du heute abend schon was vor?
  – Nein, ich bleibe zu Hause.
  – Willst du bei mir CDs anhören?

  – Oh ja, nicht schlecht. Ich bringe auch ein paar mit.
  – Ja, gut. Also, bis dann.
  – Tschüs.

8 – Trudi Schmidt.
  – He, Trudi! Hier ist Silke.
  – Salut. Was gibt's denn Neues?
  – Ich gehe heute abend zu Gabis Party. Du auch?
  – Moment mal …
  – Wieso?
  – Ich gehe auch zu einer Party. Aber nicht bei Gabi.
  – Wo denn?
  – Bei Ilse.
  – Ach was! Die ist nächste Woche. Heute ist die Party bei Gabi.
  – Wirklich? Mensch, gut daß du mich angerufen hast!
  – Kommst du also später mit zu Gabi?
  – Ja, natürlich.

Solution:

1c **2**a **3**b **4**c **5**b **6**b **7**a **8**c

So eine Woche!

Listening
Speaking
Reading
Writing

An information-gap activity, in which students must exchange invitations and note down details given by their partner about the events to which they are inviting them. Students A and B take turns at inviting each other to the various events/functions in their respective diaries. Each student should fill in the blanks on his/her diary as the information is supplied. Ask students to compare their diary entries once they have exchanged all of their information. Talk them through the model dialogue before they begin the activity.

Teacher: *Partnerarbeit. Jeder Partner/jede Partnerin macht vier Einladungen. Schreibt die fehlenden Informationen in eure Terminkalender. Heute haben wir Sonntag, den 17. Juli. Morgen ist also Montag, der 18. Juli, usw.* (At the end of the activity:) *Vergleicht jetzt eure Terminkalender. Stimmt das? Habt ihr alles richtig aufgeschrieben?*

Solution:

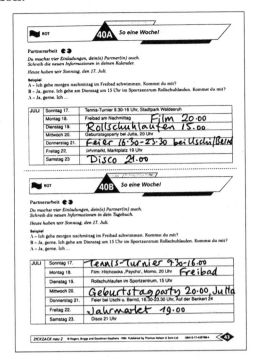

Students may now attempt the *Lernziel 1* activities in the *Selbstbedienung* section on pages 62 and 63 of the students' book. See page 81 of this book for further details.

Revision of language (prepositions with the dative case)

Listening
Speaking

Revise the prepositional phrases used in deciding on a meeting place (*vor, in, an, hinter* etc.), before asking students to move onto the next *Lernziel* material.

Wir gehen aus

Listening
Speaking
Reading

A selection of advertisements and invitations accompanied by recordings. Students must first listen and identify who is going to which of the events advertised. If necessary, write up the young people's names to support students.

Teacher: *Hört zu. Diese Jugendlichen gehen alle aus. Aber wohin?* (Complete the example with the class to demonstrate.)

Secondly, students should listen again and identify the meeting place decided upon in each conversation.

Teacher: *Hört nochmal zu. Wo treffen sie sich? Nummer eins?*
Student: *Bei Dieters Freund zu Hause.*

Wir gehen aus

1 – Dieter ... Ich gehe zum Fußballspiel ... Berlin gegen Frankfurt. Willst du mitkommen?
 – Ja gerne. Ist das im Olympiastadion?
 – Ja, am vierten November.
 – Wo treffen wir uns?
 – Bei mir?
 – Ja, gut.

2 – Christina, kommst du zu Asafs Party am Samstag?
 – Ja. Wie ist seine Adresse?
 – Berliner Straße 60.
 – Danke. Treffen wir uns bei ihm?
 – Ja, klar. Tschüs! Bis dann.

3 – Moni, kommst du zu der Grillparty bei Meiers?
 – Wann ist das?
 – Am zehnten November ab sieben Uhr abends.
 – Ja, dann komme ich. Wo treffen wir uns?
 – An der Bushaltestelle, um halb acht?
 – Ja, gut.

4 – Asla, magst du klassisches Ballett?
 – Ja, was läuft denn?
 – *Schwanensee* in der Stadthalle. Hast du Lust, mitzukommen?
 – Ja, natürlich. Wo treffen wir uns?
 – Mein Vater holt dich mit dem Auto ab.

5 – Danny, kommst du mit zu Susis Party?
 – Hat sie Geburtstag?
 – Ja, am elften November. Kommst du also?
 – Ja, gerne. Wo treffen wir uns?
 – An der Straßenbahnhaltestelle?
 – Ja, bis dann!

6 – Hallo Jens. Kommst du zum *Pina* Konzert?
 – Ja sicher! Ich habe meine Karte schon gekauft. Soll ich bei dir vorbeikommen?
 – Ja, gute Idee.

7 – He du Kirsten! Hast du Lust, zum *Metal Hammer* Konzert zu kommen?
 – Ja, ich hab' schon eine Karte. Kommst du bei mir vorbei?
 – Ja.

8 – Wiebke, am Samstag geh' ich in die Alte Oper in Bremen.
 – Ja? Was läuft denn?
 – Die englische Gruppe *Fairplay*. Hast du Lust, mitzukommen?
 – Ja, warum nicht! Wo treffen wir uns?
 – Vor dem Opernhaus.
 – Alles klar.

Solution:

Dieter **C** Christina **A** Moni **E** Asla **B**

Danny **D** Jens **H** Kirsten **G** Wiebke **F**

1 Bei Dieters Freund zu Hause

2 Bei Asaf – Berliner Straße 60

3 An der Bushaltestelle

4 Der Vater von Aslas Freundin holt sie mit dem Auto ab

5 An der Straßenbahnhaltestelle

6 Jens kommt bei seiner Freundin vorbei

7 Kirsten kommt bei ihrem Freund vorbei

8 Vor dem Opernhaus

Follow up the activity by playing a game with the whole class, focusing on locations. Tell students you will allow them three seconds only to use the clues you give them to work out which event you have chosen to attend. Mark the scores on the board/OHP. Hand the activity over to students in groups of four or five, after practising the prepositional phrases – *in der Stadthalle, im Olympiastadion*, etc.– with them.

Teacher: *Wir machen jetzt ein Spiel. Ich gegen euch* (write up *ich* and *Klasse*). *Ihr habt nur drei Sekunden. Zum Beispiel, ich sage: ‚In der Stadthalle‘, und ihr sagt: ‚Rumänisches Staatsballett‘ oder ‚Schwanensee‘.*

 As a follow-up students could compose written invitations with illustrations using a desktop-publishing package.

Partnerarbeit. Treffen wir uns vor dem Bahnhof?

Listening
Speaking
Reading

A flow chart summarising the language relating to making and accepting or declining invitations and arranging a time and meeting place. Talk students through a model dialogue, then ask them to work in a variety of pairs and complete a number of dialogues.

Teacher: *Partnerarbeit. Macht Dialoge über Einladungen. Was? Wann? Wo? Zum Beispiel ...*

Treffpunkte

Reading
Writing

Students should identify eight places in the wordsearch grid, and then fill in the phrases relating to where to meet.

Solution:

1 Im Theater   **5** In der Sporthalle

2 Vor der Disco   **6** Im Park

3 Im Schwimmbad   **7** Vor der Bank

4 Vor dem Kino   **8** Vor dem Bahnhof

This is followed by *Welche Antwort paßt?*, a matching exercise in which students must identify pairs of questions and answers relating to invitations.

Teacher: *Lest die Fragen und Antworten, die durcheinander sind. Was paßt wozu?*

Solution:

1d 2e 3a 4c 5b

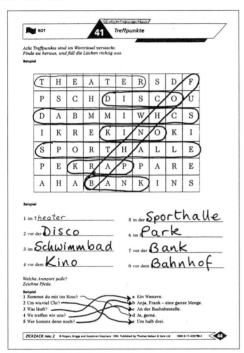

Telefonspiel

Listening
Speaking

First, revise *am* + the date and *um* + the time before starting this activity. Write up on the board/OHP a model dialogue to show how the telephone message could be conveyed:

– *Hallo. Es gibt eine Party am Samstag,*
  den zwölften März.
– *Wo denn?*
– *Bei Volker.*
– *Um wieviel Uhr?*
– *Um acht.*
– *Wo treffen wir uns?*
– *Bei mir.*

Alternatively, write up how the message could be conveyed in non-dialogue form. Then divide the class into equal groups of five or six. Each group then stands or sits in a line. Pass message 1 (see below) to the first student in each line. When the signal is given, this student makes an imaginary

phone call to the next student in order to pass on the invitation. That student then phones the next and so on, to the last in line.

The game can be made competitive if you time the teams, perhaps on a second message once they are familiar with the rules. The last student in each group can report the received message either:
a) back to the class after all the groups have finished;
or b) directly to you, if it is being timed.

Messages:

1 *Party – Samstag, 12. März – bei Völker – 8 Uhr – Treffpunkt: bei mir*

2 *Grillparty – bei Annette – Mittwoch, 1. August – ab 7 Uhr – Treffpunkt: an der Bushaltestelle*

3 *Klassendisco – Samstag, 20. Juni – in der Schule – halb acht – Treffpunkt: vor der Schule*

4 *Schwimmen – Freibad – 3 Uhr – Freitag – Treffpunkt: am Freibad*

Teacher: *1-2-3-4-5, Gruppe A, hier* (placing them in a line.) *Du-du-du-du und du – Gruppe B, dort. Diese Reihe hier, Gruppe C. Ihr fünf – Gruppe D, da drüben. Man macht Einladungen am Telefon. Ich lade die erste Person ein, die dann die zweite einlädt, und so weiter. Zum Beispiel …*

> Students may now attempt the *Lernziel 2* activities in the *Selbstbedienung* section on page 43 of the students' book. See below for further details.

Lernziel 1
Schade!

 ROT

Students should read each dialogue, and decide which option from the menu box best summarises each excuse.

Solution:

1 Es kostet zuviel Geld.

2 Ich muß für die Schule arbeiten.

3 Es ist zu kalt.

4 Ich fahre weg.

5 Ich bin krank.

Mach doch mit!

 GOLD

Students should read the three humorous cartoons, and decide which of the three possible responses is the most likely in each case.

Solution:

A2 B3 C1

Lernziel 2
Einladungen

 ROT

Students are asked to produce original ideas for invitations to a party, following the examples depicted.

Wo treffen sie sich?

 GOLD

A substitution exercise, in which students must replace the drawings with the appropriate words.

Solution:

1 Bahnhof

2 Café

3 Kino

4 Schwimmbad

5 Disco

Telefongespräch

 ROT

A jumbled telephone conversation to be re-written in the correct order.

Solution:

– Hallo Dieter! Hier ist Gisela.

– Na, wie geht's?

– Gut, danke. Hör mal, am Freitag hat Karin Geburtstag, und sie gibt eine Party. Kommst du?

– Ja, gerne. Vielen Dank. Wo treffen wir uns?

– Bei mir. Gegen halb acht, OK?

– Prima.

– Also, bis dann. Tschüs.

– Tschüs.

Ausreden

Listening
Reading

Students should listen to this humorous poem, which highlights the problem of making excuses for not wanting to go to an event, in order to preserve someone's feelings! Students can follow the text in their books.

 Ausreden

– Kommst du zu meiner Party, Werner?

– Vielen Dank! Ich möchte gerne, aber …
  … ich hab' Besuch von meinen Kusinen.

– Umso besser! Komm mit ihnen!

– Ich hab' so viele Hausaufgaben.

– Du hast nicht mehr, als die anderen haben.

– Dann gehe ich mit den Hunden spazieren.

– Kein Problem! Komm mit den Tieren!

– Ich muß Flöte üben, mit meiner Schwester.

– Toll! Dann bring das ganze Orchester!

– Ich muß auch Babysitten morgen.

– Bring das Kind mit! Keine Sorgen!
  Und noch etwas …

– Was könnte es sein?

– Vielleicht ein kleines, ehrliches ‚Nein'?

Grammar exercises 18-20 on copymasters 78 and 79 are based on the material in this chapter.

78-79
+83

The students' personal profile for this chapter is on copymaster 85.

85

After completing work on this chapter, check whether any further reinforcement is appropriate from the video material, Activity Box cards and Assessment Support Pack tasks.

Main teaching points

Lernziel 1: **Parts of the body, illness, injury and allergy**

Lernziel 2: **Seeking advice and going to the chemist's**

Language presented:

- Parts of the body
- Illness, injury and allergy vocabulary
- *Mir ist ...*
- *Was fehlt dir?*
- *Weh tun*

- *Ich habe* + illness
- *Ich bin allergisch gegen*
- *Ich darf nicht*
- *Haben Sie etwas gegen ...?*
- Medicaments vocabulary

Before beginning work on this chapter, check where the video material, Activity Box cards and Assessment Support Pack tasks will be most appropriate.

Lernziel 1
Krankheiten und Verletzungen

Sonja sagt

Listening
Speaking

Teach and practise parts of the body before playing this game, which uses mime and gesture.

Play a version of Simon Says involving parts of the body and classroom commands. To keep students alert, tell them you might either end the statement with *sagt Sonja* or start it with *Sonja sagt ...* Some commands you could use include:

Sonja sagt:
  Hört zu!
  Steht auf!
  Hebt die Hand! (Hände)
  Hebt den Fuß!
  Nickt mit dem Kopf!
  Macht die Augen zu!
  Hände 'runter!
  Legt die Hand auf den Rücken!
  Legt die Hand auf den Magen!
  Faßt ans linke Ohr.
  Legt den Finger auf die Zähne.

Die Körperteile

Reading
Writing

Students should label the parts of the body, using the vocabulary from the menu box.

83

Ich habe Kopfschmerzen ... Mein Fuß tut weh

Listening
Speaking
Reading

Present the new language dealing with illness and injuries in two sections, without the visuals initially. Using appropriate mimes, tell students you are suffering various ailments (1 to 6 on the tape transcript), then ask them to repeat these ailments individually, then chorally.

Teacher: *Ich habe Kopfschmerzen.* (Mime:) *Was habe ich?*
Student: *Kopfschmerzen.*
Teacher: *Gut. Ich habe auch Halsschmerzen ...*

For the second set of ailments (7 to 10 on the tape transcript), continue to use mime but, in order to avoid confusion over *mein/dein*, have the students mime the injury before repeating the new language.

Teacher: *Mein Fuß tut weh.* (To student:) *Du, mach so* (mime). *Was fehlt dir? Mein Fuß tut weh.*
Student: *Mein Fuß tut weh.*

Now ask students to listen to the cassette and to complete the matching activity using the photos in the students' book.

Teacher: *Hört jetzt gut zu. Welches Bild ist das? Zum Beispiel ...* (complete the first one with students).

Ich habe Kopfschmerzen ... Mein Fuß tut weh

1 – Du, nicht so laut ... Ich habe Kopfschmerzen.
  – Kopfschmerzen? Oh. Entschuldigung.

2 – Ich habe Halsschmerzen.

3 – Aua, aua. Ich habe Magenschmerzen.

4 – Was? Du kommst heute nicht in die Schule, sagst du? Warum denn?
  – Ich habe Ohrenschmerzen.
  – Das tut mir aber leid. Gute Besserung.

5 – Ich habe zuviel getanzt.
  – Wieso?
  – Ich habe Rückenschmerzen.

6 – Soll ich dir eine Tüte Bonbons kaufen?
  – Nein danke. Ich habe Zahnschmerzen.

7 – Ich muß mich hinsetzen. Mein Fuß tut weh.

8 – Mein Bein tut weh.

9 – Willst du Tennis spielen? Hast du Lust?
  – Tennis, sagst du? Leider nicht. Mein Arm tut weh.

10 – Es tut mir leid, aber ich kann meine Hausaufgaben nicht machen. Meine Hand tut weh.

Solution:

1E 2J 3C 4F 5I 6B 7G 8H 9A 10D

Was fehlt dir?

Listening
Speaking
Reading
Writing

 GOLD

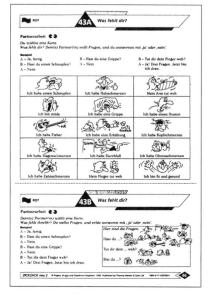

First practise the new vocabulary, preferably using an OHP version of the copymaster. Then write on the board/OHP and practise the following questions.

Hast du einen Schnupfen?
Hast du Halsschmerzen?
Hast du eine Grippe?
Hast du eine Erkältung?
Hast du einen Husten?
Hast du Fieber?
Hast du Kopfschmerzen?
Hast du Magenschmerzen?
Hast du Durchfall?
Hast du Ohrenschmerzen?
Hast du Zahnschmerzen?
Tut dir dein Finger weh?
Tut dir dein Arm weh?
Bist du müde?
Bist du fit und gesund?

Then ask students to play a pairwork guessing game. Partner A picks from the pile of illness and injury cards and Partner B has to work out which one it is by asking questions. Scores could be kept (one point for every question asked). The partner with the lowest score wins.

For a *GOLD* approach, the cut up cards could also be used in a game of bingo. Finally, the illustrations could be stuck into books and labelled.

 Using a word-processing package, students could label illustrations of one or two sickly-looking people with the appropriate ailments.

Was wird hier gespielt?

Listening
Speaking

Tell students they are going to hear a series of recordings of various sports being played and that they should identify the sports in turn. Disputes can be resolved by putting the matter to the vote. This should provide useful revision of this vocabulary area before moving on later to the flow chart activity: *Partnerarbeit. Was fehlt dir?* (see page 86).

Teacher: *Hört gut zu. Was wird hier gespielt?* (Play no. 1:) *Also, wird hier Tennis gespielt, oder ...?*
Student: *Nein, Tischtennis.*
Teacher: *Richtig. Hier wird Tischtennis gespielt.*

 Was wird hier gespielt?

1 *(table tennis)*
2 *(badminton)*
3 *(basketball)*
4 *(football)*
5 *(swimming)*
6 *(skiing)*
7 *(tennis)*
8 *(volleyball)*
9 *(roller skating)*
10 *(ice skating)*
11 *(handball)*
12 *(squash)*

Die neue Turnhalle

Listening
Speaking

Ask students to listen to the conversations of the *Clique* as they enter their new sports hall. Write the list of sports from the solution on the board, but in a jumbled order, and ask students to put them into the order in which they are mentioned in the recording. Again this provides further revision of sports in preparation for the flow chart pairwork.

Teacher: *Hört zu. Hier wird über Sportarten gesprochen. Wie ist die richtige Reihenfolge?*

 Die neue Turnhalle

– Du, hast du die neue Turnhalle schon gesehen? Schön, nicht?
– Ja, klar. Was machst du denn heute abend? Spielst du Basketball, oder ...?
– Nein. Ich laufe Ski.
– Was?! He, habt ihr das gehört, Jungs? Kurt läuft Ski.
– Warum denn nicht? Es gibt hier eine schöne Piste hinter der Turnhalle.
– Was? Echt? Das ist ja toll!
– Und was machst du, Jens?
– Ich? Ja, ich trainiere ein bißchen Judo mit Heidi.
– Mit Heidi? Ist sie so stark?
– Na, klar. Sie hat schon den braunen Gürtel.
– Den braunen Gürtel! Vorsicht, Jens. Sie ist vielleicht gefährlich.
– Wer spielt Basketball mit uns? Du, Sabine?
– Ja. Und Silvia, Guido und Ralf. Spielst du auch mit, Jutta?
– Nee, danke. Ich gehe zum Fitnessraum. Wer geht mit? Bernd? Anke?
– Zum Fitnessraum? Lieber nicht. Anke und ich spielen Badminton.
– Ja, und dann gehen wir schwimmen, nicht wahr, Bernd?
– Genau. Das macht fit: Badminton und Schwimmen.
– Guck mal, Robert. Karate!
– Ja, das weiß ich schon. Ich will mal Karate trainieren.
– Und Dirk und ich spielen Volleyball.
– Nee, Handball.
– Du, Dirk. Handball spiele ich nicht so gern.
– OK Astrid. Dann spielen wir Volleyball.

Solution:

1 Basketball	4 Fitnessraum	7 Karate
2 Skilaufen	5 Badminton	8 Volleyball
3 Judo	6 Schwimmen	

Partnerarbeit. Was fehlt dir?

Listening
Speaking
Reading

A flow chart which sets illness and injury in the context of declining an invitation to do something. First, play the recording to demonstrate how the chart works. Ask students to follow and pick out the question and answer chosen each time. Then perform dialogues with one or two students in front of the class before asking them to continue in pairs.

The dialogues could be consolidated in writing, if required.

Teacher: *Hört gut zu und lest den Text.*

 Partnerarbeit. Was fehlt dir?

1 – Wir spielen Tennis ... kommst du mit?
 – Nein, ich habe keine Lust.
 – Wieso denn?
 – Mir geht's nicht gut.
 – Was fehlt dir denn?
 – Ich habe eine Erkältung.
 – Ach, wie schade ... Gute Besserung.

2 – Wir gehen in die Disco. Kannst du mitkommen?
 – Leider nicht.
 – Warum denn nicht?
 – Ich bin krank.
 – Was ist mit dir los?
 – Ich habe Kopfschmerzen, Fieber und einen Schnupfen.
 – Du hast aber Pech. Gute Besserung! Tschüs!

> Students could word-process their own versions of the flow chart for display.

Partnerarbeit. Wer bin ich?

Listening
Speaking
Reading

 67

A deduction activity based on a number of people depicted with various ailments. Ask students to take it in turns to choose to be one of the people and invite their partner to guess who they are pretending to be. Talk students through the model dialogue before asking them to work in pairs.

Teacher: *Seht euch die Bilder an. Was hat Anton? Was fehlt ihm? Er hat ...?*
Student: *Ohrenschmerzen.*
Teacher: *Und ...?* (Continue until students are confident.) *Jetzt Partnerarbeit. Partner(in) A wählt eine Person, und Partner(in) B stellt Fragen. Seht euch das Beispiel an.* (Read through the model dialogue with students.)

Ich kann nicht ... Ich bin krank

Listening
Speaking

 68   GOLD

Tell students they are going to hear some recordings of people who give reasons for not being able to do something. They then answer a set of questions using vocabulary jumbled in a menu box. Provide practice of switching from first person to third person forms before starting this activity, if required.

Teacher: *Hört gut zu. Warum können sie das nicht machen? Wer kann nicht Fußball spielen? Warum nicht?*

The activity can be further differentiated for a *GOLD* approach by asking students simply to identify which visual matches each recorded item.

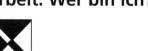 **Ich kann nicht ... Ich bin krank**

1 – Andi Braun.
 – Du, Andi. Ich kann nicht kommen. Mir geht es nicht so gut.
 – Aber, Frank. Was fehlt dir denn?
 – Mein Fuß tut weh. Ich kann heute nicht Fußball spielen.
 – Wie schade.

2 – Vati, heute kann ich nicht in die Schule gehen.
 – Wieso denn, Boris?
 – Ich habe Magenschmerzen.
 – Du armes Kind. Ich rufe den Arzt an. Du bleibst im Bett.

3 – Na, Britta. Willst du im Garten arbeiten?
 – Im Garten? Ach nein, Mutti. Ich kann nicht. Ich habe Kopfschmerzen.
 – Kopfschmerzen? Ach so.

4 – Aua ... ich kann keine Karotten essen.
 – Warum denn? Was hast du denn?
 – Ich habe Zahnschmerzen.
 – Zahnschmerzen? Dann gebe ich deinem Bruder die Tüte Bonbons.

Solution:

1 Frank. Sein Fuß tut weh.

2 Anton. Er hat Magenschmerzen.

3 Britta. Sie hat Kopfschmerzen.

4 Maria. Sie hat Zahnschmerzen.

As a follow-up ask students to work in pairs and make up their own dialogues giving reasons for not being able to do various things, as a result of illness or injury. Complete one or two dialogues with students before starting the pairwork. Refer students to the *Tip des Tages*, if necessary.

Teacher: *Jetzt seid ihr dran. Partnerarbeit. Macht weitere Dialoge.*

Wo tut es ihm weh?

A simple gap-filling activity to revise parts of the body and various illnesses. When students have completed the exercise, ask them if they can work out the meaning of *Heu* from *Heuschnupfen*. Then ask them to produce their own grids, along the lines of the illustration, to depict a different ailment. They can then swap with other students to see if they can work out each other's puzzles.

Teacher: *Füllt die Lücken aus. Was bedeutet ‚Heu'?*

Entschuldigungszettel

Ask students to read these excuse notes written to teachers to apologise for the absence of a child from school, and match them to the visuals. Although introduced here, *wegen* followed by the genitive is not intended for formal presentation. This activity will require students to refer to the word list.

Teacher: *Seht euch die Entschuldigungszettel und die Bilder an. Was paßt wozu? Schlagt die Wörter in der Wörterliste nach.*

Solution:

1E 2A 3D 4C 5B

Lieber Herr Heinemann!

A creative activity, in which students write their own imaginary letters of excuse to a teacher. There should be lots of opportunity for humour here. It might be worthwhile organising a brainstorming session on possible solutions before students tackle this activity. Write up students' suggestions on the board/OHP. One possible beginning is shown as an example.

Teacher: *Ihr seid faul und wollt nicht in die Schule gehen. Ihr müßt also einen Entschuldigungszettel schreiben. Ihr müßt den Zettel im Namen eurer Mutter oder eures Vaters schreiben.*

> Excuse notes could finally be word-processed.

Allergien

This listening activity presents the vocabulary needed to talk about allergies. Point out to students that they only have to understand the gist, not every word, to complete the task. Students should listen to the tape and match the pictures to the recorded items. The first item appears in the students' book. Whenever somebody sneezes during a lesson do not miss the opportunity to say ‚Gesundheit!'

Teacher: *Hört zu und seht euch die Bilder an. Was paßt wozu?*

  Allergien

1 – Was willst du trinken? Ein Glas Milch?
  – Nein danke. Ich darf nicht.
  – Du darfst nicht? Wieso denn?
  – Ich bin allergisch gegen Milch. Ich darf auch keinen Fisch, keinen Käse, keine Sahne und keine Bananen essen.
  – Mensch! Das ist ja schlimm!

2 – Was ist los, Oliver?
  – Ich bin krank.
  – Was fehlt dir denn?
  – Ich habe Magenschmerzen und Kopfschmerzen.
  – Hast du auch Fieber?
  – Ich glaube ja.
  – Hmm ... Kopfschmerzen und Magenschmerzen?

– Ja. Ich weiß nicht, warum ich so krank bin. Das Omelett hat mir geschmeckt!

– Hast du Allergien?

– Ja. Ich darf keine Meeresfrüchte essen, also keine Krabben und keine Muscheln.

– Du armer. Das ist es. Im Omelett waren Muscheln.

– Muscheln?

– Ja ... komm. Rufen wir den Arzt an. Mach dir keine Sorgen. Der Arzt kommt gleich.

3 – Gesundheit, Karl. Du, kommst du mit? Wir gehen spazieren.

– Danke, aber heute nicht. Am besten bleibe ich zu Hause.

– Warum denn? Es ist schön warm heute. Komm doch mit!

– Da, siehst du?

– Bist du erkältet?

– Nein. Ich habe Heuschnupfen. Bei diesem heißen Wetter ist es immer fürchterlich.

– Das tut mir aber leid. Hoffentlich geht es dir bald besser. Tschüs, Karl.

– Danke, Dieter. Tschüs.

4 – Kopfschmerzen und Halsschmerzen, sagst du? Hier, Aspirin.

– Danke. Ich darf aber kein Aspirin nehmen. Ich bin allergisch dagegen.

– Ach so. Was nimmst du dann, wenn du Kopfschmerzen hast?

– Nichts. Besonders kein Aspirin.

5 – Elsa, kommst du mit? Ich gehe zum Tierarzt. Mein Hund ist krank.

– Ich darf nicht.

– Du darfst nicht mit zum Tierarzt kommen! Du spinnst wohl!

– Nee. Ich bin allergisch gegen Tiere. Ich habe Asthma.

– Es tut mir leid.

– Ach was. Das macht nichts. Viele Leute haben Asthma.

Solution:

1D 2E 3B 4C 5A

Krank im Urlaub

Listening
Speaking

An extended listening text with illness and injury embedded. Ask students to look at the visuals and listen to the telephone conversation. Their task is simply to connect each person to his/her ailment on the copymaster, and finally to write out each person's aliment in the spaces provided at the bottom of the copymaster. It will be necessary for students to look up some vocabulary in the word list.

Teacher: *Hört gut zu und seht euch die Bilder an. Macht Linien, so* (point to the example on the copymaster).

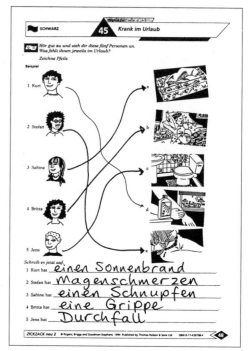

Krank im Urlaub

– Hallo, Torsten!

– Jens. Wo bist du?

– In Spanien, im Urlaub.

– Schön. Du bist nicht alleine, oder?

– Nein. Ich bin mit Sabine, Kurt, Stefan und Britta hierher gekommen.

– Toll. Das muß aber viel Spaß machen.

– Gar nicht.

– Wieso?

– Wir sind alle krank.

– So ein Pech, krank im Urlaub! Was fehlt euch denn?

– Kurt hat einen Sonnenbrand. Er hat am ersten Tag fünf Stunden in der Sonne gelegen.

– Das war dumm! Natürlich kriegt man einen Sonnenbrand, wenn man so lange in der Sonne liegt. Was fehlt Stefan?

– Er hat Magenschmerzen ... schwere Magenschmerzen.

– Oh, das ist schlimm. Was hat er gegessen?

– Paella – er wußte nicht, daß Krabben drin sind ... er ist allergisch gegen Krabben.

– Das ist wirklich Pech. Wenn man nach Spanien fährt, will man natürlich Paella essen.

– Ja.

– Die Sabine ist noch fit und gesund, oder?

– Auch nicht. Sie hat einen Schnupfen.

– Einen Schnupfen? Die Arme!

– Und Britta hat eine Grippe. Sie liegt die ganze Zeit im Bett. Sie will wieder nach Deutschland zurück.

– Wie schade. Und du, Jens? Bist du auch krank?

– Ja, eigentlich schon. Ich habe Durchfall.

– Du Jens, das tut mir ...

– Oh, nein! Ich muß dringend zur Toilette. Tschüs, Torsten.

Solution:

1d 2e 3a 4b 5c

Students may now attempt the *Lernziel 1* activities in the *Selbstbedienung* section on pages 72 and 73 of the students' book. See page 92 of this book for more details.

Lernziel 2 **Medikamente**

Partnerarbeit. Haben Sie etwas gegen Seekrankheit?

Listening
Speaking
Reading

70

Talk students through the new vocabulary for medicines presented alongside the visuals, and the new illness terms. They can then practise this new language in the pairwork task. Go through the example with them first.

Teacher: *Nun, Medikamente. Seht euch die Bilder an. Hier haben wir Tabletten gegen Seekrankheit. Wie heißt ‚Seekrankheit' auf englisch?*

Student: Seasickness.

Teacher: *Richtig. Und Hustenbonbons? etc. Jetzt Partnerarbeit. Partner(in) A wählt eine Krankheit, und fragt zum Beispiel: ‚Haben Sie etwas gegen Seekrankheit?' Partner(in) B antwortet: ‚Ja, hier. Tabletten.' Macht jetzt weiter.*

In der Apotheke

Listening
Speaking
Reading

70

Students should now be able to do the simple matching activity. Ask students to listen to the cassette and match the recorded items to the medicines depicted on page 70, which have just provided the basis for the previous pairwork activity.

In der Apotheke

1 – Guten Morgen.

– Guten Morgen. Haben Sie etwas gegen Brandwunden?

– Also, diese Salbe ist sehr effektiv. Sie kostet acht Mark.

– Danke schön.

2 – Bitte schön?

– Ich brauche etwas gegen Ohrenschmerzen.

– Gegen Ohrenschmerzen? Diese Tropfen hier sind sehr gut.

– Gut. Die nehme ich.

3 – Guten Tag. Ich fahre übermorgen mit der Fähre von Hamburg nach Harwich. Haben Sie etwas gegen Seekrankheit?

– Diese Tabletten hier. Aber Vorsicht! Sie machen müde.

– Das macht doch nichts. Ich schlafe gern, besonders auf einer Fähre auf der Nordsee!

4 – Guten Tag. Haben Sie etwas gegen Magenschmerzen?

– Haben Sie starke Magenschmerzen?

– Nein, es ist nicht so schlimm.

– Also, hier haben Sie einen Saft. Er schmeckt gut und tut gut. Das macht 12 Mark.

– Danke schön.

– Bitte schön.

5 – Ich hätte gern etwas gegen Erkältung.

– Haben Sie auch Halsschmerzen?

– Ja.

– Dann empfehle ich diese Hustenbonbons.

– Gut. Was kostet die Packung?

– Sechs Mark.

6 – Ich habe mir in den Finger geschnitten. Das blutet so und tut weh. Haben Sie etwas dagegen?

– Laß mal den Finger sehen ... ja, das ist nicht so schlimm. Hier, Pflaster.

– Danke.

7 – Guten Morgen. Haben Sie etwas gegen Heuschnupfen?

– Diese Kapseln hier, aber Vorsicht! Sie sind stark. Gehen Sie am besten zu einem Arzt.

– Danke, aber ich glaube, ich nehme lieber die Kapseln.

8 – Wir haben viele Mücken in unserem Hotelzimmer. Können Sie uns 'was empfehlen?

– Ja, sicher. Dieser Spray ist effektiv gegen Mücken. Ich weiß, wie ärgerlich Mücken sind!

Solution:

1H 2F 3A 4G 5B 6C 7E 8D

Haben Sie etwas gegen Zebrastreifen?

Reading

A brief cartoon commenting light-heartedly on the practice of sunbathing without due care and attention. Not intended for detailed exploitation.

Wundermittel

Listening
Speaking
Reading

Ask students to listen to a series of advertisements for various medicines. Students should listen to the recording, match each item to one of the products depicted in the artwork, and write out what it claims to cure.

Teacher: *Hört zu: Werbung für Medikamente. Wie heißt das auf englisch? Schaut in der Wörterliste nach. Nummer eins (play the first recorded item:) Welches Produkt ist das?*
Student: *,Heili'.*
Teacher: *Richtig. ,Heili' – Tabletten gegen …?*
Student: *Kopfschmerzen.*
Teacher: *Ja. Schreibt es auf. Macht jetzt weiter.*

Wundermittel

1 – Kaufen Sie ,Heili', das Wundermittel gegen Kopfschmerzen. Tabletten in allen Apotheken zu finden. ,Heili'.

2 – ,Ruckzuck', wirkt wie ein Wunder, wenn Sie sich verbrannt haben – ,Ruckzuck'.

3 – Kaufen Sie ,Mirgehtsbesser', das Wundermittel. Tropfen gegen Ohrenschmerzen. ,Mirgehtsbesser'. Natürlich.

4 – ,Schluckundlach', Saft gegen Magenschmerzen. ,Schluckundlach', ein echtes Wundermittel.

5 – Wenn Sie Zahnschmerzen haben, nehmen Sie ,Medikawohl'. Pillen gegen Zahnschmerzen. ,Medikawohl' und Sie fühlen sich wohl.

6 – ,Fitundfett' Wundermittel. Haben Sie Halsschmerzen? Kaufen Sie unsere Hustenbonbons. ,Fitundfett'.

7 – ,Gesundwienie'. Haben Sie zu lange in der Sonne gelegen? Haben Sie einen Sonnenbrand? Kaufen Sie diese fantastische Salbe – ,Gesundwienie'.

8 – ,Heilkraft', die wirkungsvolle Salbe gegen Rückenschmerzen. ,Heilkraft'. Ein Wundermittel.

Solution:

1 Heili – gegen Kopfschmerzen
2 Ruckzuck – gegen Brandwunden
3 Mirgehtsbesser – gegen Ohrenschmerzen
4 Schluckundlach – gegen Magenschmerzen
5 Medikawohl – gegen Zahnschmerzen
6 Fitundfett – gegen Halsschmerzen
7 Gesundwienie – gegen Sonnenbrand
8 Heilkraft – gegen Rückenschmerzen

Follow up by asking students to find out the meanings of the brand names by looking up their component parts in the word list, and to invent their own brand names, which more able students could include in a brief advert based on *Wundermittel*.

 These could be produced using desktop-publishing.

Ein guter Rat

Listening
Speaking
Reading

Students should work in pairs and offer the most suitable piece of advice for each ailment or illness depicted. Demonstrate one or two examples, before asking students to carry out the pairwork.

Was macht die Zähne kaputt?

Listening
Speaking
Reading
Writing

Ask students to look at the visuals of food and drink and decide which are good and which are bad for their teeth. When they decide, they should record the information on the copymaster. Once the activity has been completed, students give feedback, either in pairs or as a whole-class activity, and the results could be recorded on the board or OHP. You could agree or disagree with the findings, leading to discussion.

Teacher: *Seht euch die Bilder an. Was ist gut für die Zähne? Was macht die Zähne kaputt? Macht vier Listen.*

Do a few examples on the board/OHP if necessary.

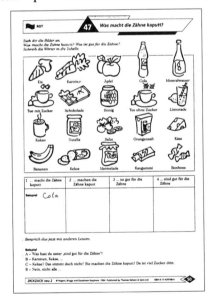

Was meinen Sie, Herr Doktor Schweiger?

   SCHWARZ

Listening
Speaking

A demanding listening text designed to help students imagine how they might react to finding themselves in a hospital in Germany listening to two doctors diagnosing the illness, without thinking that the patient might be able to understand some of what they are saying.

Write up some of the more difficult medical terms on the board, then ask students to listen to the cassette and note anything they understand in the course of the doctors' conversation, which considers using a stomach pump; whether the patient has appendicitis; and continued observation. Brainstorm with the whole class after playing the recording once or twice. Then ask students to make their notes in pairs. Finally, help students to break down words like *Blinddarm* and *Lebensmittelvergiftung* into their constituent parts.

Teacher: *Ihr seid krank und liegt im Krankenhaus. Zwei Ärzte kommen, Herr Dr. Schweiger und Frau Dr. Nagel. (Write the names on the board/OHP.) Hört gut zu. Was sagen sie? Macht Notizen in Paaren.*

Was meinen Sie, Herr Doktor Schweiger?

– Herr Doktor Schweiger, was fehlt denn diesem Patienten?

– Frau Doktor Nagel, dieser Patient aus England klagt über Magenschmerzen.

– So, was hat er denn in den letzten Tagen gegessen?

– Er sagt, er habe gestern Fisch gegessen, und der Fisch muß wohl schlecht gewesen sein.

– Hat er gebrochen?

– Ja, er hat gestern abend und heute früh ziemlich stark brechen müssen.

– Hat er denn Fieber?

– Eigentlich nicht. Er hatte gestern erhöhte Temperatur, aber nicht erwähnenswert.

– Und hat er irgendwo anders noch Schmerzen?

– Nein, eigentlich nicht ... nur im Magenbereich.

– Was meinen Sie, Herr Doktor Schweiger? Sollten wir ihm vielleicht den Magen auspumpen lassen?

– Ja, ich wäre dafür, den Magen auszupumpen, weil es mir eine normale Lebensmittelvergiftung zu sein scheint.

– Oder sollten wir operieren? Ich meine, es könnte der Blinddarm sein. Was halten Sie von einer Operation?

– Nein, Frau Doktor Nagel, davon halte ich überhaupt nichts, denn in diesem Fall ist wohl eine Lebensmittelvergiftung die wahrscheinlichste Ursache der Krankheit.

– Sie mögen Recht haben, aber wir müssen ganz sicher sein.

– Ja, ich möchte den Jungen noch weitere zwei oder drei Tage im Krankenhaus behalten.

– Ja, gut. Wir müssen aber noch seine Gastfamilie anrufen, damit sie Bescheid weiß, und seine Eltern in England ...

– Ja, sehr gut.

Points raised by doctors:

  (i) (Complaining of) stomach pains
 (ii) eaten fish (could have been off)
(iii) vomited previous evening and early that morning
 (iv) no particularly high temperature
  (v) no pain other than (around) stomach
 (vi) use a stomach pump?
(vii) could be (straightforward) food poisoning
(viii) could it be appendicitis?
 (ix) food poisoning most likely
  (x) two to three days observation in hospital
 (xi) host family + parents to be informed (by phone)

Students may now attempt the *Lernziel 2* activities in the *Selbstbedienung* section on page 73 of the students' book. See below for further details.

 Selbstbedienung **sb**

 72–73   73

Lernziel 1
Was sagt Long John Silver?

 GOLD

A light-hearted matching activity involving parts of the body.

Solution:

Long John Silver sagt: ‚Das ist mein Bein'.
Venus de Milo sagt: ‚Das sind meine Arme'.
Admiral Nelson sagt: ‚Ich sehe keine Schiffe …, aber das ist mein Auge'.
Frankenstein sagt: ‚Das ist mein Kopf'.
Van Gogh sagt: ‚Das ist mein Ohr'.
Graf Dracula sagt: ‚Das sind meine Zähne'.

Fünf Minuten später

 GOLD

A series of humorous drawings in which disasters are about to happen. The task is to predict what each person will say in five minutes' time. A menu of alternatives is provided.

Solution:

A Ich habe Kopfschmerzen.
B Ich habe Magenschmerzen.
C Mein Bein tut weh.
D Ich habe Ohrenschmerzen.
E Mein Fuß tut weh.
F Ich habe einen Sonnenbrand.

Ich bin allergisch gegen …

 ROT

Photos to cue statements about allergies.

Solution:

Paul: ‚Ich bin allergisch gegen Fisch und Tee'.
Uschi: ‚Ich bin allergisch gegen Käse und Sahne'.
Moni: ‚Ich bin allergisch gegen Zucker und Eier'.
Omri: ‚Ich bin allergisch gegen Wurst und Bananen'.
Sven: ‚Ich bin allergisch gegen Milch und Kaffee'.

Lernziel 2
Was haben Sie gegen ...?

 GOLD

Authentic advertising material plus statements for a true/false reading activity.

Solution:

1 falsch **2** richtig **3** falsch **4** falsch **5** richtig

Frank ist krank

 SCHWARZ

Students have to diagnose Frank's injuries, and then offer suggestions for remedies (any suitable ones will do!).

Solution:

Sein Bein tut weh. Schmerztabletten.
Er hat Kopfschmerzen. Pillen gegen Kopfschmerzen.
Er hat Magenschmerzen. Saft gegen Magenschmerzen.
Er hat einen Sonnenbrand. Eine Salbe gegen Sonnenbrand.
Er hat Zahnschmerzen. Kapseln gegen Zahnschmerzen.

Hypochonderlied

Listening
Speaking
Reading

A song, following the theme of the chapter, for students to listen to, and then to sing along to.

 Hypochonderlied

Herr Doktor, ich hab' einen Schnupfen.
Sogar meine Augen sind wund.
Können Sie mir etwas geben?
Ich fühle mich gar nicht gesund.

Nehmen Sie diese Tabletten.
Hoffentlich haben Sie Glück.
Und wenn Sie dann immer noch krank sind,
Kommen Sie in *fünf Tagen* zurück.

Herr Doktor, ich hab' eine Grippe.
Sogar meine Füße tun weh.
Können Sie mir etwas geben?
Dann nehme ich es mit dem Tee.

Nehmen Sie diese Tabletten.
Hoffentlich haben Sie Glück.
Und wenn Sie dann immer noch krank sind,
Kommen Sie in *fünf Wochen* zurück.

Herr Doktor, ich kann gar nicht schlafen.
Seien Sie bitte so nett ...
Ich brauche nur ein paar Tabletten,
Dann gehe ich wieder ins Bett.

Nehmen Sie diese Tabletten.
Hoffentlich haben Sie Glück.
Und wenn Sie dann immer noch krank sind,
Kommen Sie in *fünf Jahren* zurück!

Steffi

Reading

Another cartoon about the exploits of Steffi, intended for fun, not detailed exploitation.

Grammar exercises 21 and 22 on copymaster 79 are based on the material in this chapter.

 79 +83

The students' personal profile for this chapter is on copymaster 85.

 85

After completing work on this chapter, check whether any further reinforcement is appropriate from the video material, Activity Box cards and Assessment Support Pack tasks.

Main teaching points

Lernziel 1: **Planning a journey**

Lernziel 2: **Staying at a campsite**

Language presented:

- *Ich will/Wir wollen* + infinitive
- *Das ist zu* + adjective
- *Lieber/Am besten*
- *Wohin?*

- *Wie lange?*
- Travel vocabulary
- Vocabulary for holiday activities
- Camping vocabulary

Before beginning work on this chapter, check where the video material, Activity Box cards and Assessment Support Pack tasks will be most appropriate.

Lernziel 1
Wohin?

Wohin fahren sie?

Listening
Speaking
Reading

A photo story about a group of teenagers in Pinneberg, Northern Germany, planning a summer holiday. The teenagers' comments provide some background information on Helgoland, their chosen holiday destination, and there is further information about the island on page 79 in *Helgoland – Inselparadies!* The cassette version adds expression to the statements made by the teenagers and provides students with a model for their own performances/recordings. Encourage students to use the word list to find out the meanings of new items of vocabulary. Students should identify where the group is going, and how they plan to get there.

Teacher: *Diese jungen Leute vom Jugendzentrum Pinneberg planen eine Urlaubsreise. Aber wohin? Nach Spanien? Nach Italien? In die Schweiz? Und wie kommen sie dahin? (Hört zu und) lest den Text.*

Wohin fahren sie?

Herr Timm:	Also, bald sind Ferien. Fünf Tage zusammen im Urlaub. Aber wo?
Monika:	Ja, genau. Wohin fahren wir?
Stefan:	Nach Spanien – Sonne, Schwimmen und schöne spanische Mädchen!
Gabi:	Lieber schöne spanische Jungen!
Andrea:	Oder wie wäre es mit Italien?
Volker:	Aber nein! Spanien, Italien ... das ist doch alles zu teuer und zu weit! Wir haben nur fünf Tage Urlaub zusammen. Am besten fahren wir gar nicht so weit weg.
Martin:	Ja? Wohin denn?
Volker:	Nach Helgoland, zum Beispiel!
Birgit:	Helgoland? Was gibt's dort Besonderes?
Volker:	Sonne, Meer, Surfen, viele Touristen ... und keine Autos!
Herr Timm:	Das stimmt. Helgoland ist autofrei. Und das ist gar nicht so weit von Pinneberg.
Ralf:	Wo liegt das eigentlich?
Anja:	Helgoland ist eine kleine Insel in der Nordsee ... etwa 70 Kilometer von Cuxhaven entfernt.
Asla:	Gute Idee, Volker. Wie kommen wir dorthin? Mit dem Flugzeug?
Volker:	Lieber nicht. Ich habe immer Flugangst.

Asla:	Ich fliege ganz gern. Das geht am schnellsten.
Birgit:	Das stimmt, aber es kostet auch am meisten. Mit dem Schiff ist es billiger.
Martin:	Oh nein – ich werde immer seekrank!
Volker:	Du, das ist keine lange Schiffsreise, und das Meer ist ganz ruhig. Wir fahren am besten mit dem Bus nach Cuxhaven und dann direkt mit dem Schiff nach Helgoland.
Herr Timm:	Na, was meint ihr? Mit dem Bus und dann mit dem Schiff nach Helgoland?
Asla:	Ja, klar.
Martin:	Na, gut.
Birgit:	OK.
Ralf:	Toll!

Wohin fahren sie? Ein Rätsel

Reading Writing

A copymaster based on the previous item in the students' book. Students should first complete the clues to the puzzle, which shows where the young people are going on holiday. They can then match up the sentence halves, and write a paragraph of information about Helgoland.

Solution:

1 Schiff	5 autofrei	9 Nordsee
2 Pinneberg	6 Italien	10 Helgoland
3 Urlaub	7 seekrank	
4 Flugangst	8 Sonne	

Helgoland ist eine Insel.
Die Insel liegt in der Nordsee.
Sie ist etwa 70 Kilometer von Cuxhaven entfernt.
Man kommt mit dem Schiff oder mit dem Flugzeug dahin.
Auf Helgoland darf man nicht Auto fahren.
Sonne, Meer, Surfen ... alles auf Helgoland!

Wie kommt die Familie Müller nach Spanien?

Listening Speaking Reading

A discussion by the Müller family about how best to get to their holiday destination, Malaga, in Southern Spain. Ask students to look at the outline map and then go through the multiple choice items with the class. Then ask them to listen to the recording and make a note of the means of transport used for each part of the journey.

Teacher: *Die Familie Müller verbringt zwei Wochen in Südspanien in Malaga. Die Familie fährt zum Flughafen und fliegt direkt nach Malaga. Aber wie kommt sie zum Flughafen? Mit der S-Bahn? Und wie fliegt sie? Charter oder Linienflug? Hört gut zu, und kreuzt die richtigen Antworten an.*

Wie kommt die Familie Müller nach Spanien?

Frau M.:	Wie kommen wir am besten zum Flughafen? Was meinst du?
Herr M.:	Mit dem Wagen wäre es ganz praktisch. Aber es kostet so viel, am Flughafen zu parken. Ich glaube, es kostet zwanzig Mark pro Tag.
Frau M.:	Das ist eine Menge Geld. Fahren wir vielleicht mit dem Bus oder mit der S-Bahn?
Herr M.:	Nein, lieber nicht. Wir haben zuviel Gepäck. Ich glaube, am besten fahren wir mit dem Taxi dorthin. Wir sind dann in zweieinhalb Stunden in Malaga. Toll, nicht?
Michael:	Was für eine Maschine ist es eigentlich? Weißt du's?
Herr M.:	Nee. Aber es ist ein normaler Flug. Kein Charter.
Jutta:	Wie kommen wir vom Flugplatz in Malaga zum Hotel?
Herr M.:	Das ist alles ganz einfach. Wir werden mit einem kleinen Bus abgeholt.

Frau M.: Hast du auch ein paar Rundfahrten gebucht?

Herr M.: Nein. Am besten organisieren wir das, wenn wir dort unten sind. Die Frau meint, am besten macht man eine Tour mit dem Zug. Das soll viel billiger sein als mit dem Bus.

Jutta: Ich möchte auch Nordafrika besuchen. Wie kommen wir am besten dahin?

Herr M.: Mit dem Flugzeug geht es am schnellsten, aber es kostet sehr viel. Die Fahrt mit dem Schiff dauert nur ein paar Stunden und soll sehr schön sein.

Jutta: Na gut, dann fahren wir mit dem Schiff.

Solution

1b 2b 3c 4d 5a

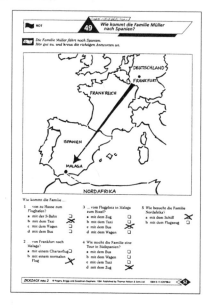

Gruppenarbeit. Und du?

Listening
Speaking
Reading

Ask students to work in groups and discuss possible holiday destinations and means of transport. Refer them to the *Tip des Tages* on page 77 for support. Help them focus on *lieber* and *am besten*. Work through the example, and begin the activity as a whole class discussion, writing up the key expressions for students' reference, before handing the activity over to them in groups. If necessary, brainstorm with the class and write up suggestions for holiday destinations and the means of transport alongside reasons for saying no or yes.

Teacher: *Und ihr? Was sagt ihr, wenn ihr einen Urlaub plant? Wohin? (To one student:) Nach*

Schottland? Oder lieber nicht?

Student: *Lieber nicht.*

Teacher: *Warum? Zu weit? Zu kalt?*

Student: *Zu kalt.*

Teacher: *OK. Nach Spanien?*

Student: *Ja!*

Teacher: *Wie kommen wir dahin? Mit dem Auto?*

Student: *Nein, es ist zu ... Am besten fliegen wir.*

Teacher: *(Handing over to groups:) Gruppenarbeit. Ihr macht Urlaubspläne. Wohin? Und wie kommt ihr dahin?*

Mit dem Flugzeug nach Helgoland

Listening
Speaking
Reading
Writing

Ask students to look at the information about flights to Helgoland and listen to the recording. Then ask them to listen again and answer the questions.

Teacher: *Wollen wir nach Helgoland fliegen? Dann gehen wir zum Reisebüro Mailänder (hier ganz unten) und buchen einen Flug. Hört gut zu und beantwortet die Fragen.*

Mit dem Flugzeug nach Helgoland

– Reisebüro Mailänder. Guten Tag.

– Ich möchte nach Helgoland fliegen. Kann ich bei Ihnen buchen?

– Ja, natürlich. Wann wollen Sie fliegen?

– Am dritten April.

– Das ist kein Problem. Das ist ja in der Vorsaison.

– Was kostet ein Flug – hin und zurück, bitte?

– Wenn sie an einem Tag hin- und zurückfliegen kostet es 350 Mark. Der normale Hin- und Rückflug kostet aber 400 Mark.

– Ist das ein Charterflug?

– Nein, Linienflug.

– Ah gut. Um wieviel Uhr ist der erste Abflug von Hamburg?

– Um 08.15 Uhr. Der fliegt non-stop nach Helgoland und kommt um 8.55 Uhr an.

– Das ist nicht lang!

– Nein, der Flug dauert nur 40 Minuten.

Solution:

1 Am 1. April.
2 Ja.
3 Um 08.15.
4 DM400,-/DM350,-
5 40 Minuten.
6 (0 47 25) 566

Mir geht's nicht gut!

Reading
Writing

Two cartoons to consolidate *Ich habe Flugangst* and *Ich bin seekrank*. Not intended for detailed exploitation, although some students may wish to produce display-size versions and/or alternative text and artwork.

Wir fahren nach England

  GOLD

Listening
Speaking
Reading

A discussion between four teachers of English from Pinneberg about their preferred means of travelling with their exchange group from Germany to Bristol. Ask students to identify the route each one chooses by looking at the alternatives A–D.

Teacher: *Vier Englischlehrer an einer Realschule in Pinneberg planen einen Austausch mit einer Schule in Bristol. Hört gut zu. Was sagen die Lehrer? Wie wollen sie nach Bristol fahren? Seht euch A, B, C und D an. Wer ist A? Herr Fichte? Oder Frau Heinemann? Oder ...?*

 Wir fahren nach England

1 Herr F.: Was meinen Sie, Frau Ziegert? Wie kommen wir am besten nach Bristol?

Frau Z.: Ich glaube, am besten fahren wir mit dem Bus nach Ostende. Das ist alles Autobahn. Und dann mit der Fähre nach Dover. Das sind nur vier Stunden auf dem Schiff. Und von Dover können wir dann direkt mit dem Bus nach Bristol fahren. Es gibt eine Autobahn um London herum – die M25 und dann die Autobahn nach Bristol – die M4, glaube ich.

2 Herr F.: Und Sie, Frau Heinemann? Was meinen Sie?

Frau H.: Am besten fliegen wir. Das geht viel schneller. Und ein Charterflug kostet auch nicht viel. Der Flug dauert nur anderthalb Stunden nach London. Also, ich schlage vor, wir fahren mit der S-Bahn zum Hamburger Flughafen. In London gibt's auch eine U-Bahn zur Stadtmitte. Wir fahren also mit der U-Bahn in die Innenstadt und dann mit einem Intercityzug weiter nach Bristol.

3 Herr F.: Was meinen Sie, Herr Gerecht?

Herr G.: Am besten fahren wir mit dem Schiff nach Harwich. Es ist zwar eine lange Überfahrt – so zwanzig Stunden – aber es gibt eine Disco und ein Kino an Bord. Das ist bestimmt viel besser für die Schüler, als acht Stunden im Bus zu sitzen. Also, ich meine, wir fahren mit dem Bus nach Hamburg und mit dem Schiff nach Harwich. Dann wieder mit dem Bus nach London. Von London nach Bristol würde ich lieber mit dem Zug fahren. Das geht nämlich viel schneller. Was meinen Sie, Herr Fichte?

4 Herr F.: Ich fliege auch lieber. Aber nicht Charter. Am besten fliegen wir also Lufthansa Hamburg–Heathrow. Und es ist viel besser, wenn die Eltern ihre Kinder mit dem Wagen zum Flugplatz bringen. Von Heathrow nach Bristol kann man dann mit dem Bus fahren. Es gibt eine Autobahn.

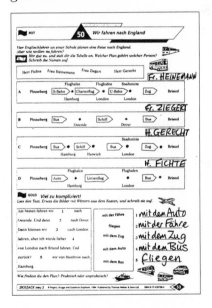

Solution:

A Frau Heinemann   C Herr Gerecht
B Frau Ziegert   D Herr Fichte

The *GOLD* follow up text (*Viel zu kompliziert!*) describes a most complicated travel plan. Students should substitute phrases from the menu box for pictures. They are then asked whether they think the travel plan is practical or not.

Solution:

1 mit dem Auto   4 mit dem Bus
2 mit der Fähre   5 fliegen
3 mit dem Zug

Helgoland-Inselparadies!

Listening
Speaking
Reading

Information about the facilities and activities available in Helgoland for tourists. Ask students to read the text, which is interspersed with visuals replacing key words. These words are listed in the students' book jumbled beneath the text. Students could use the word list to help them write out the text in full and/or listen to Volker on cassette giving the full text – enjoying his holiday, despite the fact that he has broken his leg!

Teacher: *Seht euch den Text und die Bilder an und hört zu. Was fehlt hier? Ersetzt die Bilder mit den passenden Wörtern vom Kasten. Schreibt dann den ganzen Text in eure Hefte.*

Helgoland – Inselparadies!

– Schönen Gruß aus Helgoland. Ich bin's, der Volker. Ich habe mir zwar das Bein gebrochen, aber Urlaub ist Urlaub, nicht? Wie ihr seht, sitze ich hier bequem und lese einen Prospekt über Helgoland. Wollt ihr mitlesen?

1. Helgoland ist eine kleine Insel in der Nordsee. Sie besteht aus drei Teilen: Oberland, Unterland und Düne. In Oberland sieht man die schönen roten Felsen am Meer.

Toll, nicht?

2. Im Südosten liegt Unterland, und im Osten befindet sich die zweite, kleinere Insel von Helgoland, Düne. Hier ist der Sand schön weiß, und viele Leute schwimmen, surfen, segeln und angeln. Es gibt sogar einen Strand, wo sich die Leute nackt sonnen und schwimmen!

3. Aber auch wenn die Sonne scheint, ist es aber oft windig am Strand, und viele Leute sitzen im Strandkorb oder in den Dünen und sonnen sich.

4. Auf Helgoland kann man Minigolf und Tennis spielen. Abends kann man auch in die Disco gehen.

5. Außerdem ist Helgoland autofrei und zollfrei. Viele Touristen besuchen Helgoland nur für einen Tag und machen Einkäufe, denn Tabak, Wein, Kaffee, Tee, Parfüm, Käse und Fleisch sind dort billiger als in Deutschland.

Für mich ist Helgoland ein Inselparadies – auch wenn ich mir das Bein gebrochen habe!

Solution:

1 Insel; Felsen

2 Sand; surfen; angeln; Strand

3 Sonne; Strandkorb; Dünen

4 Minigolf; Tennis; Disco; autofrei; zollfrei; Wein; Kaffee; Parfüm; Käse

Some students may be interested in the (relatively recent) history of Helgoland, particularly the fact that it was held by the British for most of the 19th century before being handed back to Germany in 1894, in exchange for control over the island region of Zanzibar, in East Africa. The use of the Helgoland by the Germans during the Second World War led to heavy bombardment by the British forces, who took control again and only returned the island to German control well after the end of the war. The town and port were rebuilt in the 1950s. Helgoland is now used mainly in navigation and as a centre for scientific research, especially in the study of birds. There may also follow some general discussion about offshore duty-free rights, as in the Channel Islands and the Isle of Man.

Students could word-process information about Helgoland as part of a displayed project. If resources are available, information from remote data-bases or software packages could be used to add to the detail. A spoken commentary could be added on audio cassette, or the whole integrated into a CD-ROM version.

Students may now attempt the activities relating to *Lernziel 1* in the *Selbstbedienung* section on page 82 of the students' book. See page 102 of this book for further details

Lernziel 2
Camping macht Spaß!

Welcher Campingplatz?

Listening
Speaking
Reading

Details of six campsites for students to match to the
stated requirements of the holidaymakers. Introduce
the notion of choosing campsites by asking students
to imagine they are going to a campsite themselves.
Ask them what they want to find in and around the
campsite. Revise leisure activities, if necessary, and
write them up. Then ask students to listen to the
recording and read the brief outlines of the facilities
available in each of the six sites listed. Refer
students to the wordlist for new items of vocabulary,
such as *Einrichtungen* and *Trimm-dich-Pfad*. You
can now ask them to work out the most suitable site
for each group of people in the photos. Read through
the requirements with students, emphasising the use
of *will* and *wollen,* and/or play the recording,
pausing after each statement.

Teacher: *Wir wählen einen Campingplatz. Was für
einen Campingplatz wollen wir?* (To one student:)
*Was willst du zum Beispiel? Willst du schwimmen
oder wandern? Ich will ...*
Student: *Ich will schwimmen.*
Teacher: *Gut, du willst schwimmen. Wir wählen
also einen Campingplatz mit Schwimmbad oder an
der See.* (To another student:) *Was noch? Willst du
angeln? Willst du andere Teenager treffen?*
Student: *Ich will angeln.*
Teacher: *Seht euch diese Campingplätze an. Was
gibt's hier? Waschräume, beheiztes Schwimmbad,
Minigolf? Schlagt in der Wörterliste nach. Und diese
Leute hier* (point to the photos and text in the book).
*Was paßt am besten? Welcher Campingplatz ist für
die Familie Leiser geeignet? Lest die Texte (und hört
zu).*

Welcher Campingplatz?

1 – Wir sind alle sehr sportlich. Ich will Tennis
spielen. Mein Sohn Markus will angeln und
mein Mann auch. Meine Töchter wollen reiten,
und ich will jeden Tag schwimmen.

2 – Ich will andere junge Leute treffen. Meine
Freundinnen Asla und Jutta auch. Das ist sehr

wichtig für uns. Wir schwimmen auch alle sehr
gern.

3 – Wir wollen einen schönen Campingplatz finden,
wo unser vierjähriger Sohn Philip ruhig spielen
kann. Wir bringen auch unseren Hund Max mit.
Ich will ein paar Wanderungen machen.

4 – Ich will unbedingt viel Sport treiben, und meine
Freundin Meike will viele Wanderungen
machen. Wir sind nämlich sehr sportlich. Wir
hassen aber Discos!

5 – Ich will die Gegend besuchen und Ausflüge
machen. Wir wollen aber auf dem Campingplatz
essen – wir kochen nicht so gern!

6 – Meine Tochter und mein Sohn schwimmen sehr
gern und wollen Wassersport treiben. Wir
wollen lieber einen Campingplatz an der See.
Mein Mann und ich sind keine Discofans. Am
liebsten wollen wir einen kleineren, ruhigen
Campingplatz.

Solution:

1 Familie Leiser – Campingplatz Schöndorf
2 Drei Teenager – Campingplatz Rosenstadt
3 Familie Blumenauer – Campingplatz Ruhewald
4 Zwei Teenager – Campingplatz Zauberberg
5 Zwei Studenten – Campingplatz Donauinsel
6 Familie Strotmann – Campingplatz Kleiner Blausee

Follow up the activity by asking students to say
which campsite they would choose and why. They
could prepare their answers in pairs before
answering the question in front of the class. You
could also conduct an informal survey to find out
which of the six campsites appeals most and why.
Students could also take it in turns to be one of the
speakers in *Welcher Campingplatz?* and play *Wer
bin ich?* Perform a model dialogue with a student
and write up some of the key words/expressions,
such as:

– *Willst du ...?*
– *Schwimmst du/kochst du gern?*
– *Hast du einen Hund/ein junges Kind?*

Partnerarbeit. Auf dem Campingplatz

Listening
Speaking
Reading
Writing

Students can now find out how to book into a
campsite, and answer questions about their
requirements. Refer them to the extract from the
campsite brochure. Allow them time to look up new

vocabulary before asking them the meaning of the key words (*Erwachsene, je, Stellgebühren, PKW, Zelt*). Some students may well be able to work out some of the meanings without using the word list. The model dialogue in the students' book is intended to provide the opportunity for students to introduce their own variants. Ask them to work in pairs, replacing the options with others of their own choice. The model dialogue is, in fact, the first dialogue in the next activity, *Camping ist billig, oder?* You may wish to play the cassette version first to students before asking them to tackle the dialogues.

Teacher: *Jetzt kommt ihr am Campingplatz Nürnberg an. Lest den Text. Wie heißt auf englisch 'Erwachsene', usw? Was sagt man, wenn man am Campingplatz ankommt? Partnerarbeit. Macht Dialoge auf dem Campingplatz. Ersetzt die Worte in Blau durch andere Worte, zum Beispiel ...*

Camping ist billig, oder?

Listening
Speaking
Reading

Recordings of a number of people booking into a campsite. Ask students to listen to the recording and complete the details of people's requirements on the grid.

As a follow-up, students practise conversations in pairs. The example given (the first item in the recording) is the same example that students have worked on in the previous activity, but this time instead of inventing their own dialogues, they should now reconstruct the recorded dialogues using the information they have written on the grid.

Teacher: *Hört zu. Ihr hört jetzt Leute auf dem Campingplatz Nürnberg. Was wollen sie? Schreibt die Antworten in die richtigen Kästchen.* (For the pairwork activity:) *Partnerarbeit. Seht euch die Tabelle nochmal an und macht Dialoge. Was hat man gesagt?* (Write up some clues/key words for the receptionist's role, if necessary.)

Camping ist billig, oder?

1 – Guten Tag. Haben Sie noch Plätze frei?
– Ja. Wie lange wollen Sie bleiben?
– Eine Nacht.
– Und wie viele Personen sind Sie?
– Zwei Erwachsene und zwei Kinder.
– Wie alt sind die Kinder?
– Acht und dreizehn.

– Haben Sie einen Wohnwagen?
– Nein, wir haben ein Auto und ein Zelt.
– Also, zwei Erwachsene und zwei Kinder mit Auto und Zelt für eine Nacht – das macht 35 Mark 50.

2 – Guten Abend. Wir haben nicht reserviert. Ist noch was frei?
– Für wie viele Leute?
– Wir sind zwei, mein Freund und ich.
– Haben Sie ein Zelt?
– Nein, einen Wohnwagen.
– Wie lange wollen Sie bleiben?
– Eine Nacht.
– Also, zwei Personen, ein Wohnwagen und das Auto, für eine Nacht ... macht 26 Mark 50.

3 – Guten Abend. Mein Name ist Krull. Wir haben eine Reservierung für heute nacht.
– Wie heißen Sie nochmal?
– Krull, K–R–U–L–L.
– Ja, ich hab's schon. Also, das ist für zwei Erwachsene und zwei Kinder mit Zelt und Auto. Stimmt das?
– Nein, wir haben drei Kinder.
– OK, danke schön, das macht dann also 40 Mark.

4 – Guten Tag.
– Guten Tag. Kann ich Ihnen helfen?
– Haben Sie noch Platz für einen Campingbus für heute nacht?
– Ja, es ist im Moment noch viel frei. Wie lange wollen Sie bleiben?
– Drei Nächte.
– Ja, gut. Wie viele Personen sind Sie?
– Meine Frau und ich und die zwei Kinder.
– Sind die Kinder unter fünfzehn?
– Ja, die sind erst dreizehn und vierzehn.
– Also, zwei Erwachsene, zwei Kinder, ein Campingbus, für drei Nächte, das macht 106 Mark 50.

5 – Haben Sie noch 'was frei?
– Ja, wie viele Leute sind Sie?
– Nur ich. Ich bin allein.
– Also, ein Erwachsener mit Zelt und PKW.
– Nein. Ich habe kein Auto. Ich bin mit dem Bus gekommen.
– Also, ein Erwachsener mit Zelt für eine Nacht. Das kostet 16 Mark.

Solution:

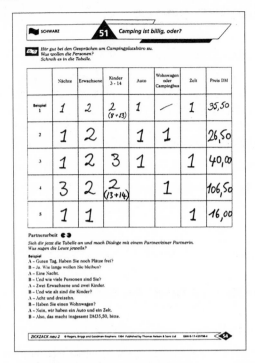

SCHWARZ — 51 — Camping ist billig, oder?

Hör gut bei den Gesprächen am Campingplatzbüro zu.
Was wollen die Personen?
Schreib es in die Tabelle.

	Nächte	Erwachsene	Kinder 3 - 14	Auto	Wohnwagen oder Campingbus	Zelt	Preis DM
Beispiel 1	1	2	2 (8 + 13)	1	✓	1	35,50
2	1	2		1	1		26,50
3	1	2	3	1		1	40,00
4	3	2	2 (13+14)		1		106,50
5	1	1				1	16,00

Partnerarbeit
Sieh dir jetzt die Tabelle an und mach Dialoge mit einem Partner/einer Partnerin.
Was sagen die Leute jeweils?

Beispiel
A – Guten Tag. Haben Sie noch Plätze frei?
B – Ja. Wie lange wollen Sie bleiben?
A – Eine Nacht.
B – Und wie viele Personen sind Sie?
A – Zwei Erwachsene und zwei Kinder.
B – Und wie alt sind die Kinder?
A – Acht und dreizehn.
B – Haben Sie einen Wohnwagen?
A – Nein, wir haben ein Auto und ein Zelt.
B – Also, das macht insgesamt DM35,50, bitte.

ZICKZACK neu 2   © Rogers, Briggs and Goodman-Stephens 1994 Published by Thomas Nelson & Sons Ltd   ISBN 0-17-439798-X   54

Students could enter details of numerous campsites – real or imaginary – in a database for others to access. If resources are available, they could also question remote databases for comparative information on campsites.

Using desktop-publishing, they could design publicity material for a campsite, including a labelled plan of the site and photographs and drawings of the area.

Students may now attempt the activities relating to *Lernziel 2* in the *Selbstbedienung* section on page 83 of the students' book. See below for further details.

Bist du ein Genie in Mathe?

   **SCHWARZ**

Listening
Speaking
Reading
Writing

Ask students to look again at the price list for the campsite at Nürnberg and work out what it would cost each family depicted. Some students could set their own puzzles for partners to solve, using similar symbols. As a *SCHWARZ* alternative, they could work out and write down the details for themselves and then challenge their partners to work out from the total cost only what the individual details are, i.e. number of people/days, facilities required, etc.

Teacher: *Könnt ihr gut rechnen? Was kostet es für diese Familien auf dem Campingplatz Nürnberg? Jetzt seid ihr dran. Schreibt ähnliche Rätsel für eure Partner.*
(SCHWARZ:) Partnerarbeit. Sagt eurem Partner/eurer Partnerin, was die Gesamtsumme ist, und stellt die Fragen: Wie viele Personen sind das? Für wie viele Nächte? Mit Zelt oder ...?

Solution:

1 DM 62,00

2 DM 34,50

3 DM 130,50

4 DM 106,00

5 DM 80,00

Selbstbedienung ◄ sb

Lernziel 1
Mein idealer Urlaub

 GOLD

Students are asked to draw and label a poster for their dream holiday destination.

Lieber nicht!

 ROT

Two cartoons about means of travelling to different holiday locations. Students must complete the empty speech bubble and suggest further possible cartoons of a similar kind.

Solution:

Ich werde immer seekrank./
Ich fliege lieber./
Lieber mit dem Flugzeug.

Bus-Schiffsreise nach London

 SCHWARZ

A text about a bus trip to London from Frankfurt am Main, on special offer. Students must read the text, complete the four statements summarising the text and put them into the correct order.

Solution:

D (Bus)

A (Calais)

C (Dover; Mittag)

B (Frankfurt am Main)

Lernziel 2
Campingplatzregeln

 SCHWARZ

Four visuals with jumbled text dealing with regulations at a campsite. Students should construct likely captions for each picture, using the jumbled text. Students could then think up and illustrate other regulations for different groups of people.

Solution:

A Keine laute Musik

B Nicht schneller als 10 km fahren

C Eltern haften für ihre Kinder

D Ab 22 Uhr absolute Ruhe

Camping – ja oder nein?

 SCHWARZ

Students are asked to give their opinions on camping and campsites, arguing for or against.

Wir haben eine Reservierung

 GOLD

Jumbled questions and answers relating to booking in at a campsite.

Solution:

1e 2g 3a 4h 5d 6b 7f 8c

Bildvokabeln.
Auf dem Campingplatz

Reading
Writing

Further campsite facilities for students to learn and label on the copymaster.

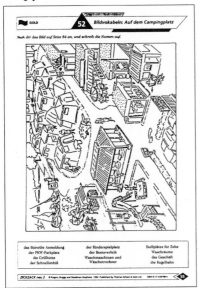

Grammar exercises 23 and 24 on copymaster 80 are based on the material in this chapter.

The students' personal profile for this chapter is on copymaster 85.

After completing work on this chapter, check whether any further reinforcement is appropriate from the video material, Activity Box cards and Assessment Support Pack tasks.

Urlaubszeit

Listening
Speaking
Reading

A poem about spending holidays on a campsite. Students can learn the poem by heart and recite it to the rest of the class, possibly after practising their pronunciation in pairs or groups.

Some might like to reproduce the text on word-processor and illustrate it for display.

 Urlaubszeit

Die Welt ist weit
Urlaubszeit.
Keine Arbeit,
Glückseligkeit.

Sonnenlicht
Im Gesicht.
Denke nicht,
Kein Unterricht.

Wenig Geld,
Altes Zelt,
Freies Feld,
Weite Welt.

Main teaching points

Lernziel 1: **Shopping in a department store**

Lernziel 2: **Buying presents and stamps**

Language presented:

- *Billig/teuer*
- *Im ersten/zweiten Stock* etc.
- *Für* + accusative
- *Gefallen*
- Gifts vocabulary
- *Eine Briefmarke zu ...*

Before beginning work on this chapter, check where the video material, Activity Box cards and Assessment Support Pack tasks will be most appropriate.

Lernziel 1
Im Kaufhaus

Presentation of language (articles available in department stores)

Listening
Speaking

Vocabulary relating to shopping in a department store. Present the new items in groups of three or four, as usual, calling upon students to repeat individually and chorally. Then move on to asking simple, obvious questions to cue the new vocabulary.

Teacher: *Ist das eine Postkarte?* (Show box of chocolates.)

Student: *Nein, das ist eine Schachtel Pralinen.*

Conclude this introductory section by referring students to the photos of a department store in the students' book and summarise what can be bought there, thus:

Teacher: *Hier kann man fast alles kaufen – Postkarten, T-Shirts, Andenken, Fußballschuhe, Blumen, Pralinen, Schals, Notizblöcke, Schreibpapier, Portemonnaies, Radiergummis,*

Bleistifte – ja, fast alles. Was ist das? Genau, das ist ein Kaufhaus. Wie heißt das auf englisch? Bei uns haben wir (name of local department store). *Das ist ein Kaufhaus.*

Wegweiser

Listening
Speaking
Reading
Writing

Tell students that you are going to play them a few dialogues which take place in a department store and ask them to say what they are about. Bring out the point that department stores are often huge places and therefore customers need clear guidance as to where goods are to be found. Then ask students to look at the *Wegweiser* and say what they think it is. Play the recordings again and use the pause button after the question each time. Give students time to locate the item on the *Wegweiser*, then play the answer and ask students to repeat it. Note that some of the items requested come under more general terms on the *Wegweiser*. Continue similarly with the other dialogues, emphasising the use of *im* used with floors of the department store.

Teacher: *Wir hören jetzt ein paar Dialoge.* (Play one or two.) *Worum geht es hier? Wo sind die Personen? Ja, in einem Kaufhaus. Hört zu. In welchem Stock findet man jeden Artikel?*

Wegweiser

1 – Entschuldigen Sie, bitte. Wo kann ich hier
    Kassetten bekommen?
  – Im Erdgeschoß.

2 – Bitte, wo kann ich hier Pflanzen bekommen?
  – Pflanzen? Also, die sind im Untergeschoß,
    hinten rechts.

3 – Wo gibt es hier Andenken, bitte?
  – Ja, hier im Erdgeschoß.

4 – Wo gibt es hier Pralinen, bitte?
  – Unten – im Untergeschoß.
  – Danke schön.

5 – Entschuldigen Sie. Wo kann ich hier
    Fußballschuhe bekommen?
  – Im Erdgeschoß. Die Sportabteilung ist im
    Erdgeschoß.

6 – Wo kann ich hier einen Schal bekommen?
  – Einen Schal? Mal sehen. Den finden Sie im
    ersten Stock.

7 – Wo gibt es hier Blumen, bitte?
  – Im zweiten Stock. Nein, nein – im
    Untergeschoß.

8 – Wo kann ich hier einen Radiergummi
    bekommen?
  – Einen Radiergummi? Bei den Schreibwaren im
    Erdgeschoß.
  – So. Danke schön.

9 – Wo kann ich hier ein Portemonnaie
    bekommen?
  – Portemonnaies finden Sie bei den Andenken im
    Erdgeschoß.

10 – Wo gibt es hier T-Shirts, bitte?
  – Für Herren oder Damen?
  – Für Kinder.
  – Ach so . . . ja, da gehen Sie in den ersten
    Stock.

Solution:

1 Im Erdgeschoß	6 Im ersten Stock
2 Im Untergeschoß	7 Im Untergeschoß
3 Im Erdgeschoß	8 Im Erdgeschoß
4 Im Untergeschoß	9 Im Erdgeschoß
5 Im Erdgeschoß	10 Im ersten Stock

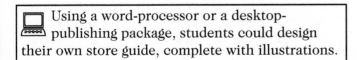 Using a word-processor or a desktop-
publishing package, students could design
their own store guide, complete with illustrations.

Partnerarbeit. Wo kann ich hier ... bekommen?

Listening
Speaking
Reading

 86

Pairwork follow up to the previous activity. Partner A works at the information desk in the department store, and has access to the *Wegweiser*. Partner B makes enquiries about where certain items are to be found. Students should change roles frequently so that both partners practise both asking and responding. If required, refer students to the *Tip des Tages* on page 87.

Teacher: *Partnerarbeit. Ihr macht Dialoge im Kaufhaus. Partner/in A arbeitet im Kaufhaus, und Partner/in B bitte um Hilfe. Zum Beispiel ...* (refer to the example in the students' book).

Ich hätte gern ...

Listening
Speaking

Tell students you are going to play them some dialogues recorded in different departments of the store. Ask them to match the recordings to the visuals on the copymaster. Look at the visuals carefully, then go through the first dialogue together.

Teacher: *Hört gut zu!* (Play the first dialogue.) *Also, welches Bild ist das?*
Student: *(Bild) B – Andenken.*
Teacher: *Richtig. Nun, hört zu.*

 Ich hätte gern ...

1 – Darf ich Ihnen helfen?
  – Ja, ich hätte gern einen Schreibblock.
  – Ja, bitte, hier an der Kasse.

2 – Ich möchte ein Portemonnaie, bitte.
  – Ein Portemonnaie? Ja, also, hier gibt es eine
    große Auswahl.

3 – Was kosten die Fußballschuhe, bitte?
  – Fußballschuhe? Ab siebzig Mark.

4 – Ich hätte gern eine Pflanze.
  – Ja, was für eine Pflanze?
  – Also, sie darf nicht sehr teuer sein.

5 – Ich hätte gern einen Schal.
  – Welche Farbe? Ein blauer Schal, vielleicht?
  – Ja, der blaue Schal gefällt mir gut.

6 – Kann ich hier Postkarten bekommen?
  – Ja, natürlich. Die sind gleich hier.

7 – Bitte schön?
– Ich hätte gern ein paar Blumen. Narzissen vielleicht.

8 – Ich hätte gern einen Radiergummi. Einen von diesen hier.
– Ja, die Tiere. Welches Tier soll es denn sein? Das Kaninchen oder der Elefant?
– Der Elefant, bitte.

9 – Was darf es sein, bitte?
– Einen Riegel Marzipan, bitte.
– Lübecker Marzipan?
– Ja, bitte.

10 – Ich möchte ein T-Shirt.
– Welche Größe?
– Größe ‚M‘, bitte.

11 – Was für Andenken haben Sie?
– Andenken? Tja, alles mögliche – Schlüsselanhänger, Puppen, Bilder, Postkarten, alles …

12 – Bitte schön?
– Ich hätte gern die neueste Kassette von Evi Bamm.
– So, bitte schön. Dreißig Mark.

Solution:

1B 2H 3D 4C 5E 6A 7C 8B 9H 10F 11A 12G

Partnerarbeit. Wo …?

Listening
Speaking
Reading

A cross section of a *Kaufhaus* drawn in open-plan style, providing opportunities for further practice of the language, and introducing some new vocabulary.

Ask students to study the visual and familiarise them with the names of the items by playing various games. In pairs they could play *Ich denke an einen Artikel*, with one partner asking questions to find out which item his/her partner is thinking of. Alternatively, you could time students to see how long it takes them to spot the items you name, or you could give them a short time limit for team members to come up with the answer.

Teacher: *Das ist ein großes modernes Kaufhaus. Partnerarbeit. Partner(in) A denkt an einen Artikel. Partner(in) B stellt Fragen. Partner(in) A antwortet mit ‚ja‘ oder ‚nein‘. Seht euch das Beispiel hier im Buch an.* (For the class game:) *Jetzt habt ihr nur drei Sekunden. In welchem Stock sind die Gummistiefel?*

Der Kunde ist König

Listening
Speaking
Reading

An information-gap activity focusing again on the transactional language. This time the items being sought by the customer are drawn on partner B's half of the copymaster.

Teacher: *Partnerarbeit. Partner(in) B stellt Fragen über Artikel im Kaufhaus. Partner(in) A beantwortet die Fragen. Zum Beispiel* (complete the model dialogue on the copymaster).

Solution:

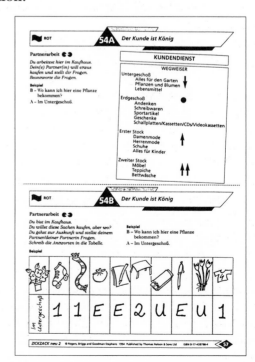

Preissensationen

Listening
Speaking
Reading
Writing

Students are told they have won a thousand marks to spend in the department store. They must draw up a list of the items they want, using only those items depicted on the page and not exceeding their limit. Practise pronunciation of new vocabulary. Then ask some students: *,Was kaufst du?'*

Draw students' attention to the correct use of the articles in the accusative, using the table in the *Tip des Tages*.

Zwölf Unterschiede

Listening
Speaking
Reading

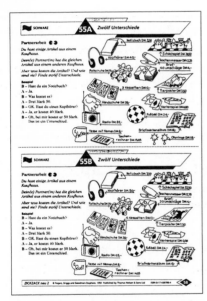

A spot-the-differences pairwork activity, focusing on purchases from a department store. By telling each other about the items on their cards, students can identify the twelve differences between cards A and B and make a note of them. Perform a model dialogue. Take the part of student B and choose someone from the class to be student A.

Teacher: *Seht euch den Arbeitsbogen an. Partner(in) A hat zwölf Artikel von einem Kaufhaus. Partner(in) B hat dieselben Artikel von einem anderen Kaufhaus. Aber was kosten diese Artikel? Wie sind die Artikel? Findet die zwölf Unterschiede heraus. Macht Dialoge. Zum Beispiel (to a student who has sheet A): Hast du ein Notizbuch?*

Student: *Ja.*
Teacher: *Was kostet es?*
Student: *Drei Mark 50.*
Teacher: *OK. Hast du einen Kopfhörer?*
Student: *Ja, (er kostet) 40 Mark.*
Teacher: *Nein, (bei mir kostet er) 50 Mark. Das ist ein Unterschied.* (Write *Unterschiede* on the board/OHP and make two columns, as below. Write in the first entry *Kopfhörer* as shown.) *Jetzt Partnerarbeit.*

Solution:

A	B
Kopfhörer DM 40	Kopfhörer DM 50
3 Kassetten	4 Kassetten
Radio DM 85	Radio DM 95
Taschenrechner DM 15,95	Taschenrechner DM 14,95
Schachspiel DM 36,50	Schachspiel DM 32,50
40 Briefumschläge	20 Briefumschläge
Taschenmesser DM 12,25	Taschenmesser DM 12,75
Kartenspiel DM 6,90	Kartenspiel DM 9,90
Briefmarkenalbum DM 18	Briefmarkenalbum DM 19
Ohrringe	Keine Ohrringe
Heike auf der Tasse	Rudi auf der Tasse
Tierposter mit Pferd	Tierposter mit Katze

Billig oder teuer?

Listening
Speaking
Reading

Ask students to look at the pictures of department store goods and the prices. First, they must apply their economic awareness, decide whether they think the prices given are cheap or dear, and tick the appropriate column on the copymaster. Then tell students that they are going to hear people commenting on the prices of the things shown and that they should listen for other expressions for *billig* and *teuer,* and again tick the appropriate column. Use the pause button as a signal for repetition. Give the meaning, and practise pronunciation of *Wucher*. Refer students to the *Tip des Tages* on page 88 of the students' book afterwards.

Teacher: *Seht euch die Bilder und die Preise an. DM 15 für eine Flasche Wein. Ist das zuviel?*
Student: *Ja.*
Teacher: *Ja, das ist teuer! Das sind sechs Pfund. 190 Mark für ein Fahrrad. Ist das teuer?*
Student: *Nein.*
Teacher: *Nein, das ist billig. Wie findet ihr die Preise? Schreibt es auf.* (For the recording:) *Ihr hört jetzt ein paar Leute im Kaufhaus. Sie sprechen über die Preise. Schreibt auf, wie sie die Preise finden.*

Billig oder teuer?

1 – 400 Mark für einen Computer. Wie findest du das?
  – Das ist billig.
2 – 15 Mark für eine Flasche Wein. Wie findest du das?
  – Das ist viel zu teuer.
3 – 190 Mark für das Fahrrad! Das ist preiswert!
4 – Drei Mark 50 für die Bonbons. Was meinst du?
  – Tja, ein bißchen teuer.
5 – Guck mal. 2 000 Mark für den Ring.
  – Das ist Wucher!
6 – Hier ist eine CD für 15 Mark 50. Wie findest du das?
  – Das ist billig.
7 – Wieviel kostet das?
  – Das T-Shirt? 50 Mark.
  – Nee, das ist viel zu teuer.
8 – Du, nur vier Mark für die Ohrringe!
  – Mensch, das ist sehr billig!
9 – Zehn Mark für einen Stadtplan? Ein bißchen teuer.
10 – Ein CD-Spieler für 4 000 Mark.
  – Das ist ja Wucher!
11 – Eine Mark 20 für ein Eis. Was meinst du?
  – Ja, das ist preiswert.
12 – 200 Mark für die Schuhe. Wie findest du das?
  – Das ist ein bißchen teuer.

There are also opportunities here for drama work. Students could produce their own dialogues in department stores and invent the prices. Other students can then ask the prices and respond accordingly. Students might also make a collage of items from magazines, newspapers etc. for which they know the German and make a separate price list in German currency. The collages can then be used as prompts for pairwork, incorporating the drama element. Monitor the students' performances and invite a few pairs to perform in front of the class.

		Deine Meinung		Die Meinung der Jugendlichen	
Artikel		billig	teuer	billig	teuer
Beispiel 1				✓	
2					✓
3				✓	
4					✓
5					✓
6				✓	
7					✓
8				✓	
9					✓
10					✓
11				✓	
12					✓

Using word-processing and illustrations from German magazines, students could set up a comparative study on the cost of certain items in Germany and their own local stores. Results could be displayed and/or stored in a data-base.

Frank und Erika im Kaufhaus
Listening Speaking

SCHWARZ

Tell students that they are going to hear a dialogue between Erika and Frank in a department store, and they must decide which of these two people they would rather go shopping with and give their reasons. The text itself is lengthy and fairly demanding, but the task allows for a variety of individual responses, e.g. one student might prefer to go shopping with Frank because he is interested in music. Another student might prefer to go with Frank because he does not like spending a lot of time in shops. In discussing the students' reasons, it should be possible to build up a fuller picture of the text.

Teacher: *Erika und Frank sind in einem Kaufhaus. Hört gut zu. Wollt ihr mit Erika oder mit Frank einkaufen gehen? Warum? Warum nicht?*

Frank und Erika im Kaufhaus

Erika: So, wo sind hier die Schuhe?

Frank: Weiß nicht.

Erika: Wo ist ein Wegweiser? ... Ah, da ist einer ... Nun, laß uns mal sehen. Da, Schuhabteilung. Im zweiten Stock. Und? Kommst du mit?

Frank: Was? Schuhe kaufen? Nein, danke!

Erika: Wartest du denn hier?

Frank: Wie lange brauchst du denn?

Erika: Ich weiß nicht. Eine Viertelstunde vielleicht?

Frank: Ach, dann gehe ich lieber in die Musikabteilung.

Erika: Du, ich will aber auch noch in die Sportabteilung.

Frank: Und wie lange brauchst du da?

Erika: Nicht lange. So zwanzig Minuten.

Frank: Zwanzig Minuten!

Erika: Ja, und dann komme ich zu dir in die Musikabteilung. Wo ist die? ... Da! Musik, im ersten Stock.

Frank: Nein, nein. Das dauert mir viel zu lange. Hier drin ist es so warm! Ich warte dann lieber draußen.

Erika: OK. Draußen, am Eiskiosk.

Frank: In dreißig Minuten.

Erika: Also, um zwölf. OK. Ich tue mein Bestes. Tschüs!

Students may now attempt the activities relating to *Lernziel 1* in the *Selbstbedienung* section on pages 92-93 of the students' book. See page 113 of this book for further details.

Lernziel 2
Schenken und Schicken

Partnerarbeit. Geschenke

Listening
Speaking
Reading
Writing

A flow chart designed to promote pairwork discussion about things to buy in a department store. The activity consolidates the use of *für* with possessive adjectives in the accusative case, and revises subject/verb inversion. Perform a model dialogue with a student in front of the class to demonstrtate.

Teacher: *Partnerarbeit. Ihr seid in einem Kaufhaus mit eurem Briefpartner/eurer Briefpartnerin. Ihr wollt Geschenke kaufen, aber welche? Zu welchem Preis? Für wen? Macht Dialoge. Zum Beispiel ...*

Students can follow up the activity by writing a list of presents to buy for various people and word process the list.

Vor Weihnachten im Kaufhaus
Listening
Speaking
Writing

   **SCHWARZ**

Continue with the theme of buying presents for people. Tell students you are going to write up six categories of people for whom they must choose any Christmas gifts available in a department store. Ask them to brainstorm in groups and write down their answers. Allow them also to use the word list, if necessary. Then ask all groups to say how many items they have managed to come up with, category by category.

 These lists could be word-processed.

Teacher: *Es ist bald Weihnachten* (draw a Christmas tree on the board/OHP). *Es ist bald der 25. Dezember. Toll! Man bekommt Geschenke. Gruppenarbeit. Ihr kauft Weihnachtsgeschenke für folgende Gruppen* (write up):

1 Kleine Kinder unter vier Jahren.
2 Kinder zwischen vier und acht Jahren.
3 Kinder zwischen acht und zwölf Jahren.
4 Teenager.
5 Männer.
6 Frauen.

Macht eine Geschenkliste für jede Gruppe. Zum Beispiel für Kinder unter vier Jahren ... ein Bilderbuch und ...?

Then you can ask students to listen to the department store announcement to find out what Christmas gifts are on offer for the various groups. Ask them to note as much detail as they can, referring to glossaries and dictionaries as appropriate. You may choose to play the cassette version first before asking students to complete their groupwork task.

Teacher: *Hört zu. Es ist Dezember, und das Kaufhaus ist voll mit Geschenken für Weihnachten. Was für Geschenke gibt es für die folgenden Gruppen?*

 Vor Weihnachten im Kaufhaus

– Sehr geehrte Kunden, sehr geehrte Kundinnen. Wir wünschen Ihnen frohe Weihnachten. Im Warenhaus gibt es eine große Auswahl an Weihnachtsgeschenken für die ganze Familie. Die Abteilung für kleine Kinder ist im vierten Stock. Hier finden Sie alles für das ein- bis vierjährige Kind. Es gibt Duplo-Steine, Stofftiere, Bilderbücher ... Alles für das kleine Kind.

Im vierten Stock gibt es auch Geschenke für Kinder zwischen vier und acht. Zum Beispiel Puzzles, Puppen und Bücher. Im dritten Stock sind Geschenke für ältere Kinder zwischen acht und zwölf. Es gibt Fahrräder, Badmintonschläger, Zelte. Alles mögliche.

Im dritten Stock gibt es auch alles für den Teenager. Alles für den Sport ... Turnschuhe, Trainingsanzüge, Tennisschläger. Alles für die Freizeit ... CDs, Kassetten, Jeans, Pullover.

Im zweiten Stock finden Sie alles für Ihren Mann, Ihren Freund, Ihren Onkel oder Ihren Vater. Wir haben Handschuhe, Schals, Rasierapparate, Hosen und so weiter. Die Auswahl ist unbegrenzt.

Suchen Sie etwas für Ihre Freundin, Ihre Frau, Ihre Mutter oder Ihre Tante? Sie finden alles im ersten Stock. Make-up, Parfüm, BHs, Kleider, Schals, Bücher und Schmuck. Sie finden einfach alles! Wir wünschen Ihnen einen angenehmen Tag bei uns.

Wenn Sie hungrig werden, vergessen Sie nicht das Restaurant im Erdgeschoß. Dort gibt es eine große Auswahl an ...

Partnerarbeit. Gefällt es dir?

Listening
Speaking
Reading

This section introduces the language of liking and disliking. Students in pairs should look at the visuals of different clothes, and make positive and negative comments about them. Show students how the construction with *gefallen* works, and practise one or two examples with them before they embark independently on the pairwork. Some students may find the construction with *gefallen* a difficult one to use, but language support is given in the *Tip des Tages* on the same page.

Teacher: *Seht euch die Bilder an. Gefällt dir die Bluse? Wie heißt ,gefällt' auf englisch?*
Student: Like.
Teacher: *Richtig. Die Schuhe gefallen mir. Gefallen dir die Schuhe? usw. Jetzt Partnerarbeit. Macht Dialoge.*

Und die Geschenke?

Reading
Writing

This activity puts the theme of liking in the context of receiving presents. Students should look at the visuals of people and their presents, and write whether each person likes his/her gift or not. Refer students to the *Tip des Tages* for language support.

Teacher: *Seht euch die Bilder an. Wer mag sein/ihr Geschenk? Wer mag es nicht? Schreib es auf. Zum Beispiel ...*

Wo bekomme ich Briefmarken?

Listening
Speaking

The following section of material deals with purchasing stamps at a post office. Ask students to listen to this first dialogue, then ask them to try and say what it is about, and where the post office is.

Teacher: *Hört gut zu! Was passiert hier?* (Play the first section of the recording, then ask:) *Was kann man im Kaufhaus nicht kaufen? Wo kauft man Briefmarken?*

 Wo bekomme ich Briefmarken?

– Entschuldigung.
– Ja?
– Wo bekomme ich hier Briefmarken?
– Briefmarken? Im Kaufhaus verkauft man fast alles, aber keine Briefmarken.
– Wo bekomme ich denn Briefmarken?
– Auf der Post. Die ist hier in der Hauptstraße. Geh hier geradeaus bis zur Ampel, dann bieg nach links ab. Die Post ist dann auf der rechten Seite.
– Ist es weit von hier?
– Nein, so etwa drei Minuten.
– Danke schön.
– Bitte schön.

Auf der Post

Listening
Speaking
Reading

Now tell students they are going to hear five dialogues in the post office, which they should match to the visuals of letters and postcards in the students' book.

Teacher: *Jetzt sind wir auf der Post. Seht euch die Briefe und Postkarten an.* (Complete the first example with students.) *Ist das A, B, C, D oder E?*
Student: *D.*
Teacher: *Richtig. Hört zu!*

Auf der Post

1 – Was kostet eine Postkarte nach Frankreich, bitte?
– 80 Pfennig.
– Und ein Brief?
– Eine Mark.
– Also, eine zu 80 Pfennig und eine zu einer Mark.

2 – Was kostet ein Brief nach England, bitte?
– Eine Mark.
– Eine dann, bitte.
– Eine Briefmarke zu einer Mark … Bitte schön.

3 – Bitte schön?
– Eine Postkarte nach Schottland, was kostet das, bitte?
– 80 Pfennig.
– Aha … zwei, bitte.
– Eine Mark 60, bitte.

4 – Meine Brieffreundin wohnt in Amerika. Was kostet ein Brief nach Amerika, bitte?
– Drei Mark.
– Danke. Und eine Postkarte?
– Zwei Mark.
– Also, eine Briefmarke zu drei Mark und zwei Briefmarken zu zwei Mark.

5 – Ein Brief nach Österreich kostet eine Mark, oder?
– Ja, genau.
– Also, drei Stück, bitte.
– Bitte schön. Drei Mark.
– Vielen Dank. Auf Wiedersehen.

Solution:

1D **2**A **3**E 4B **5**C

Students may now practise the transactional language in pairs. Refer them to the model dialogue in the students' book then ask them to reproduce dialogues in a post office, with the envelopes and postcards to guide them.

Teacher: *Jetzt seid ihr auf der Post. Lest den Text* (complete a reading with a student, to demonstrate). *Partnerarbeit. Seht euch die Briefe und Postkarten an und macht Dialoge.*

Once students are confident with the language, introduce an element of drama into the dialogues. Tell students they are in various states of mind as they buy their stamps, and that they must speak accordingly.

Teacher: *Jetzt seid ihr nochmal auf der Post, aber ihr* (write up:) *seid: müde, krank, ärgerlich; ihr habt es eilig, wollt lange auf der Post bleiben usw. Was sagt ihr und wie?* (Perform one or two examples.)

Was kaufen sie auf der Post?

Listening
Speaking
Writing

    GOLD

A series of short dialogues at the post office. Students listen for the number of stamps, the individual price and the total price, and fill in the details on the copymaster.

Teacher: *Wie viele Briefmarken kaufen diese Leute? Was kosten die Briefmarken? Was macht alles zusammen? Hört gut zu!* (Play the first dialogue and do the first question on the board with the whole class.)

Was kaufen sie auf der Post?

1 – Guten Tag. Zwei Briefmarken zu 80 Pfennig.
– Zwei zu 80. Eine Mark 60, bitte.

2 – Zehn Briefmarken zu 60, bitte.
– Zehn zu 60. Das macht sechs Mark.

3 – Acht Briefmarken zu 30 Pfennig.
– Das macht zwei Mark 40. Sonst noch etwas?
– Nein, danke.

4 – Vier Briefmarken zu 50 Pfennig, bitte.
– Vier zu 40?
– Nein, zu 50.
– Das macht zwei Mark.
– Moment, das habe ich klein.
– Danke.

5 – Ja, bitte?
– Fünf Briefmarken zu einer Mark, bitte.
– Sonst noch etwas?
– Nein, danke.
– Also, fünf Mark, bitte.

6 – Eine Briefmarke zu fünf Mark, bitte.
– Für ein Paket?
– Ja.
– Soll ich es wiegen?
– Nein, das ist nicht nötig.

7 – Zwanzig Briefmarken zu 80 Pfennig.
– Zwanzig?
– Ja.
– Das macht sechzehn Mark.
– Danke schön.

8 – Fünfzehn Briefmarken zu 50, bitte.
– Sonst noch etwas?
– Zwei Briefmarken zu 80.
– Das macht dann insgesamt neun Mark zehn.
– Danke.

Solution:

(see reduction of copymaster below)

The *GOLD* follow-up (*Nach welchem Land?*) requires students to look at the addresses on the envelopes, and write in which country each is being sent to.

Solution:

1 ENGLAND

2 FRANKREICH

3 AMERIKA

4 ÖSTERREICH

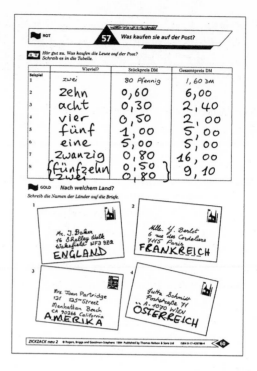

Informationen am Briefkasten *Listening Speaking Reading*

Photos of a post box, giving details of collection times. Comprehension is tested by true/false questions.

Teacher: *Jetzt wollt ihr Briefe und Postkarten schicken. Ihr sucht einen Briefkasten aus. Wie heißt auf englisch ‚Briefkasten‘? Gut. Bevor man Briefe oder Postkarten einsteckt* (mime posting a letter), *liest man die Informationen am Briefkasten. Wie ist es richtig? Lest die Sätze und schreibt ‚richtig‘ oder ‚falsch‘ auf.*

Solution:

1 richtig **2** richtig **3** falsch **4** falsch **5** falsch

As a follow-up, the lower panel on the post box giving details of alternative post boxes could be discussed.

Some students might be prepared to produce a cardboard German letterbox with the various pieces of information on it. The box could then be used on occasions in lessons, particularly as part of drama work.

> Students may now attempt the *Lernziel 2* activities in the *Selbstbedienung* section on page 93 of the students' book. See below for further details.

Selbstbedienung sb

 92–93 74

Lernziel 1
Was ist das?

 GOLD

A number of wrapped items from a department store. Students must select from the menu what they think each item is.

Solution:

1 Fußballschuhe
2 eine Pflanze
3 ein Badmintonschläger
4 ein Portemonnaie
5 ein Bleistift
6 eine Puppe

He Axel, was kostet ...?

 SCHWARZ

A gap-filling activity cued by visuals and based on *Preissensationen* (students' book page 88).

Solution:

– He Axel, was kostet der Fernseher?
– Vierhundertzwanzig Mark.
– Das ist aber teuer! Und die Skier?
– Sechshundert Mark. Du, der CD-Spieler ist aber preiswert!
– Du hast doch einen CD-Spieler!
– Ja, stimmt. Achthundert Mark für die Videokamera, das ist Wucher!
– Was kostet denn der Computer?
– Tausend Mark.
– Mensch das ist alles so teuer! Und ich mit meinen zwanzig Mark Taschengeld!

Tierheim

 **GOLD**

A tree providing homes for a number of animals at different levels. Students must write down the 'floor' on which each animal lives.

Solution:

Das Kaninchen wohnt im Untergeschoß.
Die Maus wohnt im Erdgeschoß.
Der Specht wohnt im ersten Stock.
Das Eichhörnchen wohnt im zweiten Stock.
Die Eule wohnt im dritten Stock.
Der Storch wohnt im vierten Stock.

Kaufhaus BILLIG

 GOLD

A poster-designing activity, in which students must advertise a department store, highlighting, as in the example, the letters of the adjectives describing the store (*preiswert, teuer* or *Wucher*).

Lernziel 2
Was kaufst du für ...?

 ROT **SCHWARZ**

Students write sentences to say which present they buy for each person depicted.

Solution:

1 Für meine Mutter kaufe ich eine Pflanze.
2 Für meinen Bruder kaufe ich eine Kassette.
3 Für meine Stiefschwester kaufe ich ein Portemonnaie.
4 Für meinen Onkel kaufe ich ein Buch.
5 Für meine Großmutter kaufe ich eine Schachtel Pralinen.

As a *SCHWARZ* follow up students decide from the expressions on the faces whether or not each person liked his or her present.

Solution:

Die Pflanze gefällt meiner Mutter.
Die Kassette gefällt meinem Bruder nicht.
Das Portemonnaie gefällt meiner Stiefschwester.
Das Buch gefällt meinem Onkel nicht.
Die Pralinen gefallen meiner Großmutter.

Briefmarken

 ROT

Students must read the jumbled dialogue at a post office and rewrite it in the correct order.

Solution:

– Guten Tag.
– Guten Tag. Was kostet ein Brief nach Wales?
– Nach Wales?
– Ja.
– Eine Mark.
– Und eine Postkarte?
– 80 Pfennig
– Eine Briefmarke zu 80 Pfennig und zwei zu einer Mark.
– Bitte schön – das macht zwei Mark 80.
– Danke schön. Auf Wiedersehen.
– Auf Wiedersehen.

Kleiner Mensch

Listening
Speaking
Reading
Writing

A song based on the chapter's theme. Students listen first, then sing along.

 Kleiner Mensch

Letzte Woche hatte ich Geburtstag.
Man hat mir einen neuen Walkman geschenkt.
Plötzlich sah ich einen kleinen Menschen,
Der sagte mir, was er darüber denkt.

‚Denke
Nicht immer an Geschenke,
Denke
Nicht immer nur an Geld.
Was haben dir
Deine Eltern gegeben?
Das Leben! Ja, das Leben!
Das beste Geschenk auf der Welt!'

Letzte Woche sah ich meinen Onkel.
Er hat mir ein Computerspiel geschenkt.
Plötzlich hörte ich den kleinen Menschen.
Der sagte mir, was er darüber denkt.

‚Denke
Nicht immer an Geschenke,
Denke
Nicht immer nur an Geld.
Was haben dir
Deine Eltern gegeben?
Das Leben! Ja, das Leben!

Das beste Geschenk auf der Welt!'
Letzte Woche war ich bei Verwandten.
Man hat mir hundertneunzig Mark geschenkt.
Plötzlich sah ich da den kleinen Menschen.
Ihr wißt schon, was er darüber denkt.

‚Denke
Nicht immer an Geschenke,
Denke
Nicht immer nur an Geld.
Was haben dir
Deine Eltern gegeben?
Das Leben! Ja, das Leben!
Das beste Geschenk auf der Welt!'

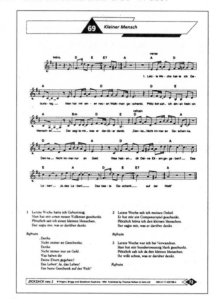

Grammar exercises 25-27 on copymaster 80 are based on the material in this chapter. 80 +83

The students' personal profile for this chapter is on copymaster 85. 85

After completing work on this chapter, check whether any further reinforcement is appropriate from the video material, Activity Box cards and Assessment Support Pack tasks.

Main teaching points

Talking about what you have done and where you have been throughout the year

Language presented:

- The perfect tense with *haben* and *sein*
- *war/waren*

> Before beginning work on this chapter, check where the video material, Activity Box cards and Assessment Support Pack tasks will be most appropriate.

Sabines Jahr

Listening
Speaking
Reading

In this chapter the perfect tense is introduced for the first time. This activity presents a summary of Sabine's year. Ask students first of all to read the jumbled captions relating to what Sabine did each month, and listen to the cassette. See if they can work out for themselves what some of the captions mean. Point out the two parts of the perfect tense, and how the past participle goes to the end of the sentence each time. Once the pattern of the sentences has been established, students can work out the other captions. They should then match each caption to its appropriate photo.

Teacher: *Lest den Text und hört gut zu. Das war Sabines Jahr.*
(Pause the cassette and ask after each statement:)
‚Wann hat sie das gemacht?' Seht euch die Fotos an. War das im Januar? Im Februar? etc.

Sabines Jahr

– Letztes Jahr ... naja ... was habe ich gemacht?
1 – Ich bin zu einer neuen Schule gegangen.
2 – Ich habe auch einen Job als Babysitter bekommen.
3 – Ja ... was noch? Ich bin mit meiner Familie in den Schwarzwald gefahren.
4 – Und ja ... ich habe zum Geburtstag ein neues Fahrrad bekommen.

5 – Und was noch? Ich bin nach Australien ins Barossatal zu meiner Großmutter geflogen.
6 – Ich habe mir beim Skifahren das Handgelenk gebrochen. Das war der Tiefpunkt für mich.
7 – Ich habe Omri kennengelernt! Das war der Höhepunkt für mich.
8 – Ich habe auch eine Klassenfahrt nach England gemacht.
9 – Ich habe Weihnachten gefeiert.
10 – Ich habe viel Tennis gespielt.
11 – Ich habe für die Schule viel gearbeitet.
12 – Ich habe für Partys neue Klamotten gekauft. Das war ein tolles Jahr!

Solution:

Januar **5**	Mai **10**	September **11**
Februar **12**	Juni **3**	Oktober **8**
März **6**	Juli **7**	November **2**
April **4**	August **1**	Dezember **9**

Sabine features periodically throughout the chapter, commenting again on events from her past year.

Partnerarbeit

Listening
Speaking
Reading

Ask students to take it in turns to pretend to be Sabine and answer questions about her year. Demonstrate a few examples using the model dialogue before asking students to work in pairs.

Students can refer to the *Tip des Tages* for language support. If required, provide further practice of word order by writing the words of sentences in the perfect tense on separate cards. Ask students to work in pairs to put the sentences in the correct order.

Teacher: *Jetzt Partnerarbeit.* (To a student:) *Du bist Sabine, und ich stelle Fragen. Zum Beispiel …*

Ich bin zu einer neuen Schule gegangen
Listening
Speaking
Reading
Writing

A matching activity based on *Sabines Jahr*, requiring students to put the correct past participle at the end of each sentence. Play the recording of *Sabines Jahr* first for support and/or afterwards for students to check their answers.

Solution:

1 gegangen	7 kennengelernt
2 bekommen	8 gemacht
3 gefahren	9 gefeiert
4 bekommen	10 gespielt
5 geflogen	11 gearbeitet
6 gebrochen	12 gekauft

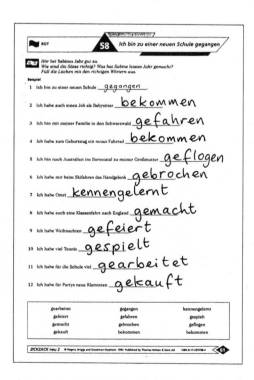

Presentation of language (the perfect tense)
Listening
Speaking
Reading
Writing

You may wish with some classes to draw students' attention more formally to the form of the perfect tense at this stage. This can be tackled in a number of ways, for example: *Wie sagt man das auf deutsch?*

Provide students with English translations of some of the sentences and ask them to find the German equivalent in the text.

Teacher: *Seht euch diese Sätze an. Wie schreibt man das auf deutsch?*

Alternatively, the following copymaster could be used.

Deutsch-Englisch Domino
Reading

The copymaster, based on *Sabines Jahr*, can either be cut up as straightforward domino cards or into separate English and German sets for a memory game or for a game of snap (*Dasselbe!*).

Im Februar

This section practises the perfect tense with *haben* and regular verbs.

Was hast du heute gekauft?
Listening
Reading
Speaking

A number of young people talking about what they have bought in town. Ask students to listen to the conversations, look at the pictures and say what each person has bought. Note that for some speakers, more than one item applies.

Teacher: *Hört gut zu. Was haben sie gekauft? Was sagen sie?*

Was hast du heute gekauft?

1 – Hallo Heike. Wie geht's?
– Hallo Birgit. Mir geht's gut, danke.
– Wo warst du denn heute?
– In der Stadt. Ich habe ein neues Make-up gekauft. Es war ganz billig. Es hat nur zehn Mark gekostet. Ich habe auch diese Kassette gekauft.
– Auch billig?
– Ja, wirklich.
2 – Grüß dich, Peter. Was machst du denn hier?
– Grüß dich, Bernd. Ich gehe jetzt nach Hause.
– Hast du 'was Interessantes gekauft?
– Ja, einen Computer. Letzte Woche hatte ich Geburtstag.
3 – Hallo, Gabi.
– Hallo, Susi. Gehst du in die Stadt?
– Nein, ich habe kein Geld mehr.
– Wieso denn nicht?
– Ich habe diese Ohrringe gekauft und ein paar Sachen für die Schule.
4 – Hallo, Rachel.
– Hallo, Rebekka. Wie geht's?
– Nicht gut. Ich bin ein bißchen müde. Ich war den ganzen Tag in der Stadt.
– Hast du viel gekauft?
– Ja, und ob! Ich habe diese Hose gekauft.
– Die gefällt mir gut. War sie teuer?
– Nein, es geht ... Ich habe auch diesen Pullover und diese Turnschuhe gekauft.

Solution:

Heike: H, E

Peter: C

Gabi: A, F

Rachel: D, G, B

Follow up the activity by using the visuals in the following way to practise the perfect tense.

Teacher: *Ich habe eine Kassette gekauft. Wie heißt das auf englisch?* (To a student:) *Du bist Peter* (point to visual). *Was hast du heute gekauft?* (Point out to students the use of the accusative form for the articles here.)

Use flashcards from previous chapters to cue similar dialogues. Encourage students to ask the question as soon as possible: ‚*Was hast du (heute) gekauft?*‘ This could become a written activity for consolidation by placing several flashcards of items bought in a row, and asking students to write complete sentences.

Partnerarbeit. Was hast du gestern gekauft?
Listening
Speaking
Reading

A pairwork activity to further consolidate using the perfect tense with *haben* and regular verbs. Students take it in turns to say which day it is, and ask their partner what (s)he bought on the previous day.

Teacher: *Heute ist Mittwoch. Gestern war Dienstag. Wie heißt ‚gestern' auf englisch?*
Student: Yesterday.
Teacher: *Richtig. Was hast du gestern gekauft?*
Student: *Ich habe gestern Ohrringe gekauft.*
Teacher: *Gut. Jetzt Partnerarbeit.*

Einkaufskettenspiel
Listening
Speaking

Divide the class into groups of about eight. The first person must say what (s)he has bought. The second person must repeat the purchase of the first person and then add another, and so on. This activity emphasises the position of *gekauft*.

Teacher: (To a student:) *Du fängst an. Du warst in der Stadt, und du sagst, was du gekauft hast. Du sagst zum Beispiel: ‚Ich war heute in der Stadt und habe eine Hose gekauft.'* (To another student:) *Du machst dann weiter. Du sagst: ‚Ich war heute in der Stadt und habe eine Hose und einen Pullover gekauft.'* (Continue until students have understood.) *Jetzt Gruppenarbeit!*

Im April

This section extends work on the perfect tense to include some strong verbs which have an irregular past participle.

Was hast du zum Geburtstag bekommen?

Listening
Speaking

Tell students they are going to hear eight people saying what they received for their last birthday. They should try and identify what each one received. Write up the names in the order they speak on the cassette. Highlight the use of *bekommen*.

Teacher: *Ihr hört gleich acht junge Leute. Sie sprechen über ihren letzten Geburtstag. Hört gut zu. Was für Geschenke haben sie bekommen? Bücher? Kassetten? Geld?*

Was hast du zum Geburtstag bekommen?

Monika: Ich habe von meinen Eltern Kleider bekommen.
Michael: Ich habe ein paar Bücher, ein paar Kassetten und viel Geld bekommen.
Oliver: Von meinen Eltern habe ich einen Drucker für meinen Computer bekommen.
Angelika: Ich habe eine Gitarre bekommen.
Susi: Zu meinem Geburtstag habe ich einen neuen Tennisschläger, einen Walkman und etwas Geld bekommen.
Raphael: Ich habe einen CD-Player bekommen.
Brigitte: Ich habe Geld bekommen.
Sven: Ich habe Geld von meinem Onkel und einen Rucksack von meinem Vater bekommen.

Solution:

Monika: clothes
Michael: books, cassettes, money
Oliver: printer
Angelika: guitar
Susi: tennis racquet, Walkman, money
Raphael: CD player
Brigitte: money
Sven: money, rucksack

Partnerarbeit. Was hast du zu deinem Geburtstag bekommen?

Listening
Speaking
Reading

A cumulative game to practise the verb *bekommen* and to draw attention to the position of the past participle in a German sentence. Present the question ‚*Was hast du zu deinem Geburtstag bekommen?*' Quote two or three of the answers from the previous listening activity, e.g. *Ich habe eine Gitarre bekommen; Ich habe Geld bekommen.* Then draw students' attention to the visuals and work through the model dialogue, so that students get the idea that they must add to what has gone before.

Teacher: *Kettenspiel. Was hast du zu deinem Geburtstag bekommen? Seht euch die Bilder an. Partner(in) A fängt an und sagt: ‚Ich habe eine Gitarre bekommen.' Partner(in) B macht weiter und sagt: ‚Ich habe eine Gitarre und einen Tennisschläger bekommen.' Macht weiter.*

Students could also add extra items of their own invention after working through all the visuals in the book.

Was hast du an deinem Geburtstag gemacht?

Listening
Speaking
Reading

Ask students to look at the visuals and the speech bubbles about what the eight named people did on their birthday. Then play the recording and ask students to match the visuals and the text. This activity introduces the perfect tense of a number of common strong verbs.

Teacher: *Seht euch die Bilder und die Texte an und hört gut zu. Was paßt wozu?*

Was hast du an deinem Geburtstag gemacht?

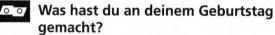

Sabine: Ich habe eine Party gegeben.
Michael: Ich bin mit meiner Freundin ins Kino gegangen.
Tulai: Also, ich habe in der Stadt ein paar Freunde getroffen, und wir haben zusammen ein Eis gegessen.
Miriam: Ich habe Tennis gespielt.

| Jutta: | Ich bin zu einer Freundin gegangen. Wir haben Kuchen gegessen. |
| Kai: | Nichts Besonderes. Ich bin zu Hause geblieben, hab' ferngesehen. |

Solution:

Sabine D; Michael F; Tulai C; Miriam B; Jutta E; Kai A

Ich habe eine Party gegeben

Listening
Reading
Writing

An activity using the previous text, in which students should decide each time between *ich bin* and *ich habe* and also supply the correct past participle. Play the recording for support or for students to use to check their answers. There is space at the bottom of the copymaster for students to write at least three sentences about what they did for their last birthday.

Solution:

Im Juli

This section continues to practise strong verbs with *haben*, particularly focusing on *kennengelernt,* and descriptions of people's physical features and clothes.

Hast du die Betti kennengelernt?

Listening
Speaking
Reading

An activity for extended listening and reading for enjoyment.

This cartoon story incorporates physical descriptions, descriptions of clothing and comments about character. It introduces the perfect tense forms of *kennenlernen, sprechen, finden* and *tragen.* Play the recording and ask students to follow the text. Students could act out the story afterwards, making any changes they wish to the physical descriptions.

Teacher: *Seht euch die Bilder an. Hört gut zu und lest den Text.*

Hast du die Betti kennengelernt?

Konrad:	Tag, Oliver. Wie geht's dir?
Oliver:	Nicht so gut. Wie war die Party?
Konrad:	Toll.
Oliver:	Hast du die Betti kennengelernt?
Konrad:	Betti? Nee. Wieso?
Oliver:	Die ist meine neue Freundin.
Konrad:	Wie sieht sie aus?
Oliver:	Sie hat kurze, braune Haare ...
Konrad:	Glatt?
Oliver:	Ja. Hast du sie kennengelernt?
Konrad:	Ja, sie war mit Susanne zusammen.
Oliver:	Sie ist nett, nicht?
Konrad:	Naja, ganz OK. Aber ... sie ist ein bißchen groß für dich, oder?
Oliver:	Groß? Die Betti? Nein. Was hat sie denn getragen?
Konrad:	Ich weiß nicht mehr. Vielleicht einen Rock?
Oliver:	Nein, Betti trägt immer Jeans.
Konrad:	Und sie hat kurze, braune Haare, sagst du?
Oliver:	Ja. Und sie ist klein. Naja, macht nichts. Mit wem hast du denn getanzt?

Konrad: Du, ich habe ein tolles Mädchen
kennengelernt. Ich habe mit ihr den
ganzen Abend getanzt.

Oliver: Wie heißt sie?

Konrad: Petra.

Oliver: Petra! Wie sieht sie aus?

Konrad: Mittelgroß, dunkelbraune Haare, blaue
Augen. Sie ist toll. Wir gehen morgen
zusammen aus.

Oliver: Du Schwein! Das ist die Betti! Das ist
meine Freundin!

Konrad: Nee, nee. Sie heißt Petra.

Oliver: Ja! Petra Bettinski heißt sie. Ihre Freunde
nennen sie alle Betti!

Treff-spezial-Ferien

Reading
Writing

Six personal adverts, in which young people are each
trying to get in touch with someone they met on
holiday. Students should match each advert to the
appropriate illustration. Encourage students to refer
to the word list and/or the teacher should read
through the adverts with students and bring out the
meaning of new vocabulary.

Teacher: *Lest die Texte und seht euch die Bilder an.
Was paßt wozu? Schlagt die Wörter in der
Wörterliste nach.*

Solution:

1B **2**C **3**F **4**A **5**D **6**E

Students could follow up the activity by inventing
their own personal adverts. With drawings, these
could make an interesting and amusing classroom
display.

Was hast du gesehen?

Listening
Speaking

A visual memory game. Students are shown a picture
of five people for a short time, then they have to say
what they can remember about the people to build
up as full a picture as possible. The game is probably
best played in teams of about four. When the time
allocation has passed, remove the pictures and issue
teams instead with a copy of the grid from the
bottom half of the copymaster, where they should
record all the details they can remember about the
five people. Then collate all the information on the

board or OHP, awarding one point for each piece of
information reported. There are about 46 details in
total. Encourage students to give feedback by using
complete sentences, for example:

*Ich habe ein kleines Mädchen gesehen. Sie hat
kurze, glatte, blonde Haare ...*

Teacher: *Gruppenarbeit. Seht euch das Bild an. Ihr
habt 30 Sekunden. Was habt ihr alles gesehen?
Schreibt dann alles auf. Ihr bekommt einen Punkt
für jede Information.*

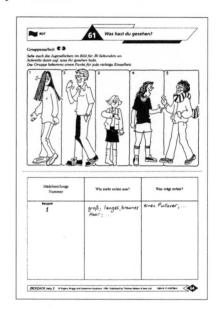

Im Oktober

In this section, verbs which use the auxiliary *sein* in
the perfect tense are introduced, as well as *war* and
waren.

Wie ist Lars zum Schwimmbad gekommen?

Reading
Writing

Students practise using sentences with *ist ...
gekommen*, by writing sentences to show how each
young person arrived at the swimming pool. A model
is given as a guide.

Solution:

Lars ist mit dem Rad zum Schwimmbad gekommen.
Michael ist mit dem Bus zum Schwimmbad
gekommen.

Martina ist mit dem Mofa zum Schwimmbad gekommen.

Francesca ist mit der S-Bahn zum Schwimmbad gekommen.

Thomas ist mit der U-Bahn zum Schwimmbad gekommen.

Sandra ist mit dem Auto zum Schwimmbad gekommen.

Ich bin gut angekommen   *Reading*

Two postcards about a journey to England. Ask students to read the postcards and to decide whether the statements which follow are true or false.

Solution:

1 richtig **2** falsch **3** richtig **4** falsch
5 richtig **6** falsch **7** falsch

Wie war die Reise?   *Listening*
     Speaking

A telephone conversation between Sabine, who is on an exchange in England, and her mother. Ask students to listen to the recording and work out what it is about. Play the recording in sections and collate the information on the board/OHP.

Teacher: *Sabine ist mit der Schule in Großbritannien, bei einer britischen Familie. Sie telefoniert mit ihrer Mutter in Deutschland. Hört gut zu.*

Then ask questions to check understanding:

1 Wo ist Sabine?
2 Wie ist ihre britische Familie?
3 Wie war die Fahrt mit der Bahn in Deutschland?
4 Wie war es auf dem Schiff?
5 Wie ist Sabine nach London gefahren?
6 Wie ist sie von London nach Bristol gekommen?

Wie war die Reise?

– Hallo Mutti, ich bin's.
– Ah, hallo Sabine! Wie geht's dir denn? Alles in Ordnung?
– Ja, klar. Mir geht's gut. Die Familie ist sehr nett.
– Wie war denn die Reise?
– Die Fahrt mit der Bahn war ganz gut, aber die vier Stunden auf der Fähre waren fürchterlich.

Die See war so stürmisch, und wir waren alle seekrank. Ich habe dann im Bus nach London geschlafen.
– Seid ihr nicht mit dem Zug gefahren?
– Doch, von London nach Bristol mit einem Intercity ... Mutti, jetzt bin ich aber müde. Ich gehe sofort ins Bett. Tschüs. Schöne Grüße zu Hause.
– Tschüs. Bis bald. Mach's gut!

Katjas Tagebuch   *Listening*
     Reading
     Writing

Katja's diary is incomplete. Ask students to listen to her talking to her friend Dieter about their stay in England and ask them to fill in the gaps on the copymaster.

Katjas Tagebuch

Katja: Wir sind am Montagvormittag in die Schule gegangen, nicht?

Dieter: Ja, und nach dem Essen haben wir Tennis gespielt.

Katja: Was haben wir am Abend gemacht?

Dieter: Ich bin mit dem Bus zu einem Jugendzentrum gefahren, aber du bist ins Kino gegangen.

Katja: Ja, richtig. Ich habe einen Kung-Fu-Film gesehen. Und dann am Dienstag sind wir alle mit dem Zug nach London gefahren.

Dieter: Am Mittwoch waren wir alle in Brighton. Erinnerst du dich noch, wie schlecht die Fahrt war? Mit dem alten Bus?

Katja: Ja, und ob! Und am Abend? Was haben wir da gemacht?

Dieter: Wir sind spät in Hailsham angekommen. Ich glaube, im Bus haben wir Karten gespielt.

Katja: Was haben wir am Donnerstag gemacht?

Dieter: Keine Ahnung! Moment mal ... ich glaube, ja genau ... wir sind zur Schule gegangen. Von neun bis vier. Das war ein langer Tag!

Katja: Ja, richtig. Und am Abend sind wir dann mit dem Zug zu einem Jugendzentrum in Eastbourne gefahren. Zu einer Grillparty.

Dieter: Am Freitag haben wir Sport getrieben. Zuerst haben wir Tennis gespielt, und dann sind wir zum Schwimmbad gefahren. Ja, und am Abend hast du in der Schuldisco mit Debbie getanzt.

Katja: Am Samstagvormittag bin ich in die Stadt gegangen, und am Nachmittag habe ich eine Kassette gekauft. Um acht Uhr bin ich dann mit meinem Partner zu einer Party gegangen.

Dieter: Was hast du am Sonntag gemacht?

Katja: Wir sind alle mit der Bahn nach Windsor gefahren.

Dieter: Ja, und am Montag?

Katja: Das ist einfach. Wir sind um 9 Uhr nach Harwich gefahren, und um 16.30 Uhr sind wir mit einer Fähre nach Hamburg zurückgefahren.

Solution:

5 Sie ist zu einer Party gegangen.

6 Am Mittwoch und am Donnerstag.

7 Sie ist zu Hause geblieben und hat Schularbeiten gemacht.

8 Er hat blonde, lockige Haare und blaue Augen.

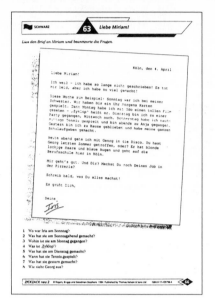

Liebe Miriam!

Reading
Writing

63
SCHWARZ

A letter for reading comprehension, drawing together much of the language presented throughout this chapter.

Teacher: *Lest den Brief an Miriam und beantwortet die Fragen.*

Solution:

1 Am Sonntag war sie bei ihrer Schwester.

2 Sie hat Karten gespielt.

3 Sie ist ins Kino gegangen.

4 Ein Film.

Deine Woche

Reading
Writing

64
SCHWARZ

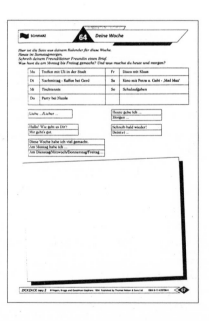

Students should use the week's diary entries to write a letter to a penfriend describing what they did last week and what they are going to do for the rest of the weekend. For help with the beginning, ending and sentence structure, students should be redirected to the letter *Liebe Miriam!* (on copymaster 63).

Teacher: *Seht euch den Kalender an und schreibt einen Brief an einen Brieffreund/eine Brieffreundin. Beschreibt, was ihr letzte Woche gemacht habt.*

Using word-processing or a desktop-publishing package, students could compile their own album of significant events over the past year. They could incorporate drawings, realia and photographs. They could also word-process letters to exchange partners or classes to tell them about their year and ask them to reply in similar fashion.

Students may now attempt the activities in the *Selbstbedienung* section on pages 104 and 105 of the students' book. See below for further details.

Kannst du einen Satz bilden?

 GOLD

Jumbled sentences in the perfect tense.

Solution:

1 Er hat Brötchen und Kuchen gekauft.
2 Ich bin um sechs Uhr in Hamburg angekommen.
3 Ich habe im Bus nach Stuttgart geschlafen.
4 Wir sind mit dem Bus nach München gefahren.
5 Gestern abend habe ich Tennis gespielt.

Wie ist es richtig?

GOLD

A word puzzle.

Solution:

Warst du in der Stadt? Was hast du gekauft? Einen Pullover, eine Hose und ein Eis.

Lieber Kurt!

 ROT

A letter with gaps, which students should fill in by selecting the correct word each time from the menu.

Solution:

Ich bin gut nach Hause gekommen. Ich habe im Zug geschlafen, dann habe ich im Speisewagen gegessen: das Essen hat mir aber nicht gut geschmeckt. Die Überfahrt von Hamburg nach Harwich war fürchterlich. Die Nordsee war stürmisch, und ich war seekrank. Ich bin um 16 Uhr in Harwich angekommen. Natürlich war ich sehr müde, aber jetzt geht es mir wieder besser.

Schreib bald wieder.

Wo ist das Ende?

 GOLD

A number of sentences which require a correct past participle, which students should select from the menu.

Solution:

1 Ich habe eine Pizza gegessen.

2 Ich bin zu einer Party gegangen.

3 Ich habe einen Film gesehen.

4 Ich habe Jeans getragen.

5 Ich habe eine Party gegeben.

6 Ich habe ein Glas Milch getrunken.

7 Ich habe ein neues Fahrrad bekommen.

8 Ich habe Tennis gespielt.

9 Ich bin mit der Straßenbahn gefahren.

10 Ich bin nach Amerika geflogen.

Lieber Karl-Heinz!

 SCHWARZ

Two postcards for reading comprehension followed by a number of questions.

Solution:

1 Axel und Claudia.

2 Axel.

3 Swansea.

4 Er hat Tennis gespielt oder ist zu Hause geblieben und hat ferngesehen.

5 Sie hat lange Haare und blau-grüne Augen.

6 Zu einer Party.

7 Ein Glas Cola.

8 Noch drei Tage.

Grammar exercises 28-30 on copymaster 81 are based on the material in this chapter.

The students' personal profile for this chapter is on copymaster 85.

After completing work on this chapter, check whether any further reinforcement is appropriate from the video material, Activity Box cards and Assessment Support Pack tasks.

page/copymaster numbers	Kapitel 1	Listen AT1	Speak AT2	Read AT3	Write AT4
SB6-7	Meine Stadt	3	2	3	1
SB7	Richtig oder falsch?	2	1	3	1
CM1	In meiner Stadt	2	2	1	1
SB8	Partnerarbeit. Stadtspiel	2	2	2	-
CM2	Wo wohnst du?	3	-	2	-
	Wo ist das bitte?	2	-	-	1
SB8	Stadtrundfahrt	4	3	2	-
CM3	Stadtrundgang	5	2	5	-
SB9	Im Verkehrsamt	4	2	3	-
SB9	Partnerarbeit	3	3	3	-
CM4	Ich kenne die Stadt nicht	3	2	2	-
SB10	Wie findest du Osnabrück?	3	3	3	3
SB11	Schön, oder ...?	2	2	2	2
CM5	Wie denn?/Liebe Asla!	2	2	3	4
SB12	Straßenschilder	-	-	3	1
SB12	Und deine Stadt?	-	-	4	3
SB12	Lieber Andreas!	-	-	3	4
SB13	Was kann man hier machen?	-	-	2	3
SB13	Halb und halb	-	-	3	-
SB13	Müllstadt	-	-	2	2
SB13	Meine Stadt	-	-	2	2
SB14/CM6	Bildvokabeln. In der Stadt	-	-	2	2
	Kapitel 2				
	Wo ist hier die nächste Post?	2	2	-	-
SB16	Stadtplan	2	2	2	1
SB16	Partnerarbeit. Was ist das?	2	2	2	-
SB17	Wer spricht?	2	2	2	-
SB17	Wie ist es richtig?	2	2	2	-
SB18	Partnerarbeit. Ist hier ein Kino in der Nähe?	3	3	3	-
CM7	Wegbeschreibungen	3	3	3	1
SB18	Partnerarbeit. Erste Straße links	3	3	2	-
CM8	Die Post? Das ist ganz einfach	4	2	1	-
CM9	Wo ist das Jugendzentrum?	3	3	3	-
SB19	Wo ist das, bitte?	3	2	1	-
SB19	Partnerarbeit	2	2	-	-
CM10	Vor dem Museum	2	2	-	-
SB20	Ist das weit von hier?	3	3	3	3
SB20	Partnerarbeit	3	3	-	-
CM11	Ein Kilometer	3	2	2	-
SB21	Wo ist das Schwimmbad?	4	3	4	-
CM12	Ein Brief an David	-	-	5	-
SB22	Spiegelbilder	-	-	1	1
SB22	Wo ist das Museum?	-	-	3	3
SB22	Wo ist hier das nächste Kino?	-	-	4	-
SB23	Im Restaurant	-	-	3	-
SB23	Wie weit ist das Krankenhaus von hier?	-	-	2	2
SB24	Touristen	4	3	4	-
SB24	Steffi	-	-	3	-

	Kapitel 3	AT1	AT2	AT3	AT4
SB26	Partnerarbeit. Welches Geschäft ist das?	2	2	1	-
CM13	Die Geschäfte	2	1	1	1
SB21	Was kann man hier kaufen?	3	2	1	-
CM14	Das kann man alles kaufen	3	2	1	-
	Kann ich Ihnen helfen?	4	2	1	1
SB27	Partnerarbeit. Am Markt, oder?	2	2	2	-
SB28/CM15	Ralf der Räuber	4	3	4	2
SB29	Jörgs Einkaufsliste	3	3	4	2
SB29	Wo treffen sie sich vielleicht?	4	2	3	-
CM16	Mastermind	3	2	2	1
SB30	Wieviel?	3	3	3	-
SB30	Das Einkaufslied	4	3	4	-
SB31	Was kaufen die Leute im Geschäft?	3	2	2	-
SB31	Partnerarbeit. Einkaufslisten	2	2	2	2
CM17/18	Was kauft ihr für das Picknick?	3	2	2	2
CM19	Einkaufszettel	3	2	2	2
CM20	Obst- und Gemüsespiele	2	2	2	-
	Radiorezepte	5	3	3	1
CM21	Ladendieb!	8	4	3	-
SB32	Welches Geschäft ist das?	-	-	1	2
SB32	Wo sind die Sachen?	-	-	3	3
SB32	Purzelwörter	-	-	2	3
SB33	Wieviel?	-	-	2	2
SB33	Im Doofimarkt!	-	-	2	2
SB33	Meine Einkaufsliste	-	-	2	2
SB34/CM22	Bildvokabeln. Im Supermarkt	-	-	2	2
	Kapitel 4				
SB36/CM23	Wie kommst du dahin?	3	1	2	2
SB36	Wie fahren sie dahin?	2	2	2	2
SB37	Partnerarbeit. Wie kommst du zum Sportplatz?	2	2	-	-
SB37	Sonntags bin ich immer müde!	3	3	3	4
SB38	Wie fährst du?	3	3	4	4
SB39	Entschuldigung ... Ich suche den Bahnhof	3	2	3	
SB38	Partnerarbeit. Der Bus nach Schenefeld kommt	3	2	2	-
SB40	Welche Linie ist das?	4	2	4	-
SB40	Partnerarbeit	3	3	3	-
	München Hauptbahnhof	5	-	4	-
SB41	Einmal nach Pfarrkirchen, bitte	3	2	3	-
CM24	Einfach oder hin und zurück?	3	3	3	-
SB41	Partnerarbeit. Abfahrt	4	3	3	-
CM25	Auskunft	6	3	4	2
CM26	Abfahrt-Ankunft	3	4	4	-
	Zurückbleiben bitte	7	4	-	-
CM27	Einige Informationen	3	3	5	-
SB42	Gespräche	-	-	3	2
SB42	Ein Brief aus Perpignan	-	-	5	3
SB43	Was ist das?	-	-	-	1
SB43	Zweimal nach Hamburg, bitte	-	-	3	3
SB43	Wann fährt der nächste Zug?	-	-	4	2
SB44/CM28	Bildvokabeln. Am Bahnhof	-	-	1	1
SB44	Steffi	-	-	3	-

	Kapitel 5	AT1	AT2	AT3	AT4
SB46	Wer ist das?	3	2	3	-
SB47	Partnerarbeit. Haarige Probleme	3	3	3	3
CM29	Paßt das?	2	2	2	-
CM30	Wie heißen die Mädchen?	3	3	3	-
CM31	Kleider	2	2	2	2
SB48	Gruppenfoto	4	2	4	-
CM32	Ausgeflippte Kleider	3	1	2	-
SB49	Bunte Kleider	4	3	3	3
SB49	Steffi	-	-	3	-
SB50	Was hältst du von Asla?	4	3	4	3
SB50	Graffitimauer	3	3	3	3
CM33	Teenager	5	2	3	-
SB51	Partnerarbeit. Wer spricht?	3	3	3	4
SB51	Sag mir jemand, wer sie war	6	3	6	-
CM34	Austauschpartner	5	4	5	1
SB52	So ein Durcheinander!	-	-	4	1
SB52	Im Umkleideraum	-	-	3	-
SB53	Popstar	-	-	3	4
SB53	Quatsch!	-	-	3	2
SB53	Unheimlich bunt	-	-	1	1
SB54/CM35	Bildvokabeln. Im Freibad	-	-	1	1
	Kapitel 6				
SB56	Kommst du?	3	3	3	-
SB56	Partnerarbeit. Hast du Lust?	3	3	3	3
CM36	Wer hat Lust?	-	-	2	2
SB57	Wer kommt mit zur Party?	3	3	3	3
CM37	Solche Freunde!	3	-	2	3
	Tut mir leid	4	3	3	4
CM38	Leider nicht	3	2	3	1
SB58	Hallo Inge!	3	3	3	-
CM39	Wann denn?	4	3	3	-
SB59	Die Clique am Samstagabend	3	2	3	-
CM40	So eine Woche!	3	3	2	3
	Wo treffen wir uns?	2	2	-	-
SB60	Wir gehen aus	3	3	3	-
SB61	Partnerarbeit. Treffen wir uns vor dem Bahnhof?	3	3	3	-
CM41	Treffpunkte	-	-	2	2
	Telefonspiel	3	3	-	-
SB52	Schade!	-	-	3	2
SB52	Mach doch mit!	-	-	3	-
SB53	Einladungen	-	-	2	3
SB53	Wo treffen sie sich?	-	-	2	2
SB53	Telefongespräch	-	-	3	2
SB54	Ausreden	3	3	3	-
	Kapitel 7				
	Sonja sagt	2	2	-	-
CM42	Die Körperteile	-	-	1	1
SB66	Ich habe Kopfschmerzen ... Mein Fuß tut weh	3	3	2	-
CM43	Was ist mit dir los?	2	2	3	-
	Was wird hier gespielt?	2	2	-	-
	Die neue Turnhalle	4	2	-	-
SB66	Partnerarbeit. Was fehlt dir?	3	3	3	-

		AT1	AT2	AT3	AT4
SB67	Partnerarbeit. Wer bin ich?	3	3	3	-
SB68	Ich kann nicht ... Ich bin krank	3	3	3	-
CM44	Wo tut es ihm weh?	2	-	2	1
SB68	Entschuldigungszettel	-	-	4	-
SB69	Lieber Herr Heinemann!	-	-	4	4
SB69	Allergien	4	-	-	-
CM45	Krank im Urlaub	5	2	2	1
SB70	Partnerarbeit. Haben Sie etwas gegen Seekrankheit?	3	3	3	-
SB70	In der Apotheke	3	2	3	-
SB70	Haben Sie etwas gegen Zebrastreifen?	-	-	2	-
SB71	Wundermittel	3	2	3	3
CM46	Ein guter Rat	3	3	3	-
CM47	Was macht die Zähne kaputt?	3	3	2	2
	Was meinen Sie, Herr Doktor Schweiger?	6	2	-	-
SB72	Was sagt Long John Silver?	-	-	3	-
SB72	Fünf Minuten später	-	-	3	2
SB73	Ich bin allergsich gegen ...	-	-	3	3
SB73	Was haben Sie gegen ...?	-	-	3	-
SB73	Frank ist krank	-	-	2	3
SB74	Hypochonderlied	3	3	3	-
SB74	Steffi	-	-	4	-
	Kapitel 8				
SB76-77	Wohin fahren sie?	4	3	3	-
CM48	Wohin fahren sie? Ein Rätsel	-	-	3	4
CM49	Wie kommt die Familie Müller nach Spanien?	4	2	2	-
SB76	Und du? Gruppenarbeit	3	3	-	-
SB78	Mit dem Flugzeug nach Helgoland	3	2	3	-
SB78	Mir geht's nicht gut!	-	-	2	3
CM50	Wir fahren nach England	4	2	2	-
SB79	Helgoland-Inselparadies!	4	2	3	-
SB80	Welcher Campingplatz?	3	2	3	-
SB81	Partnerarbeit. Auf dem Campingplatz	3	3	3	-
CM51	Camping ist billig, oder?	3	3	3	-
SB81	Bist du ein Genie in Mathe?	3	3	2	-
SB82	Mein idealer Urlaub	-	-	-	2
SB82	Lieber nicht!	-	-	-	3
SB82	Bus-Schiffsreise nach London	-	-	4	-
SB83	Campingplatzregeln	-	-	3	3
SB83	Camping – ja oder nein?	-	-	-	4
SB83	Wir haben eine Reservierung	-	-	3	-
SB84/CM52	Bildvokabeln. Auf dem Campingplatz	-	-	1	1
SB84	Urlaubszeit	3	2	2	2
	Kapitel 9				
	Im Kaufhaus	3	2	-	-
SB86	Wegweiser	3	2	2	-
SB86	Partnerarbeit. Wo kann ich hier ... bekommen?	3	3	3	-
CM53	Ich hätte gern ...	3	2	-	-
SB87	Partnerarbeit. Wo ...?	3	3	2	-
CM54	Der Kunde ist König	3	3	3	-
SB88	Preissensationen	3	3	2	2
CM55	Zwölf Unterschiede	3	3	2	-
CM56	Billig oder teuer?	3	3	2	-

		AT1	AT2	AT3	AT4
	Frank und Erika im Kaufhaus	5	3	-	-
SB89	Partnerarbeit. Geschenke	3	3	3	3
	Vor Weihnachten im Kaufhaus	5	3	-	3
SB90	Partnerarbeit. Gefällt es dir?	3	3	3	-
SB90	Und die Geschenke?	-	-	2	3
	Wo bekomme ich Briefmarken?	3	3	-	-
SB91	Auf der Post	3	3	2	-
CM57	Was kaufen sie auf der Post?	2	2	-	-
SB91	Informationen am Briefkasten	3	2	3	-
SB92	Was ist das?	-	-	1	-
SB92	He Axel, was kostet ...?	-	-	3	2
SB92	Tierheim	-	-	-	3
SB93	Kaufhaus BILLIG	-	-	-	2
SB93	Was kaufst du für ...?	-	-	-	2, 3
SB93	Briefmarken	-	-	3	2
SB94	Kleiner Mensch	3	3	3	-
	Kapitel 10				
SB96-97	Sabines Jahr	3	3	3	-
SB97	Partnerarbeit	3	3	3	-
CM58	Ich bin zu einer neuen Schule gegangen	3	2	3	-
	Presentation of language	3	3	3	3
CM 59	Deutsch-Englisch Domino	-	-	3	-
	Im Februar	3	3	3	-
SB98	Was hast du heute gekauft?	3	3	3	4
SB98	Partnerarbeit. Was hast du gestern gekauft?	3	3	3	-
	Einkaufskettenspiel	3	3	-	-
	Im April	3	3	3	-
	Was hast du zum Geburtstag bekommen?	3	2	-	-
SB99	Partnerarbeit. Was hast du zu deinem Geburtstag bekommen?	3	3	3	-
SB99	Was hast du an deinem Geburtstag gemacht?	3	-	2	-
CM60	Ich habe eine Party gegeben	3	-	3	4
	Im Juli	3	3	3	-
SB100-101	Hast du die Betti kennengelernt?	5	3	5	-
SB102	Treff-spezial-Ferien	-	-	4	-
CM61	Was hast du gesehen?	3	4	-	4
	Im Oktober	3	3	3	-
SB103	Wie ist Lars zum Schwimmbad gekommen?	-	-	3	3
SB103	Ich bin gut angekommen	-	-	3	-
	Wie war die Reise?	4	3	-	-
CM62	Katjas Tagebuch	5	3	3	3
CM63	Liebe Miriam!	-	-	5	4
CM64	Deine Woche	-	-	5	5
SB104	Kannst du einen Satz bilden?	-	-	3	-
SB104	Wie ist es richtig?	-	-	3	-
SB104	Lieber Kurt!	-	-	4	1
SB105	Wo ist das Ende?	-	-	3	1
SB105	Lieber Karl-Heinz!	-	-	3	3

We have selected a single example from the different components of *Zickzack neu Stage 2* to demonstrate how the course matches up to the SOED 5-14 guidelines for each Attainment Target, at each of the three Levels of Attainment and across the various strands.

Listening

Strands	Elementary	Intermediate	Level E
Classroom language	Show understanding, through an appropriate response, of simple and familiar words and short phrases in the form of simple instructions and requests, given visual support, repetition, rephrasing.	Show understanding, through an appropriate response, of familiar words and phrases in the form of instructions, requests and simple explanations, given visual support, repetition, rephrasing if necessary.	Show understanding, through an appropriate response, of familiar words and phrases in the form of instructions, comments, information and explanations, where these form a more routine part of the everyday language of the classroom.
Examples	From the very beginning, the Teacher's Notes for *Zickzack neu 2* recommend using German for introducing and preparing classroom activities. For each activity, appropriate language is suggested, beginning with simple instructions and requests and gradually moving towards more complex comments and explanations. Further support for the student is provided on page 144 of the students' book, where the *Selbstbedienung* instructions are translated. Teacher's Book, Kapitel 1, Lernziel 1 **Teacher:** *Was ist das? Das ist der Dom. Bitte wiederhol: ‚der Dom'* Teacher's Book, Kapitel 9, Lernziel 2 Auf der Post **Teacher:** *Jetzt seid ihr nochmal auf der Post, aber ihr* (write up:) *seid: müde, krank, ärgerlich; ihr habt es eilig, wollt lange auf der Post bleiben usw. Was sagt ihr und wie?* (Perform one or two examples.)		

Strands	Elementary	Intermediate	Level E
Listening to establish relationships with others	Listen to others while working in pairs or groups and/or with the teacher; and show understanding of familiar words and short phrases by taking part in simple exchanges in familiar contexts.	Listen to others while working in pairs or groups and/or with the teacher and show understanding of familiar words and short phrases embedded in longer utterances, by taking part in simple conversations in familiar contexts.	Listen to others while working in pairs or groups and/or with the teacher and show understanding of familiar words and phrases, embedded in utterances which might contain new language, by taking part in simple conversations in a widening range of familiar contexts.
Examples	Students' Book, page 16, Kapitel 2, Lernziel 1, Partnerarbeit: Was ist das?	Students' Book, page 41, Kapitel 4, Lernziel 2, Umfrage	Copymaster 40, Kapitel 6, Lernziel 1, So eine Woche!

Listening for information	Show understanding of familiar words and short phrases, from a live or recorded source, supported by repetition and a structured task.	Show understanding of short items from a widening range of familiar material, from a live or recorded source, supported by repetition and a structured task.	Show understanding of material from a live or recorded source, supported, if required, by repetition and a structured task. This material may contain some items of unfamiliar language.
Examples	Students' Book, page 20, Kapitel 2, Lernziel 2, Ist das weit von hier?	Students' Book, page 79, Kapitel 8, Lernziel 1, Helgoland – Inselparadies	Students' Book, page 48, Kapitel 5, Lernziel 1, Gruppenfoto

Speaking

Strands	Elementary	Intermediate	Level E
Classroom language	Use simple and familiar words and phrases as part of classroom activities, with teacher support	Use the target language readily, to participate in familiar classroom activities, with some teacher support if required.	Use the target language to participate in and contribute to most classroom activities.
Example **Example**	Copymaster 1 of Stage 1 provides students with a list of useful classroom language and encourages them to ask for help, explain problems and organise classroom activities in German. *Zickzack neu 1* Copymaster 1, Kapitel 1 *Darf ich auf die Toilette?* *Ich habe keinen Bleistift.* *Du bist dran.* This approach is continued in Stage 2. Many of the games suggested also encourage the use of the target language. Teacher's Book, page 8, Introduction, **Games to practise classroom language**		

Strands	Elementary	Intermediate	Level E
Speaking to establish relationships with others	Take part in simple exchanges using familiar words.	Take part in simple conversations in familiar contexts, occasionally initiating as well as responding, with support as necessary.	Take part in conversations and simple discussions, initiating and responding and going beyond the minimum response where appropriate.
Examples	Students' Book, page 26, Kapitel 3, Lernziel 1, Partnerarbeit. Welches Geschäft ist das?	Students' Book, page 51, Kapitel 5, Lernziel 2, Partnerarbeit. Wer spricht?	Students' Book, page 61, Kapitel 6, Lernziel 2, Partnerarbeit. Treffen wir uns vor dem Bahnhof?

Strands	Elementary	Intermediate	Level E
Speaking on a topic	Say a few short sentences about oneself with preparation and prompting.	Say a few sentences on a familiar topic with preparation and prompting.	With preparation and prompting as required, talk on a familiar topic from a widening range.
Examples	Teacher's Book, page 19, Kapitel 1, Lernziel 1, Was gibt es in deiner Stadt zu sehen?	Teacher's Book, page 55, Kapitel 4, Lernziel 1, Wie fährst du?	Teacher's Book, page 55, Kapitel 4, Lernziel 1, Wie fährst du?

Strands	Elementary	Intermediate	Level E
Asking for support	Use familiar words and phrases to ask for help with the language, in a restricted range of familiar circumstances.	Use familiar words and phrases to ask for help with the language in a wider range of familiar circumstances.	Use familiar words and phrases accurately and fluently to ask for help with the language, in the context of a range of activities, using appropriate register.

Example	Copymaster 1 of Stage 1 provides students with a list of useful classroom language and encourages them to ask for support in German. *Zickzack neu 1* Copymaster 1, Kapitel 1 *Ich verstehe nicht* This approach is continued in Stage 2. Many of the games suggested also encourage the use of the target language to ask for help and support.
Example	Teacher's Book, page 8, Introduction, **Games to practise classroom language**

Pronunciation and intonation	In all of the above targets, speak with increasingly accurate pronunciation and intonation. Throughout *Zickzack neu 2* students are encouraged to use correct pronunciation and intonation through listening to and repeating model dialogues, rhymes, tongue-twisters, songs etc.
Example	Students' Book, page 74, Kapitel 7, Hypochonderlied

Knowledge about language	Use an increasing knowledge of the language structure and register to communicate with clarity and courtesy in a range of circumstances. During the course of *Zickzack neu 2*, students are introduced to the conventions of *du* and *Sie* and are encouraged to use conventions such as *bitte*, *Entschuldigung/Entschuldigen Sie* and *danke/danke schön*.

Reading

Strands	Elementary	Intermediate	Level E
Reading for information	Understand words, phrases and simple sentences of familiar language, presented in a familiar context.	Understand short, straightforward texts, consisting of familiar language, in a familiar context.	Understand straightforward texts which may include some unfamiliar language, though in a familiar context.
Examples	Copymaster 29, Kapitel 5, Lernziel 1, Paßt das?	Students' Book, page 42, Kapitel 4, Selbstbedienung, Gespräche	Students' Book, page 68, Kapitel 7, Lernziel 2, Entschuldigungszettel

Strands	Elementary	Intermediate	Level E
Reading for enjoyment	Read words, phrases and simple sentences, with the support of illustrations, word lists and help from the teacher.	Read short, straightforward texts with growing confidence, using as necessary word lists and help from the teacher.	Read a variety of materials with increasing confidence and independence, checking on new words and phrases as necessary.
Examples	Students' Book, page 88, Kapitel 8, Urlaubszeit	Students' Book, page 24, Kapitel 2, Steffi	Students' Book, page 64, Kapitel 6, Ausreden

Strands	Elementary	Intermediate	Level E
Pronunciation and the written word	Show a developing understanding of the relationship between the printed word, pronunciation and meaning:		
	read aloud familiar words, phrases and short sentences.	read aloud familiar words, phrases and short sentences, pronouncing them sufficiently accurately so as to convey their meaning readily.	read aloud familiar text with fluency; scan and read aloud a short unfamiliar text, with accent and intonation sufficiently accurate so as to convey meaning readily.
Examples	Copymaster 20, Kapitel 3, Lernziel 2, Obst- und Gemüsespiele	Copymaster 34, Kapitel 5, Lernziel 2, Austauschpartner	Students' Book, page 81, Kapitel 8, Lernziel 2, Partnerarbeit. Auf dem Campingplatz

Strands	Elementary	Intermediate	Level E
Using reference sources	Make use of word lists, glossaries and dictionaries with increasing accuracy and independence, to check the meaning of new words and phrases introduced in the context of a unit of work or personal reading activities. Throughout Zickzack neu 2 students are encouraged to make use of the comprehensive German-English, English-German glossary at the back of the Students' Book.		
Example	Teacher's Book, page 110, Kapitel 9, Lernziel 2, Vor Weihnachten im Kaufhaus … Ask them to note as much detail as they can, referring them to glossaries and dictionaries as appropriate. …		

Writing

Strands	Elementary	Intermediate	Level E
Copying	Copy familiar words and phrases.	Copy words and phrases, including new material, with increasing accuracy.	
Examples	Copymaster 10, Kapitel 3, Lernziel 2, Vor dem Museum	Copymaster 62, Kapitel 10, Katjas Tagebuch	
Writing from memory			Write familiar words and phrases from memory, using the correct written form with increasing consistency.
Example			Copymaster 45, Kapitel 7, Lernziel 1, Krank im Urlaub
Continuous writing	Write a few familiar words within a guided framework.	Write a few words or simple sentences, with support, guidance and reference materials.	Write a few simple sentences with support, guidance and reference materials if required, using the correct written form with increasing consistency.
Examples	Copymaster 61, Kapitel 10, Was hast du gesehen?	Copymaster 64, Kapitel 10, Deine Woche	